Quentin McDermott is an award-winning investigative journalist who has worked in magazines, newspapers and television. Following six years at Granada Television in the UK, he joined the ABC as the supervising producer on *Lateline* before joining *Four Corners* in 2000 as a senior investigative reporter and producer. He is the ABC producer of the critically acclaimed and award-winning documentary *Stop at Nothing: The Lance Armstrong Story*. At *Australian Story* his story on Kathleen Folbigg helped trigger a judicial inquiry in 2018 and he has covered her story for the ABC and *The Australian* ever since.

MEADOW'S LAW

Quentin McDermott

ABC BOOKS

The ABC 'Wave' device is a trademark of the Australian Broadcasting Corporation and is used under licence by HarperCollins*Publishers* Australia

HarperCollins*Publishers*
Australia • Brazil • Canada • France • Germany • Holland • India
Italy • Japan • Mexico • New Zealand • Poland • Spain • Sweden
Switzerland • United Kingdom • United States of America

HarperCollins acknowledges the Traditional Custodians of the lands upon which we live and work, and pays respect to Elders past and present.

First published on Gadigal Country in Australia in 2025
by HarperCollins*Publishers* Australia Pty Limited
ABN 36 009 913 517
harpercollins.com.au

Copyright © Richard Quentin McDermott 2025

The right of Quentin McDermott to be identified as the author of this work has been asserted by him in accordance with the *Copyright Act 1968*.

All rights reserved. Apart from any use as permitted under the *Copyright Act 1968*, no part may be reproduced, copied, scanned, stored in a retrieval system, recorded, or transmitted, in any form or by any means, without the prior written permission of the publisher. Without limiting the exclusive rights of any author, contributor, or the publisher of this publication, any unauthorised use of this publication to train generative artificial intelligence (AI) technologies is expressly prohibited. HarperCollins also exercises its rights under Article 4(3) of the Digital Single Market Directive 2019/790 and expressly reserves this publication from the text and data-mining exception.

HarperCollins*Publishers*
Macken House, 39/40 Mayor Street Upper
Dublin 1, D01 C9W8, Ireland

A catalogue record for this book is available from the National Library of Australia

ISBN 978 0 7333 4291 2 (paperback)
ISBN 978 1 4607 1579 6 (ebook)

Cover design by Hazel Lam, HarperCollins Design Studio
Front cover image by Robert McKell / Newspix
Back cover image by Christian Gilles NewsWire / Newspix
Author photograph by Georgie Greene Photography
Typeset in Bembo Std by Kirby Jones

Printed and bound in the United States

For Tracey and Oscar, my partners in crime

'The time has come,' the Walrus said,
'To talk of many things:
Of shoes — and ships — and sealing-wax —
Of cabbages — and kings —
And why the sea is boiling hot —
And whether pigs have wings.'

Lewis Carroll

To the living we owe respect;
to the dead we owe only the truth.

Voltaire

CONTENTS

Prologue 1

PART 1
1   'I'm Sorry Darling, I Had to Do It' 5
2   Neglected and Destitute 8
3   Charming and Seductive 18
4   'Mixed Feelings' 27
5   'The Cheekiest One Ever' 36
6   'This Last One Has Broken Me' 46
7   'The Biggest Party Ever!' 53
8   'I've Had Three Go Already!' 60
9   'Four is Fucking Murder!' 70
10 'Obviously, I'm My Father's Daughter' 81
11 'All Night I've Been Thinking, Maybe I Killed the Kids'   91
12 'With Three, You Yell "Murder!"' 98
13 'I Couldn't Leave the Lady in the Lurch' 107

PART 2
14 The Trial 117
15 'Honest to God' 126
16 The Verdict 136
17 Behind Bars 145
18 The Champion Bridge Player 158
19 Mothers in the Dock 162
20 'A Scholar of Bias' 169
21 The Fightback Begins 176
22 The Petition 185
23 'An Eminently Fatal Case of Myocarditis' ... 196
24 'That's, as Mothers, What You Do' 204
25 Eureka! 209

PART 3

26	An Inquiry at Last	221
27	'It is an Appalling Situation'	227
28	'She Could be Part of that Small Number'	237
29	The CALM Before the Storm	243
30	Under Siege	254
31	'The Ordinary, Plain Meaning'	264
32	'Hope Can Destroy One's Soul'	275
33	Europace	285
34	A Nobel Cause	294
35	'Dear Mr Speakman ... Please Soften Your Heart'	307
36	'It's Time'	313
37	Waiting for Mr Speakman	321
38	It's All in the Genes	332
39	Free at Last	353

Epilogue	364
Bibliography and Further Reading	368
Acknowledgements	386

PROLOGUE

The most grievous miscarriages of justice can have terrible outcomes.

On Friday, 16 March 2007, Sally Clark, an English solicitor wrongly convicted of murdering two of her three young boys, was found dead at her family home in Essex. She was forty-two years old and was later judged to have died from accidental alcohol intoxication. Unwittingly, and in terrible pain, she had drunk herself to death.

Her own personal history was tragic. In 1996, her firstborn, Christopher, who was eleven weeks old, died suddenly. Two years later, her second child, Harry, also died suddenly when he was only eight weeks old.

One month after Harry's death, Sally Clark was arrested, and charged with murdering her infants. At her trial, a prominent British paediatrician, Professor Roy Meadow, gave evidence that the chance of two cot deaths happening in an affluent family like hers was 1 in 73 million.

But he was wrong.

The professor's belief was that in a single family: 'One sudden infant death is a tragedy, two is suspicious and three is murder, until proved otherwise.' His theory became known colloquially as Meadow's Law, and based in part on his evidence, the jury convicted Sally Clark, and several other innocent mothers. Sally Clark received two life sentences for killing her children.

A first appeal failed, but a second appeal in early 2003 found that the statistical evidence offered up by Professor Meadow was wildly inaccurate, and Sally Clark emerged from the High Court in London a free woman, her husband Steve by her side, her face pale and gaunt, her expression that of a mother haunted by personal tragedy and by the vilification she had suffered in prison. She had been exonerated, but by then, the damage was done, and she never fully recovered from her ordeal.

As other mothers who Roy Meadow had helped to put behind bars were acquitted on appeal, Sally Clark's words on her own release echoed down the years: 'Today is not a victory. We are not victorious. There are no winners here. We have all lost out.'

Speaking to *The Guardian* after her death in 2007, Sally Clark's solicitor John Batt said: 'I don't think you can ever recover from something like that. Imagine being in jail where everyone thinks you are the scum of the earth, the lowest human being that walks the earth. The thick end of it is that she lost five to six years of her life in what was state-sponsored torture.'

Two months after Sally Clark's acquittal in 2003, another mother went on trial in Australia for the murder of all four of her children. Her trial too was tainted by Meadow's Law, and she too came to be regarded as the scum of the earth, and the lowest of the low.

Like Sally Clark, the bereaved mother would end up a victim of state-sponsored torture, losing decades of her life to one of the worst miscarriages of justice ever recorded. She would still be in prison now, if not for the heroic battle fought on her behalf by her closest friends, the scientists who rescued her, and her loyal legal team.

Her name was Kathleen Folbigg, and this is the story of her case.

PART 1

1
'I'M SORRY DARLING, I HAD TO DO IT'

On a humid summer's evening in December 1968, in a quiet back street in the Sydney suburb of Annandale, a middle-aged man was seen cradling the blood-drenched body of a woman he had just stabbed twenty-four times in an act of uncontrolled violence.

Thomas Britton was a vicious thug – an underworld hitman who worked as a wharfie on Sydney's Balmain docks. The woman breathing her last in his arms was his 'de facto' wife, Kathleen Donovan, a factory worker.

The frightful scene was reminiscent of a cheap pulp fiction novel. As Kathleen lay dying on the footpath, a shocked neighbour saw Britton bend over and kiss her.

'I'm sorry darling, I had to do it,' he told her lifeless body. He turned to the neighbour: 'I had to kill her because she'd kill my child.'

The murder was premeditated. Another neighbour saw the couple talking six days earlier and heard Britton tell Kathleen: 'If I see you on the street alone, I will put a knife between your ribs.' Britton had been drinking heavily that afternoon and had brought the knife with him from home and lain in wait for her.

Kathleen Donovan was a gambler and a heavy drinker. But Thomas Britton, a Welshman who had migrated to Australia years earlier, was far worse. He was an extremely violent man. His associates were notorious, murderous members of Sydney's underworld, and Britton himself was a habitual wife-beater. In 1954, he received a twelve-month prison sentence for maliciously wounding his former wife, Margaret Britton, a nineteen-year-old nurse, by slashing her with an eight-inch steel blade, leaving her with deep gashes in her right upper arm and forearm.

She told him that their marriage was over; she didn't want to take any more beatings, and the attack was so violent that Britton thought he had killed her. Luckily for her, she survived, but in 1968, he succeeded in his latest deadly endeavour.

In a statement Britton gave to the police on the night he killed Kathleen Donovan, he attempted to justify his unforgivable act.

Two weeks earlier, he said, Kathleen had abandoned him and their eighteen-month-old daughter Kathy at Sydney's picturesque Nielsen Park, where they were having a picnic. 'I objected to her drinking so much with the child present,' he explained. 'She told me she would drink what she liked, when she liked and with whom she liked. I then told her that she wouldn't.' Following further argument, he said that she 'just grabbed her bag and went. She left the child with me.'

Kathleen Donovan did have an unfortunate habit of abandoning her children. She had left two older daughters with the men who had fathered them, and one girl ended up in an orphanage in New Zealand.

In the days following their bust-up, Thomas Britton found out where Kathleen lived. He pleaded with her to come home but she refused, telling him she didn't want anything more to do with him or their daughter. He demanded to know if she had slept with a man who was also living in the house, and she denied it. 'It was from then that it all started to boil up inside me,' he admitted. 'I gave her a smack in the mouth, and I told her I didn't believe her.'

On the night he stabbed Kathleen, Britton waited for the police to arrive, acting as if he was protecting the woman he had killed.

'When she was on the ground, I rearranged her clothes as I did not want anyone seeing her like that. The bloke upstairs told me to get away from her and I told him to go to buggery as

I did not want anyone to see her underclothes. I done what I done and threw the knife on the ground. I couldn't realise that she was dead, and I kissed her and cradled her in my arms. I then told the two people looking to ring the police as I had thought I had done my wife some harm.'

Not only had Britton fatally harmed his wife. He had also destroyed his daughter's chances of a happy family life with her parents.

Little Kathy grew up to be Kathleen Folbigg. And for her, it was the beginning of a nightmare that lasted fifty-five years.

2
NEGLECTED AND DESTITUTE

In the raw aftermath of her mother's brutal murder, the infant Kathy was taken to Minda Children's Court in western Sydney. Her appearance there could have featured in a Dickensian novel. She was described – grimly but accurately – as a 'neglected, destitute child' and was formally made a ward of the state and placed in the care of her maternal uncle Kerry Platt and his wife Mary, who lived nearby with Kathy's grandmother. The family was given five dollars a week to take care of her.

At first, the Platts were keen to give Kathy a home. They had stepped in as soon as they heard the news of her mother's murder. Kathy had stayed with them before, and Kathleen Donovan had even agreed to allow them to adopt her, but later changed her mind.

Given the horror of what had just occurred, the Platts decided to erase all traces of Kathy's parentage and in 1969 she was baptised under a completely new name: Lisa Platt.

The following month, Thomas Britton went on trial, and almost unbelievably, pleaded 'not guilty' to the charge of murdering Kathleen Donovan.

The court was told that Britton believed Kathleen had left him for another man, and witness statements painted him as a man overcome with remorse for having killed her, rather than as the abusive, self-pitying thug revealed in his interview with the police and in his constant violent behaviour towards women. He was duly found guilty of murder and sentenced to 'penal servitude for life', a sentence that would end when, thirteen years later, he was released and deported back to the UK.

'Lisa' knew none of this as she settled into her new home; she was viewed as a nice, bright girl and was making good progress, considering what had occurred. But in May 1970, a few weeks before her third birthday, Mrs Platt reported a dramatic decline in her behaviour. 'Lisa' was having temper tantrums and was extremely aggressive towards other children who visited. She would scream and cry and, most seriously of all, was exhibiting alarming signs of sexual abuse.

Kathy was taken to a child health clinic where a Dr Spencer reported that Mrs Platt, whether justifiably or not, had described her as 'virtually uncontrollable' and as 'a disruptive influence on her marriage'. The doctor considered it likely that Kathy had been sexually abused by her father, writing euphemistically that: 'It seems that Lisa was misused by her father during infancy.'

Later, Mrs Platt claimed that 'Lisa' was 'still very brutal' to other children and that, when her behaviour was corrected, she would scream and cry as a means of retaliation.

Kathy was undoubtedly headstrong. She told her friends that her uncle bred budgerigars and how, on one occasion, she'd opened a cage and let them all out. Scores of birds flew away, never to be seen again.

In June 1970, three days before Kathy's third birthday, Mrs Platt gave up the battle and asked the authorities to take her away. There was no way that Kathy's father could care for her. The most he could do, locked up in Long Bay Gaol, was to sign a short, official statement confirming that Kathy was his daughter.

With no one else she knew willing to give her a home, Kathy was placed in a forbidding orphanage – Bidura Children's Home in the Sydney suburb of Glebe – where she was described as a 'very disturbed little girl ... a fair haired, delicate looking child with a pretty, but very emotionally flat face'. She was unresponsive and withdrawn and rarely smiled or spoke.

Soon afterwards, she was moved to Corelli Babies' Home, in Sydney's inner western suburbs. There, orphaned kids were lined up to meet prospective foster parents. The couples would walk along a line of children and choose which one to take away with them.

One former resident in the home would later describe what it felt like to stand in line while adult strangers looked them up and down.

'We were too young to understand what the couples were saying, but after a few line-ups we kind of worked out what was happening. Occasionally one of us would disappear and so it dawned on us that this odd ritual was about leaving the orphanage to go and live with a man and a woman.'

At Bidura, Kathy was described – quite wrongly – as 'borderline retarded' with an IQ of 77. At Corelli – again, wrongly – she was classified as being in 'the dull to normal range'. It was only later, when she was seven years old, that her IQ was assessed at 110, which put her in the 'above average to superior' range.

At the age of three, she had lost her entire family, had lost her name, had suffered the lonely rigours of life in two orphanages, and she carried the scars of emotional and probable sexual abuse. No child's life could have started off more painfully than hers.

But, as luck would have it, hope was on the horizon.

In September 1970, Kathy met her new mother and father for the first time. It was a momentous day for her.

Sitting in the back seat of their car, driving further and further away from the orphanage, she was able to look out at the trees of Ku-ring-gai Chase National Park, north of Sydney, as they flew past on the way to her new home, a house nestled in the city of Newcastle's small garden suburb of Kotara.

Her new mum and dad were Deidre and Neville Marlborough, who had two adult children of their own: Russell was twenty-one when Kathy arrived, and his sister Lea was seventeen years old and newly married. Kathy felt safer here and more settled, with her own bedroom and toys and a bike to ride, and dogs and cats to play with.

'She was this little girl with blonde, curly hair, the biggest smile, and just a really happy little girl who just craved for love,' her sister Lea recalled later. 'She was just everything I had ever wanted. I had always wanted a sister, and I got a sister.'

Neville Marlborough had a Super 8 movie camera and took hours of film of Kathy growing up. The early footage shows Kathy playing happily at home.

But the dead hand of the state's bureaucracy hung over her like a cloud. As a ward of the state, she would have been categorised as 'illegitimate' and, until she turned eighteen, she was subject to regular visits from child welfare officers.

By the age of six, Kathy no longer spoke about her past life and regarded Neville and Deidre as her real parents. She was shy, pleasant and intelligent; and Deidre, though strict, was affectionate to her young foster child. When her older brother, Russell, got married that same year, Kathy was bridesmaid. Russell described her later as pretty, cute, funny and awkward, and said she 'appeared to be always seeking acceptance from Mum'.

At primary school, Kathy was a loner and a bit of a tomboy, running around with the boys, but at times, feeling solitary and sad. School photos show her sitting quietly and obediently alongside her classmates, like any other young schoolgirl. But her own memory is that she 'skirted' through primary school, feeling disengaged and disconnected.

It's believed that when Kathy was nine years old, Neville and Deidre lied to her – telling her that they had adopted her. It was untrue, and it put the social workers in a quandary. Kathy needed to know she was being fostered, but they worried that if they told her she wasn't adopted, it would shatter her illusions of security.

It wasn't until the following year that Deidre finally summoned up the courage to tell Kathy that she wasn't adopted, and it hit her hard. The conversation was difficult and emotional, and for Kathy, extremely distressing because she had always assumed that Neville and Deidre wanted to adopt her. It was difficult to understand why they hadn't.

Even more shocking was the treatment being handed out to Kathy by Deidre. Kathy's foster sister Lea believes that she 'never got on with my mother, and my mother never got on with her'. In Lea's view, her Mum was too old to have adopted a toddler. And when Lea gave birth to a son, Ward – Deidre's first grandchild – 'he took up all the time and her love, and Kathy got none'. Russell, too, thought that Kathy always seemed to take second place to Ward.

According to Lea, whenever Kathy was naughty, she would get a 'belting' from Deidre. Lea's husband Ted Bown ascribes this in part to the favouritism shown by Deidre towards her grandson. 'She was a normal little girl, and she should have been treated like a normal little girl, but unfortunately, because my son was there, she was pushed to the side. It was her job to look after him, make sure he didn't get into trouble. If he did anything wrong, he would just turn round, and say: "Kathy did it," and she'd get belted for it.' Russell confirmed this, saying that Ward was 'the wonderboy' who never put a foot wrong, in Deidre's eyes.

In later life, Kathy would describe Deidre as 'controlling to an excessive degree'. After speaking at length to Kathy, a psychiatrist wrote that Deidre 'was intent on teaching her domestic chores and having her perform these in the household. She said her mother was someone who wanted her to be seen so that she could be shown off as someone who had been well raised by her foster mother.'

The young, orphaned girl was cast in the role of a latter-day Cinderella. Deidre would punish her by slapping her or hitting her with a feather duster handle, a wooden spoon or a belt if she didn't carry out her list of household chores.

'Her mother's physical punishment could result from any perceived misbehaviour,' her psychiatrist reported. Kathy described her mother as unpredictable, moody and domineering.

By contrast, Kathy's foster father Neville was 'a shadow in the background'. At work, he did the accounting and bookkeeping for a wholesale food business. To Kathy, he was a closed book who didn't give a lot away.

One of Kathy's oldest friends, Megan Donegan, has remained close to her since their childhood. She recalls how 'Kathy did tell me a couple of times about things that had happened when her father had to hold her mother back, over some very small indiscretion'. From what she observed, Kathy was treated 'like a slave' by her foster mother.

To escape the rigours of her harsh home environment, Kathy read books and walked the dog in a park over the road. But she needed friends she could relate to, and at primary school, she met another girl who would become her lifelong friend – Tracy Chapman.

Tracy, whose home, overrun with animals, resembled a farm more than a city dwelling, helped Kathy to forget the ordeals she suffered at home and just be a normal kid, running around with her mates, playing games, or spending time just sitting and chatting.

Both girls enjoyed the outdoors. 'She wasn't the sort of kid that you would see in a library reading a book. We would all be out exploring. The school had logs and trees around and you could go and sit on a log and play tag around the bushes.' Tracy relished the fact that Kathy was vivacious, fun and mischievous. 'She loved animals, and we had lots of animals around the house, so there were interactions with dogs and birds and spiders and snakes – and a duck – Ziggy the Duck!'

The girls went to Kotara Primary School, and one particularly happy memory stands out. Tracy's parents bought her a cassette recorder, and 'I got the soundtrack to *Grease* on tape. I still remember us dancing around the schoolyard to *Grease* and having a great old time.'

In Year 5, Tracy left and they lost contact for a while, but reunited in high school. 'She was in a circle of friends that are still my friends to today,' Tracy says. 'From Year 8 onwards, we were all quite inseparable.'

In her teenage years, despite her tight circle of girlfriends, Kathy remained – in her own words – a 'lone wolf'. Her relationship with Deidre deteriorated further, as the two repeatedly clashed over Kathy's requests to go out with her friends. She complained that her mother tried to keep her 'boxed in the square'.

But there were good times too. 'Kath and I first met in Year 7 and we were close through the whole of high school,' Megan Donegan recalls. 'She often accompanied my family on trips. There were Sunday drives with my nieces and nephews, and christenings, and we'd have her at our place a lot. She always had a big laugh.'

Megan says Kathy was extroverted, 'but there was always something that was holding her back'.

When Kathy was fifteen years old, she had her first boyfriend, a lad she described as a 'science nerd'. He was undemanding and she enjoyed his sense of humour. They would sit together at school, and he welcomed her into his group of friends. Over the next two years they grew closer, but the relationship ended when he went overseas to visit relatives. He didn't tell her he was going, and she felt abandoned and betrayed.

That same year, her foster father Neville fell on hard times. He had been off work for some time and despite his best efforts was unable to get a job. He was on the dole, but in one way he was fortunate. Because Kathy was still a ward of the state, the unemployment benefit he received was topped up with a ward allowance to pay for Kathy's care, together with a 'double orphan pension', which they were entitled to receive because both of Kathy's natural parents were no longer there to care for her.

If Neville and Deidre had adopted Kathy, the wardship would have ended, and they would have had to pay for her upkeep with their own money. There was a clear financial motive not to adopt her.

Also in 1982, unbeknown to Kathy, Thomas Britton was released from Long Bay Gaol and deported back to the UK. From London he travelled to Abersychan, near Pontypool, the Welsh town where he was born and grew up. He never told his family and friends there what had happened, and never made any effort to contact his daughter. She wasn't even aware that he was alive.

According to a report written many years later in *The Times*: 'Residents of the Welsh village of Abersychan, near Pontypool, recall Thomas John Britton as Jack the Slipper, a lovable old rogue with a twinkle in his eye, who was too infirm to put on his shoes for the fifty-yard shuffle to the pub.'

Two years later, despite all the arguments and disagreements at home, Kathy asked for the surname on her birth certificate to be changed from Britton to Marlborough. But not long after her seventeenth birthday, Kathy was forced to come to grips with who she was – and who her real parents were.

In July 1984, Neville, Deidre and a child welfare officer sat her down at home and told her the shocking truth: that her father had murdered her mother in cold blood.

Kathy was devastated. It shook her to the core, and it embarrassed her; she felt that it reflected badly on her. She wondered whether it explained why her foster parents, who knew her family history, were always so guarded about her mother, and whether it explained the unpleasant comment that Deidre had once made, that 'you probably have the same temperament as your father'.

Kathy had already endured enough in her young life, and this shattering news only intensified her instinct to bottle things up. She didn't want people to think that she and her father were alike, and guarded against it by keeping her own emotions in check.

But she did tell her closest friends and for them, there was a second revelation. Kathy had known since she was ten that she wasn't adopted – but her friends had been kept in the dark. Now she told them.

Megan Donegan remembers the day this happened; Kathy was in the music class sitting at the back, looking stunned. 'Kathy told me that her father had murdered her mother. Which is how she ended up in the foster care system. And it was just whispered up the back of the music class, very matter of fact. She was holding back tears, and she was able to do that well, she had to hold back tears a lot. A great birthday present to give someone for their seventeenth. To totally shatter their world for everything they believed in for most of their life.'

Tracy Chapman, too, has her own vivid recollection of the shockwaves caused by Kathy's revelations. 'I remember just being in complete shock. There was never a hint of anything like that in her household. She was just part of the family, so I guess we were soul-searching with Kathy that day. She was very quiet, I do remember. I think she was quite thrown and rattled but, in her matter-of-fact way, which is how she's always been in her whole life that I've known her; she's just come out and said it as it was.'

Unquestionably the revelation of who her parents were, and what her father had done to her mother, affected Kathy deeply. Five days later, feeling anxious and expectant, she went to visit the Platts — her maternal uncle and aunt — in Sydney, who gave her some old baby photos and a photo of her mother Kathleen.

Megan Donegan believes that deep down, even the shock of the revelation that she wasn't adopted, and that her father had murdered her mother, didn't change Kathy. 'I don't think so, because Kathy's always just dealt with the things that have come along in her life very stoically.'

Tracy Chapman says that even as a teenager, there was no beating about the bush with her. 'Kath just says it like it is. Sometimes it can be blunt, but it's not intended to be blunt.'

Not long before her eighteenth birthday, there was a further domestic drama. Kathy ran away from home following a family disagreement about seeing a boyfriend. She stayed with a girlfriend's family for a while and when she returned, she told her parents that she wanted to leave school and get a job. She was true to her word. Shortly afterwards, she handed in her schoolbooks and left Kotara High School, announcing that she wanted to find work or go on the dole and take some time to think. It meant that she wouldn't complete Year 12, her final year at school.

Nothing Deidre and Neville could say would change her mind, and reluctantly, they accepted it.

Lea, who was close to Kathy for many years, felt bitter about the way her mother behaved: 'I blame my mother for the way she treated Kathy,' she said later. 'My mother was very manipulative, and she only ever had love for her grandson, my son. It was all for him. Everything was him.'

She eventually fell out with Deidre and didn't speak to her for years until she died. Kathy by contrast never disowned her, and in the years before Deidre died, demonstrated her abiding love by reconciling with her. Her astonishing ability to forgive those who had wronged her would emerge as a quality much admired by those who knew her best.

She expressed the view that her biological parents, Thomas and Kathleen, were irrelevant to her upbringing. 'They have actually got nothing to do with how I grew up,' she told Tracy Chapman. 'The ethics, morals, values and everything that was instilled in me as I was growing up, they had nothing to do with that because they weren't around. They weren't there.'

She added: 'I don't remember my mother; I can't remember my father. I've only got second or third hand information on both of them. So, to me, they're an irrelevant piece of information.'

Most significantly of all, Kathy insists that she was imbued with the highest moral values by her foster family. There were certain ways to behave and there were certain ways you didn't behave. 'We were brought up with a very strict idea of what was right and what was wrong. You don't tell lies, you help others, you know? All that sort of stuff.'

It was a moral compass that, in time, would be severely tested.

3
CHARMING AND SEDUCTIVE

It was 1985 and for the young, life in Australia seemed bright; Bob Hawke was Prime Minister, a new TV soap opera called *Neighbours* was launched, and *Mad Max 3* was on at the movies.

In June, on her eighteenth birthday, Kathy's life turned a corner. That very day, she heard that she had been offered a job as a console operator in the vehicle hiring section of a large Shell service station near where she lived. She was overjoyed. She was offered a wage of $136 a week, working Monday to Friday. It meant that she could finally break the shackles of her foster home and begin a new life of her own.

The shock of learning the awful truth about her father Thomas Britton had passed, and she was excited to spread her wings and live more independently. She had left high school six months before completing her final exams, and even Neville and Deidre were happy to learn that she would be earning a wage and not living on the dole – it meant that they wouldn't have to support her.

And for Kathy there was another huge and welcome development – as she turned eighteen, she was finally discharged from her wardship. She was no longer subject to the oversight of the state or, more importantly, subservient to the rules laid down by Deidre at home. Now at last she could run her own show.

For a brief period, Kathy remained at home, but by now she was wise to her mother's outbursts. She could see them building and knew that they would end with an argument or even a slap in the face. The final breakdown in their relationship followed an incident where she caught her mother's hand and stopped her in mid-slap. She warned Deidre never to do that again and left home, to go and live with a friend.

Nightclubs in those days were packed with partygoers with big hair, lots of hairspray, dressed to impress and dancing feverishly to recent hits like 'Crazy for You', 'Power of Love' and 'Take on Me'. It was then that Kathy met a young man in a Newcastle club, danced with him and fell in love with him. His name was Craig Folbigg.

Craig was tall, good looking and adept at complimenting Kathy. She described him as 'extremely charming', with 'the gift of the gab', and she fell for him hard. It was, by all accounts, a whirlwind romance, fuelled no doubt by Kathy's desire to break away from home, make her own decisions, and chart her own destiny.

He was twenty-four, six years her senior, and unlike Kathy, who had no blood relatives at all in her day-to-day life, Craig came from a large family of nine children. He had a well-paid job as a mobile crane operator at the local BHP steelworks. Kathy was smitten and impressed. He was her 'knight in shining armour'.

Craig, too, was smitten. 'I immediately felt attracted to Kathy as she was brash, cheeky, confident, sexy and attractive. We hit it off and started seeing each other on a regular basis,' he said.

A photo of the couple taken on an early date showed the two of them beaming, Kathy wearing a dark blouse with a yellow sweater and a pearl necklace, Craig in a white shirt and red sweater, his arm around her shoulder.

Kathy told him that she had a strained relationship with her foster mother, and when he met her parents, he thought they were strange. 'Deidre was dominating and bombastic, and Neville was quiet and subdued. Neither of them showed any affection towards Kathy and this was something that I was not used to seeing from family members,' he said later.

Tracy Chapman remembers the romance as being all-consuming. Kathy was gushing over Craig and had fallen head over heels in love. 'And I think it was the same for him with her as well.'

Tracy didn't see much of Kathy for a while after that. She wasn't keen on Craig and kept herself at a distance. 'I know she loved him. She was raving about him, so you just kind of withdraw because you want them to be happy.'

Kathy's foster sister Lea, by contrast, was happy with the love match. 'Kathy and Craig were just so suited for each other,' she says. 'Craig spoiled Kathy. He absolutely idolised her.'

In January 1986, Kathy moved in with Craig. And in August, just eight months later, Craig proposed to Kathy, and she accepted.

The young couple were able to buy a home in the Newcastle suburb of Mayfield, near the steelworks site where Craig was employed. They moved there in May 1987. It was a small two-bedroom weatherboard house, with a dining room, loungeroom and a sunroom at the front, and it was there that they planned their wedding.

Craig and his family, not unnaturally, wanted a big wedding, and when Neville and Deidre opposed this, it caused a painful split, which escalated to such an extent that none of Kathy's family, apart from Deidre, came to their marriage in September that year. And Deidre wasn't invited — she slipped into the marriage ceremony unannounced. Craig would later take responsibility for this, admitting that his relationship with Neville and Deidre had broken down.

Tracy Chapman, despite her dislike of Craig, wasn't even slightly surprised when Kathy married into his big, welcoming family. 'She just wanted to be part of a family. She loved kids, and my brothers and sisters were younger, so she fussed over them. I wasn't surprised when I found out she was engaged to be married really quickly.'

Kathy was just twenty years old, but even so, she wanted a family of her own. Tracy never had any doubts that she would have children, and lots of them. 'She always wanted to be a mum. So, from my perspective, she was just always destined to be a mother with children around her.'

Kathy and Craig started married life as so many couples do – with the wind in their sails and with high hopes for the future. 'Life was good, we were married, and we had heaps of fun,' Craig said later on.

The following year, to Kathy's great surprise and excitement, she fell pregnant. It wasn't planned, and later she would joke with Tracy that 'most women of the world are probably going to hate me for this, but I had perfect pregnancies. There were never any problems. I didn't even have morning sickness.'

In November, before she gave birth, Craig was awarded a compensation payout from BHP for an injury he had suffered and was able to use the money to pay off the mortgage to their home and other debts – no mean feat for such a young, newly married man. By this time, he was working at a local firm as a used car valuer.

There was one complication during Kathy's pregnancy – a 'fainting episode' resulting in a brief admission to hospital. The following day she had a 'rigor' – a shivering fit accompanied by a fever – and felt unwell.

But on 1 February 1989, her first child – a boy – was safely delivered at the Western Suburbs Hospital in Newcastle. The happy couple called him Caleb – derived from the Hebrew for 'faithful' or 'whole-hearted'. The birth itself wasn't easy – a sixteen- to eighteen-hour labour, followed by a forceps delivery with the help of an epidural, which Kathy would later describe as being 'a bit of a rough one'.

In a conversation with Tracy, Kathy described the moment she held Caleb, her heart racing, for the very first time: 'Seeing him, I just thought that's what I was on the planet for. I just thought I was supposed to meet a fella, get married, have a household, be a wife, have a dog, do the family. And I guess because of being a foster kid and a state ward, and all that sort of stuff, I thought family was supposed to be the ultimate important thing.'

Kathy felt very protective of Caleb. She would look at his face repeatedly and say to herself, 'I did it!' With Caleb, she felt complete. She had the husband, the home and a beautiful baby. 'I remember looking at him and thinking, "Oh, he's going to be a little me",' she told Tracy.

About fourteen hours after Caleb was born, he was examined in the hospital by a consultant paediatrician, Dr Barry Springthorpe, who noted that he had developed 'respiratory distress which required some oxygen through the night. This is quite a common occurrence in newborn children.' A chest X-ray was performed, which was clear, and his condition improved over the next couple of days.

Four days after he was born, on 5 February, Kathy and Craig took their brown-haired, blue-eyed boy home and he slept in a white cane bassinet which they had set up in the sunroom at the front of the house, next to their bedroom.

From the get-go, it wasn't Craig getting up in the middle of the night to take care of their newborn baby. Kathy later remarked, drily: 'You could let a bomb off under Craig and he would stay asleep. He's a very heavy sleeper once he's out.'

Kathy decided not to breast-feed Caleb and instead he was bottle-fed with Enfalac infant formula. But Craig had some concerns. He noticed that Caleb appeared to have trouble feeding and breathing at the same time. He would suck the teat, then stop to inhale a breath of air. 'To me, this appeared that he couldn't breathe and feed at the same time,' he remarked later.

Kathy, too, was concerned: 'While we were in hospital, we discovered it took him a little bit longer to actually feed than a normal baby ... he couldn't rely on his nose to give him all the air that he wanted. He would have to stop and start, and you would have to wait a minute for him to catch his breath and then he would start again.'

Two and a half weeks after he was born, on 17 February, Kathy took Caleb to see Dr Springthorpe again. The doctor noted that Caleb had an 'inspiratory stridor, so a stridor on breathing in, and some recession, which is sinking in of the chest cage, but no change of colour, no cyanosis, no gagging associated with it'. The stridor, or noisy breathing, he concluded, was 'very, very mild'. It was most marked when Caleb was upset or lying flat on his back. Significantly, Dr Springthorpe felt that the stridor was due to a 'soft larynx, so-called laryngomalacia', colloquially known as a 'floppy larynx'.

A handwritten diary Kathy kept at the time demonstrated the meticulous preparations she made for her newborn baby's arrival, and the equally meticulous way she cared for him, hour by hour.

On Saturday, 18 February, Kathy recorded seven periods of sleep, interspersed with feeds. There was no obvious indication from her notes that anything was wrong with her baby.

The next day, Kathy and Craig took Caleb to visit Craig's brother John and his family at their home at Charlestown. They arrived home at around 8 pm that night, with Caleb asleep. Kathy changed him into a cloth nappy, a singlet and a yellow jumpsuit. She put him into his cot in the sunroom.

At about 10 pm or 10.30 pm, Craig and Kathy went into the sunroom, where Caleb was asleep in his cot. He was wrapped in a 'bunny' rug with a white blanket over him. It was February – Australia's summer – but the house was cold and draughty. 'I kissed Caleb on the forehead as did Kathy and we went to bed,' Craig said later. 'The door adjoining our room and the sunroom was left open. There was a lamp in the sunroom which we left on all night for when Kathy had to get up to feed Caleb.'

Kathy would sit on a loungeroom chair with Caleb when she fed him, and that night was no exception. 'He was asleep in my arms before I had gotten out of the chair ... by the time I had stood up off the lounge and walked into the bedroom to go and lay him down he was asleep.' She placed him in the bassinet, went back to bed and drifted off to sleep.

At around 1 am on Monday 20 February, Kathy wrote the words: 'Put back to sleep?' and 'a bit restless', in her diary, before adding the words 'Finally Asleep!!' at 2 am.

About fifty minutes later, she stirred and went to check on Caleb. 'You can hear babies breathing, they are very definite in how they take a breath,' she said later. 'So, when I didn't hear that, I thought, "What have you done, have you rolled over or something?" And I just placed my hand on his chest and didn't feel it rise ... he just didn't seem to be moving, didn't stir, didn't do anything. So, I flicked on a light and noticed that he wasn't breathing and then it was just panic from there.'

Kathy said that there was blood and froth around his nose and that Caleb was 'blue around the lips and pale, and for him that was totally unusual because he was a bit like me, he had a dark, olivey skin'. She remembers throwing the covers off him, wrapping her arms around him and grabbing him, scooping him out of the bassinet.

In his own formal statement made later on, Craig gave a slightly different account of what occurred:

'After going to sleep, the next thing I remember is waking up in bed and hearing Kathy screaming: "My baby, something is wrong with my baby!" I jumped out of bed and ran into the sunroom, where I saw Kathy standing over the cot in her pyjamas. She was just standing there, screaming and holding her hands on her forehead.

'I ran up to the cot and saw Caleb laying on his back and he was still wrapped in the "bunny" rug. He had a blue colouring to his lips around his mouth and his eyes were closed. I picked him up by placing my hands underneath his head and buttocks. As I picked him up, I felt that his skin was still warm. As he laid in my arms, I placed my mouth over his mouth and blew into his mouth. At that time, I didn't know the correct CPR procedures. While I was doing that, I said to Kathy: "Just ring the ambulance." She was just standing there screaming.

'Kathy ran into our bedroom, and I heard her talking on the telephone. I don't remember her exact words, but she said that her baby wasn't breathing, and she said our address. I carried Caleb into the loungeroom, and I placed him on the lounge. I kneeled over him and continued blowing into his mouth.'

Dave Hopkins was one of the officers in the ambulance that raced to the scene after Kathy had raised the alarm, arriving at 2.59 am. He quickly established that Caleb had suffered a cardiac arrest, was unconscious and no longer breathing; there was no pulse. He noted that Caleb's body was still warm to the touch – but another ambulance officer reported it as being cold to the touch.

Mr Hopkins found Caleb's airway was 'obstructed', possibly by fluid or saliva, which needed to be cleared before a Guedel airway could be inserted in a last-ditch attempt to bring Kathy's baby back to life. But all attempts to revive the nineteen-day-old infant failed, and an ECG monitor showed that Caleb's heart had stopped beating.

'At this time the young man and woman appeared totally distraught,' Mr Hopkins reported. 'They were both crying. We continued resuscitation attempts until it became clear that a successful outcome was not possible.'

Dave Hopkins encouraged Kathy to hold her baby for a final time. He completed his ambulance report, indicating that in his opinion, the cause of death was Sudden Infant Death Syndrome, or SIDS. 'I did not see or hear anything that night that raised any suspicion towards the parents of the baby,' he reported.

A few hours later, in a brief, sad statement signed at Mayfield police station, Kathy said: 'On the 2 February 1989, I gave birth to Caleb, this morning at around 1 am I fed Caleb, I then put him to bed. About 2.50 am I checked him, I usually do this a few times through the night however this time I found him to be cold and I called my husband, and we then called the Ambulance.'

In a poignant postscript, she said: 'Caleb was always healthy, I had no problems with him, I took him to see Dr Springthorpe on the 17th of this month, he was alright, the doctor said he had a Lazy Larynx, he said it was nothing to worry about.'

Underneath were typed the words: 'I DO/DO NOT Desire an inquest.' The word 'DO' was crossed through, and Kathy's signature was next to it. No inquest would take place, but a postmortem examination of the body was performed at Newcastle City Morgue.

The findings were that Caleb, a brown-haired, blue-eyed boy, was a well-developed, well-nourished infant whose stomach contained a large quantity of curdled milk. There were no external signs of injury, and the forensic pathologist who conducted the postmortem said that Caleb appeared to have been well cared for. The cause of death was given as SIDS.

Less than three weeks later, Craig wrote a letter to his boy. It was filled with despair, but also, imbued with hope for their family.

Kathy, grief-stricken, retreated from everyone around her. In a terrible attempt to console her, a priest told her, 'Your child was chosen by God as an angel.' Caleb's ashes were interred in the local crematorium's Remembrance Wall, and while Craig visited them often, Kathy never did.

To begin with, she felt numb, in a state of disbelief and detachment. Then, she channelled her energy into day-to-day activities. She started doing up the house, she took their two dogs on long walks, and later, went back to work at an Indian restaurant.

No one suspected foul play, and no one blamed Craig or Kathy for what had happened.

Kathy found the strength to spend time with a neighbour who had a newborn child, and she and Craig received grief and genetic counselling, as well as advice about SIDS, at Waratah Hospital. They were told there was no reason to expect that a second child would die.

4
'MIXED FEELINGS'

The grief of losing Caleb so suddenly and soon after he was born was only ameliorated by the tentative discussions Craig and Kathy had about having a second child. The general consensus among family and friends was that 'it only happens once', and Kathy's close friend Megan, who saw a lot of her at the time, remembers telling her that.

So when Kathy, unexpectedly, fell pregnant again, she felt apprehensive, but also excited. As she later explained it to Tracy, her second child 'was actually a mistake. We weren't planning another one straight away. So, he wasn't anticipated, but we were extremely happy, and we thought: "Okay, we get another chance, this is good."'

For Craig, a strong reason to go ahead was that: 'We felt that we needed this to get over Caleb's death. This was not an attempt to replace Caleb, but we wanted a family and we wanted to be happy.'

Kathy and Craig set to work renovating their home, and by the time their second child was born, it was freshly painted, with a new garage, new floors and carpeting, and a new window in the sunroom.

'We were helping each other as couples with renovating houses, knocking down sheds and garages and stuff when she was pregnant,' Megan recalls. 'And there was lots of visiting backwards and forwards; big dinners at each other's house depending on who was helping who.'

Kathy was anxious to ensure that any risks associated with

SIDS would be lessened. She saw a different obstetrician, bought better bedding and carefully prepared the nursery.

She even explored the health risks posed by the fact that the house they lived in was close to the BHP steelworks at Mayfield, and the contaminated site around it. As with Caleb, she was taking every possible precaution to ensure that her baby, when he arrived, would be healthy and thrive.

On 3 June 1990, Kathy gave birth to her second son, Patrick, at the same Newcastle hospital where Caleb was born. 'Kathy and I were overcome with happiness,' Craig said later. The baby was blond-haired and blue-eyed, and they thought he looked like Craig.

The birth itself was easier than Caleb's, but Craig had gone off to work that morning and when Kathy went into labour, she couldn't reach him, so she called his brother who lived around the corner, and he came over in his Volvo and drove her to hospital.

Some time afterwards, Kathy wrote in her diary that this was the day Patrick Allan David Folbigg was born. She remarked that she had 'mixed feelings' whether she was going to cope, or whether she would get stressed 'like I did last time'.

She added, cryptically, 'I often regret Caleb & Patrick' but qualified the remark by saying that this was only because when you have a child, your life changes so much, and she thought perhaps she wasn't a person who liked change.

Objectively it might seem like a strange thing to write, but like everything she wrote in her journals over the years, these were her own private thoughts, not intended for public consumption.

Meanwhile, Kathy and Craig and the doctors were taking every possible precaution, and to their relief, the results of an early sleep study, on 14 June, Kathy's birthday, were normal.

In the first few months of his life, Patrick did well. He was feeding noisily and happily and was only waking up once during the night by the time he was three months old. He had a routine of going to sleep around midnight or 1 am and not waking up until 6 am.

As she had done with Caleb, Kathy monitored his sleep patterns and recorded them in a diary.

To Kathy and Craig's relief, there were no problems with Patrick's breathing, and no problems with his health in general. 'He was great,' Kathy said later. Patrick seemed well ... until the night of 17 October 1990. That evening, Kathy fed him and put him into his cot at about 8.30 pm. Patrick was wearing a cloth nappy, pilchers, singlet and a pair of cotton pyjamas.

Two hours later, Craig went into Patrick's room and saw him lying on his back in the cot, covered with a sheet and a blanket. He was asleep. 'I kissed him and went to bed with Kathy. The lamp in his room was left on in case Kathy had to get up.'

Kathy, sitting in a soft chair in the loungeroom, gave Patrick his midnight feed of infant formula, put him back to bed on his side and went back to bed herself, but later, heard him coughing and went in to settle him down. At about 4.30 am, she got up to go to the toilet.

As she did so, she checked on Patrick. 'I was listening for his breathing and noticed that it was laboured,' she explained later. Patrick was gasping for air; it was a 'very scary sound'.

'It was as if he was trying very hard to draw a breath. So I immediately flung on a light and we've gone into action from there. He was lethargic, not really responsive, the eyes were shut, and he was just trying to take a breath.' Kathy saw that he was slightly blue around the lips. 'My first thought was, "Not again!"' She remembers scooping him up and running back through the house to their bedroom, calling Craig.

Soon after this, Patrick gave a high-pitched cry. 'It was rather scary. Again, I've called for Craig.'

Craig remembered waking up in bed to the sound of Kathy screaming, and as with Caleb, his memory differed from hers:

'I rushed into Patrick's room, and I saw Kathy standing in front of the cot. The rail on the cot was in the up position. I looked into the cot and saw Patrick laying on his back ... His eyes were closed, he was pale, and his arms, legs and body were limp. I picked him up in my arms and screamed at Kathy to ring the ambulance. She ran out of the room.

'I held Patrick's mouth up to my ear and I heard faint laboured breathing. Not knowing what else to do, I laid him flat on the floor in the room and I started blowing in his mouth and nose to assist his breathing. I kept doing this until the ambulance officers arrived at my house.'

Twenty minutes after Kathy raised the alarm, the ambulance arrived, and rushed Patrick and Kathy to Mater Hospital nearby. Kathy remembers a paramedic administering oxygen and as soon as that happened, Patrick's eyes shot open. 'It must have been an instant shot of oxygen to the brain.'

At Mater Hospital at 5 am, Patrick was seen by a paediatrician, Dr Joseph Dezordi. The baby was still lethargic. Again, he was treated with oxygen, and again, according to Kathy, 'it was just like switching on a light switch. One minute he was laying on the bed in the hospital not being responsive, and the next minute it was, like, bang! He was just awake and screaming and panicking. He must have been in some sort of deep sleep state and all of a sudden there's bright lights and there's people with white coats hangin' around and things on him and things on his chest and he just sort of freaked. Then the time that we spent in hospital from there, was trying to figure out what actually happened.'

The doctors found no sign of any upper airway obstruction or pneumonia, and no indication that Patrick was suffering from any serious illness, including meningitis. Importantly, there was no evidence of any physical trauma or visible injuries.

But there were other worrying signs. He vomited three times, and he was arching his back. And tests showed a significant level of glucose – or glycosuria – in Patrick's urine, which, in the absence of a high blood sugar level, was thought by Dr Dezordi to be a response to 'an acute asphyxiating event' – in his opinion, possibly a seizure of some kind.

By the following day he seemed to have recovered, but that night in hospital he had another seizure, and further fits and convulsions ensued. One of the seizures occurred when Craig was holding Patrick in his arms. More tests followed, including a CT scan of the brain which Dr Dezordi said had an 'abnormal' result. 'It was not really clear what the cause of these unusual CT scan findings were,' he commented later.

Eleven days after his admission to hospital, Patrick was discharged; the doctors decided that he was suffering from a seizure disorder and a respiratory tract infection. But six days later, on 4 November, he was readmitted to hospital, suffering a prolonged seizure. A lumbar puncture was carried out, and a further CT scan. Dr Dezordi noted that this scan demonstrated abnormalities already seen on the previous scan – but they had worsened. It showed a 'loss of brain substance', which 'was not really clear to any of the medical staff'.

Patrick was readmitted to hospital in mid-November, after suffering yet another seizure. Two days later, Dr Dezordi forwarded the two scans and a letter to an expert radiologist at a children's hospital in Sydney, Professor Merl De Silva, to ask for his opinion.

The professor studied the scans, and the two specialists had a phone conversation. Professor De Silva said that in his opinion, the changes in the CT scans were not classic signs of encephalitis. Then he said something that stunned Dr Dezordi: 'Have you considered child abuse?'

'What do you mean?' Dr Dezordi asked.

'Such as shaking,' the professor replied.

Dr Dezordi immediately telephoned another senior doctor at the hospital, Dr Ian Wilkinson. The following morning, together with Dr Wilkinson and a third doctor, he went to the baby's ward at Mater Hospital where they spoke with Kathy and Craig.

There, on Craig's birthday they delivered the terrible news that Patrick was now officially blind. He had lost the ability to focus on faces, or to follow an object with his eyes, and had a degree of cortical blindness, which can be caused by seizures. 'So that was a great birthday present for Craig,' Kathy later recalled.

As if that news wasn't shattering enough, Dr Wilkinson then told the disbelieving parents what Professor De Silva had said. 'We are not really entirely sure what the problem has been, but the possibility of a non-accidental injury or child abuse was raised. Has there been any foul play?'

'No!' Kathy and Craig replied, indignantly. The allegation of baby shaking went no further, neither then, nor at any time thereafter.

Craig would claim in a formal statement that sometime after this he was at home when he saw an A5-sized diary with a brown cover on the bedside table next to where Kathy slept. He opened it and started reading it.

'I read that Kathy did not want to cope with what we were going through, it was all too much, and she was going to leave Patrick and I. I was totally devastated by this and that same day, I told my sister Carol about the diary, and she came over to my house. I told her what I had read, and she sat down with Kathy and I, and we discussed the fact that Kathy couldn't just run away and hide. Kathy agreed to stay and work things out. From this point on, Carol spent a fair bit of time trying to assist Kathy and I through these problem times.'

Without doubt, Patrick's brain injury and the seizures that may have caused it made life much harder for Kathy and Craig. It had left the little boy suffering from epilepsy; he was taking anticonvulsant medicine and he was – to quote Craig – 'a handful'. But Kathy devoted herself to caring for him and trying to help him thrive.

'We had to try and teach him how to feed and drink and do all the rest of it, knowing that he couldn't see. It was hard work, but Craig and I were so relieved that he had survived,' Kathy said. 'We had to take him to different specialists to try and figure out how blind he was. You'd swear he was looking at you while you were trying to talk to him and then the next minute, you'd look at him and he'd be looking through you, or past you.'

Kathy took Patrick to occupational therapists at Mater Hospital every week for physiotherapy, to help him learn how to crawl. The doctors seemed pleased with his progress, and Kathy and Craig started talking about the special schools he would need to go to later on.

At home, when he was in and out of hospital and most unwell, they would have him with them in the main bedroom, in his cot next to their bed; when he seemed to be better, they would put him in his own bedroom, to give everyone a bit of space.

As Kathy saw it, Patrick wasn't weighed down by his disabilities; on the contrary, she took joy in the fact that he was a spirited, determined boy.

'Even with all his medical issues and all of his problems with epilepsy and his blindness, I thought "he's going to be a risk taker, I can just see it" because he would just roll around the floor with no concept that he might be banging into things or going and getting himself stuck under something or just hurt himself in any fashion. He would just go for it. With him there was no stopping him from discovering things even though he couldn't see. He was very tactile and hands-on.'

Craig would later describe Kathy as suffering from 'extreme anxiety and what I thought was depression', because of the extra load placed on her by caring for Patrick. 'She wasn't coping, she had to have other people to help because she couldn't do these things herself. On occasions, Kathy would get stressed and upset over the smallest of things and I was worried about this. I was also going through a lot of emotional turmoil, but I loved both my wife and our son.'

Megan Donegan, however, who was extremely close to Kathy, disagrees with Craig's opinion of his wife's state of mind: 'Kathy was doing lots of doctor's visits, there were visits with the blind association, and she was telling me about what had happened during the day with his appointments, and there was never any anger, or frustration, or not wanting to do all that.'

Kathy acknowledged later that she thought she was 'on autopilot' a lot of the time. From her point of view, the extra care she needed to give Patrick wasn't an issue because they were so happy that he had survived the 'near-miss' event. She would look in on Craig's sister Carol after going to the hospital, and every now and then Carol would help with the occupational therapy for Patrick.

By the time he was eight months old, Patrick was sleeping from 6 pm until 6 am, when he and Craig would get up and, sometimes, have breakfast together. After Craig left for work at 7.30 am, Patrick would have a bath and be changed. He would stay close to Kathy, who didn't want to let him out of her sight.

On 12 February 1991, Patrick had a fever in the evening and Kathy and Craig wondered if he had had another seizure. But he slept well, and the next morning he had milk and toast and Vegemite for breakfast and played with his dad, before Craig left for work. Shortly afterwards, Kathy put Patrick down for a sleep.

Not long afterwards, she walked into Patrick's room to find him lying flat on his back, which made her look twice because she always used to lay him on his side in the cot, and he would stay there — he was a heavy sleeper, like his dad. 'My first thought was, "Not another fit", because we hadn't had any for a while and we seemed to be going okay.'

But he wasn't breathing.

At 10 am Craig had a telephone call from Kathy: 'It's happened again!' she screamed down the phone. 'What's happened? Another fit? Have you rung the ambulance?'

'Yes,' she answered.

Agonisingly, Kathy told Megan that the ambulances were held up because of roadworks in the area. 'She said all she could hear was the ambulances driving in the street, but they couldn't get to the house because it had recently had road changes and streets had been blocked off in that area of Mayfield. They could hear the ambulances circling but they couldn't find their way to the house, and she said it was made worse by knowing they were out there but they couldn't get to her.'

Craig raced home to see the ambulances arriving. 'I saw Patrick laying on his back in his cot. I reached down and took him in my arms. I rushed him into the loungeroom and placed him on his back on the floor. I started trying to resuscitate him by blowing in his mouth and nose. His whole body was limp, he had a blue colouring around his lips, but he was still warm to touch.'

One of the ambulance officers described the scene as she

walked in the front door with two other officers. 'I saw a woman sitting on a lounge and she was hysterical. She had her hands up to her face and she was crying out and sobbing. I walked past her and into another room. I saw a man kneeling over a small baby. I think this man was attempting CPR on the child.' As she took over from Craig, she noted that Patrick was warm to the touch and that Patrick's breathing was shallow. But the baby's respiration rate was recorded as nil, and the other two officers reported that he wasn't breathing when they were there.

As the ambulance sped on its way to Mater Hospital, Kathy was hoping desperately that the paramedics could resuscitate Patrick, but it wasn't to be. For twenty minutes, as his parents looked on, doctors tried frantically to save him, and at 10.40 am, death was pronounced. Dr Wilkinson told Kathy and Craig that Patrick had died, and it was futile to continue to try and revive him. They were inconsolable.

Dr Wilkinson believed that Patrick could have suffered an epileptic fit, resulting in obstruction of his airways, or asphyxia. There appeared to be no suspicious circumstances, and he saw no evidence of foul play.

Craig gave permission for an autopsy to be carried out. This revealed no external abnormalities, but an examination of Patrick's brain showed signs of the seizures he had suffered, and of an earlier cardio-respiratory arrest.

About a week later, Patrick was cremated, and his ashes were interred alongside Caleb's.

Kathleen, consumed by grief, retreated into herself. She had shut down emotionally and became severely depressed, convinced that she had failed as a mother. And as her depression deepened, she stopped exercising and started to put on weight.

Then one day, she walked in on Craig in a romantic clinch with one of her best friends. She reacted angrily; she was at her lowest point, and it left her feeling betrayed, unattractive and vulnerable.

But despite everything, she hadn't abandoned her desire for a family.

5

'THE CHEEKIEST ONE EVER'

Craig and Kathy's house in Mayfield, comfortable and homely as it was, was overlaid with tragedy, and after Patrick died, Kathy told her husband she wanted to move.

Dr Ian Wilkinson met up with them and told them that Patrick had most probably died from an epileptic fit, which offered some comfort to Kathy.

'Compared to Craig, I accepted the reasons that we were given for why the children died far easier than he did,' Kathy says. 'SIDS for Caleb. Patrick, we were told, it was his epilepsy, so I sort of thought, "Well, at least that's a reason that I can cling on to."'

Not long afterwards, Kathy went to work part time as a sales assistant at a retail store called BabyCo in Kotara, where she had grown up and gone to school. It was a one-stop shop for everything a pregnant mum needs in planning the arrival of a child, and for their newborn. It was a brave thing to do, so soon after losing Patrick, but in one sense it wasn't surprising.

Megan's husband, Tim – who knew Craig, having worked with him at BHP and been taught by Craig's father at high school – hired Kathy to work there.

Kathy's reasoning seems to have been that moving home would give them a fresh start and help to dissipate the unbearable flashbacks of Caleb's and Patrick's deaths. Plus, the sooner she exposed herself to other mums and dads and their babies, the sooner she might return to some sort of normal life.

Her approach to her children's deaths mirrored the way she had dealt with previous challenges. The act of internalising her grief and behaving as if everything was 'normal' was a form of self-protection and something which – from her very earliest days – she had learned to do, whenever she was faced with harsh, life-altering events.

To Craig, however, consumed for months by his own overwhelming grief, and coming as he did from a large and social family, her behaviour seemed odd at best and, at times, incomprehensible.

'She appeared to get on with her life quite easily and this worried me. I was still grieving for our dead children and Kathy never looked back,' he complained later on. 'I couldn't understand how she could work at BabyCo and deal with babies and pregnant women all the time.'

Whatever his private concerns were, Craig accepted his wife's decision, and he didn't stand in her way when Kathy told him she wanted them to leave their Mayfield home. They moved to a modest three-bedroom home in the suburb of Thornton, around twenty kilometres further out of Newcastle. It was much closer to Beresfield cemetery where Caleb's and Patrick's ashes were interred.

In late 1991, Kathy told her husband that she wanted to be a mother again. At twenty-four, she had endured more pain than most women do in a lifetime, and yet she was still young. Long discussions ensued. Craig felt very uncertain; he too wanted another child but told her: 'There were things I never wanted to see and hear again. I never wanted to see another dead baby and I never wanted to hear that scream of Kathy's.'

Eventually, things came to a head and, according to Craig, Kathy gave him an ultimatum – they would have a baby, or she would leave him. Craig agreed on the understanding that this time, they would seek help from medical experts, in an effort to prevent a third tragedy. Later on, Kathy would comment that: 'We were still flying blind, so it was a leap of faith, I suppose, in trying again.'

Kathy was making a Herculean effort to return to some kind of normality. Far from getting on with life 'quite easily', as

Craig had suggested, she never forgot her children or stopped grieving for them; a diary entry on 1 February 1992 said simply: 'CALEBS 3yrs ANNIVERSARY'.

That same month, Kathy fell pregnant. It was welcome news for her and for Craig, and they celebrated the new direction that their life together was taking.

Megan, her comrade in arms, fell pregnant soon afterwards, and both were treated by the same obstetrician, Dr Michael Holland. Megan jokes that: 'We'd make our appointments for one after each other because we couldn't tie our own shoelaces up, and after the appointment we could tie each other's shoelaces up and hang out for the rest of the day.'

Kathy finished work at the end of August and busied herself by cleaning the cupboards at home and defrosting the fridge. She was looking forward to spending more time at home. But Craig was feeling unsettled: 'Worried about Craig, he's expressed deep concern over baby etc. Getting very anxious about baby now not long to go!' Kathy wrote in her journal on 31 August.

But any doubts that Craig might have harboured about the strength of their relationship would have been dispelled if he had read the entry she wrote on 5 September: 'WEDDING ANNIVERSARY. Unbelievable 5 yrs. I've known Craig 7 years How your life goes by! No regrets, love him more now, than I ever did!'

The stress, anxiety, excitement and anticipation were building, and at 6.30 am on 14 October 1992, Kathy's third child was born at the John Hunter Hospital in Newcastle. Sarah weighed in at just over three kilograms and all the tests showed she was healthy.

To begin with, the baby was nursed on an apnoea mattress and Kathy breast-fed her. Both parents were trained in CPR and Kathy and Craig asked for an early baptism for their daughter. Everything pointed to a heightened sense of alertness and anxiety on their part, and a focused effort on the doctors' part to help prevent another tragedy.

Five days after she was born, Craig took Sarah and Kathy home to Thornton, armed with an apnoea alarm to track Sarah's breathing and heart rate when she slept. The monitor was designed to set off an alarm if her breathing stopped, or if her heart rate slowed excessively.

At home, Sarah was fed bottled formula, and to begin with, slept in a crib next to her parents' bed. Later on, she slept in a cot in her own bedroom, next to Kathy and Craig's bedroom. They put an apnoea blanket under the mattress in the cot, to detect the baby's movements during sleep, but it caused real problems, because it kept on being activated, even though there was never a crisis.

Every time they checked on her after the alarm went off, Sarah was asleep and breathing normally. Craig admitted that it was harrowing for them both when the alarm went off, but he insisted they continue to use the apnoea mattress, 'as I wanted to do everything possible to keep Sarah alive'. Every time the blanket set off the alarm, it added to Kathy's anxiety.

But their life wasn't all stressful. Kathy and Megan shared a close bond, and a similar sense of humour about their children. Megan was living in Mayfield, only fifteen minutes away from Kathy in Thornton.

'Sarah was five weeks older than my Alex,' Megan says. 'So, we hung out together when the babies were little. I got a phone call one day from Kathy saying your son's left his bib in my daughter's cot. I don't want to have him leaving anything else in my daughter's bed until he's at least eighteen! It was jokes about them being boyfriend and girlfriend when they grow up. There were plans for the future. She was a good mum.'

In Kathy, Megan saw a mother who was so protective of her daughter that she wouldn't leave her for long with anyone who didn't understand how to use the apnoea monitor. She had a hard time trusting babysitters, and she asked Alex's godmother, a registered nurse, to babysit for her while she worked at BabyCo.

But Megan also noticed a darker side to Craig's relationship with Kathy. She remembers standing with Craig on the back deck of their house in Thornton while he had a smoke. Kathy said something to him, and he replied: 'I have two fat sisters; I don't need a fat wife.' Kathy at the time was unhappy with her weight, which had increased when she was pregnant with Sarah, and she talked about it privately to Megan a number of times. Megan regarded these remarks by Craig – often in front of others – as a way of humiliating her, perhaps in an effort to shame her into losing weight.

Kathy also feared that Craig was 'sniffing around elsewhere', which Megan took to mean that he might be having affairs. But Sarah made her happy, and Kathy loved the way she behaved, saying that she 'was the cheekiest one ever – run around sticking her tongue out at you if she thought that was going to get a laugh!'

Craig suggested later that he noticed the 'ease' with which Kathy became irritated and stressed with him, with Sarah 'and our life. I constantly badgered her to mellow out, as Sarah was just a baby and how could Sarah deliberately intend to irritate anybody?'

But Megan, who spent a lot of time with Kathy, disagrees. She remembers how attentive Kathy was to her daughter's needs, and how careful she was only to leave Sarah in the hands of people who were qualified to act in an emergency.

'She was very attentive, possibly overcompensating for what had happened with Caleb and Patrick. I never looked after Sarah. I didn't have any CPR training and I didn't take any offence that she wouldn't leave Sarah with me. But she was insistent that anyone that did look after Sarah knew how to do CPR. We spent days together, but I never had Sarah on my own.'

Sarah's health in her first few months was closely monitored by doctors. An early sleep study showed very few episodes of sleep apnoea, but a month after Sarah was born, a doctor noted that she was exhibiting periods of hypoventilation or breathing at an abnormally slow rate. The doctor recommended a drug to open up the air passages in her lungs, making it easier to breathe.

Kathy remembers Sarah as a baby with definite sleep issues. 'She got nicknamed the catnapper because she wouldn't sleep for any longer than fifteen or twenty minutes at a time. She was a shocker that way. Even during the night, I would be lucky to get, probably, three hours straight out of her. Even the older she got; she was always the same.'

When she was three months old, Sarah seemed well and was developing normally, but even so, Kathy and Craig were understandably anxious, even slightly paranoid. At four and a half months, Sarah contracted a viral respiratory infection, but was otherwise thriving. Kathy asked for a further sleep study – Sarah's third. On 18 August 1993, Sarah was prescribed an antibiotic for a cold-like illness, but after a week or so, her parents stopped trying to administer it because it was too difficult to do so. A week later Sarah was seen by a doctor for a croupy cough.

Three days after that, Sarah was still under the weather with a runny nose and what Craig described as flu-like symptoms. But she didn't seem particularly unwell, and Kathy remembers it as being a really good day.

To begin with, she and Craig took Sarah to Nobbys Beach, a favourite with local Newcastle families, where you can swim, surf and, on a good day, spot the dolphins playing. Afterwards, they went to visit Craig's brother John at his home, and later, took Sarah to picturesque Maitland Park for the very first time. 'She had a ball, she was crawling around and getting into things, and so we were nice and relaxed and had a really, really top day actually,' Kathy recalls.

As the afternoon light faded, they headed home. Craig too recalled it as being a good day.

But from that point on, Kathy's and Craig's memories of the evening would diverge.

Kathy recalled the early part of the evening fondly. 'She used to have a bath of an evening. One of the fun things she used to like to do was stand at the side of the bath while I was running it, and we used to put the old bubbles in and do all that sort of routine, and she'd get all excited, and so bathtime used to be a good, fun time.'

Usually, Sarah would have dinner and then play with Craig for quite a while. 'And of course, he used to get into trouble for revving her up that much! I used to think that partly the reason why she wouldn't go to sleep happily and easily was, he used to rev her up that much, that she just decided, I want to keep playing and not go to bed.'

Craig remembers Sarah having a bath that evening and Kathy dressing her before they had dinner. Afterwards they watched television before putting Sarah to sleep.

They decided that night that Sarah should sleep in her own single bed, rather than in her cot.

They were both still paranoid about what might happen to her when she slept, and so they put the single bed in their bedroom, believing that Sarah would be safer sleeping in the same room as them. But with all the problems associated with the apnoea blanket, they had stopped using it.

Kathy's memory is that Sarah 'actually slept for a couple of hours before waking up again'. Then she got out of bed and Kathy left her with Craig in the living room and went to bed herself.

Craig's version, from a later statement he made, is that, as Kathy took Sarah into their bedroom, he heard Sarah start to cry and carry on, because she didn't want to go to bed. 'This made Kathy angry, which was evident to me by Kathy making an angry, growling noise. I heard this from where I was sitting, and I had heard it many times before with Sarah and Patrick. I went up to the room and said: "What's the problem?" Kathy said: "Nothing. Get out." I said: "How about mellowing out? She is only a bloody baby; if she doesn't want to go to sleep, just leave her be." She said: "Just go away. She'll go to sleep if I say."'

Craig said he remembered hearing a noise that sounded like Kathy stomping down the hall. 'She came into the loungeroom, and she was carrying Sarah in her arms and Sarah was crying. Kathy stood about three paces in front of where I was sitting on the lounge. She moved her arms forward and let go of Sarah, causing Sarah to fall into my lap and I had to catch her. I had never seen Kathy do this before and it alarmed me. She was definitely angry and irrational.'

Craig said that he settled Sarah down and put her into her bed in their room before 11 pm that night. 'I placed the sheet and blanket over her body and laid her on her back on the mattress. I kissed her goodnight and I got into my bed after turning off the light in the room. Kathy was either asleep or ignoring me.'

Craig, who admitted that he was an extremely heavy sleeper, would later give two radically different versions of what occurred early the next morning. In one version, he claimed – most unusually – to have woken up at 1 am to see Sarah in her bed, and Kathy out of the room, and in the other version, he said that neither Sarah nor Kathy were in the room when he woke up.

Kathy's own clear recollection was that in the early hours of the morning she got up to go to the toilet and as she did so, glanced over to where Sarah was in her bed. On the way back, she took another look and saw that Sarah hadn't moved. What particularly caught her attention was that Sarah was lying flat on her back, 'and one of her arms just seemed to be hanging out'. She went over to check that her daughter was warm enough and to cover her up, as she used to kick the covers off while sleeping.

That's when she realised that she couldn't hear Sarah breathing. She screamed, and Craig woke up and started performing CPR in yet another frantic effort to revive an apparently lifeless baby.

Kathy rang for an ambulance, and Deb Martin, the first ambulance officer to arrive, was met by Kathy, sobbing, at the front door. She told Kathy to help Craig, and Kathy started doing heart compressions while Craig breathed air into Sarah's lungs. Sarah was dressed in a little ski suit; her lips were blue and she wasn't breathing. Her heart had stopped completely.

The ambulance officer administered adrenaline, to try and restart her heart. When the paramedics arrived, they administered more drugs designed to kickstart her heart, but without success.

Craig continued CPR for five or ten minutes, while Kathy came and knelt beside him.

When more ambulance officers arrived, Craig and Kathy went into the loungeroom, distraught and in tears.

Forty minutes after Deb Martin arrived, at about 2.10 am, the paramedics knew that Sarah couldn't be saved.

As stipulated in the paramedics' protocols, the police were called, and Deb Martin cut Sarah's ski suit off her body, to give to them as evidence. There were no marks on her body. As they waited for the police to arrive, Kathy dressed Sarah in a yellow track suit and pink slippers and wrapped her in a crocheted blanket. She told the ambulance officer about her two other cot deaths: both of them boys. She added: 'They think that I have some sort of genetic abnormality in my male children, so I am surprised that I've lost a girl.'

Craig told the ambulance officer: 'We've recently moved Sarah from the apnoea monitor, which we got from the SIDS Foundation. We took her off it, because it kept alarming, she was rolling off it.'

By the time the police arrived, Sarah's skin was a pale cream colour, and her eyes were closed. An inverted U-shaped mark on the bridge of her nose had been made by the oxygen mask which was used to try and revive her. Craig, sitting on the lounge, was holding her. One of the officers, a senior constable, said that Kathy and Craig appeared 'genuinely very distressed and the emotional withdrawal of the mother Kathleen during the time of attendance at the home was distressing to witness'.

The officers questioned Craig and Kathy about the circumstances leading up to Sarah's death, noting that their home was 'clean and well presented'. Craig told the police that Sarah had been considered as a high risk of SIDS, following the deaths of Caleb and Patrick. He handed an officer a bottle containing a small amount of an antibiotic medicine which they had been giving Sarah for the flu-type illness she had been suffering from.

Deb Martin took Sarah's body in her ambulance to Maitland Hospital and handed her over to the nursing staff, where at 4.30 am, she was pronounced deceased.

Later, the body was taken to the New South Wales Coroner's Court in Sydney, where a postmortem was carried out by one of the state's pre-eminent forensic pathologists, Professor John Hilton.

Professor Hilton gave the cause of death as SIDS, and subsequent microscopic examination of samples taken from the body confirmed that the lungs showed some congestion and oedema — fluid in the air sacs which make it difficult to breathe and can be caused by heart problems.

Kathy hadn't written in her diary since January, but for 30 August 1993 she recorded a time, prefaced by three forlorn words: 'Sarah left us. 1 am.'

Sarah was ten and a half months old when she died, and like Caleb and Patrick before her, she was laid to rest in Beresfield Crematorium.

A couple of days after Sarah died, Craig asked Kathy what had happened that night before she woke him, screaming. She replied: 'I had been to the toilet and just flicked on the light to check on the baby, and the rest you know.'

Later, what exactly happened that night would become the subject of intense and prolonged evidentiary and legal argument.

6

'THIS LAST ONE HAS BROKEN ME'

Even now, Megan weeps whenever she talks about Sarah's passing.

'We got the phone call early in the morning; it was still dark. And I ended up heading into work anyway and was sent home within half an hour. I was a mess. I was given two Valium and knocked out for twenty-four hours. And I couldn't attend the funeral. I was too distraught.'

Megan did everything she could to support her lifelong friend. In the days after Sarah died, and before the funeral, Megan and her husband Tim asked if they could visit her with Alex, and Kathy said yes. When they got there, Craig pointed to Sarah's handprints on a sliding glass door – the door Sarah had leant on when she stood up and steadied herself – and told them that Kathy didn't want to clean them off; she wanted to preserve the prints as a physical memory of Sarah. Megan regarded it as a sign of how deeply distressed Kathy was, even though she was trying to hold it together in public.

In mid-October 1993, seven weeks after Sarah's death, Megan and her husband Tim invited Kathy and Craig to go on a trip with them, to celebrate Megan's father's sixty-fifth birthday. They drove to Barrington House, a grand old Edwardian villa in the beautiful national park of Barrington Tops, north of Newcastle. Kathy could hardly eat but put on a brave face. There, a striking photo was taken of her, in a rare moment of joy, laughing, holding Megan's boy Alex and covered in rosellas – the flamboyantly colourful Australian parrots which are a feature of the local bird population.

Kathy and Craig experienced grief over Sarah's death in different ways. Kathy shut down, and Craig became severely depressed. 'I was confused and overcome with grief,' he said later. 'Kathy appeared devastated also, but she has always been stronger than me. I become consumed with grief, and Kathy seems to manage not to let grief control her, like it does with me.'

In a sign of how overcome he was by his emotions, Craig insisted on bringing the ashes of their three children home with him. When Kathy finally and reluctantly agreed to this, the ashes were interred in a drawer of a specially constructed ebony table.

During the day, Craig buried his grief in his work, setting off for Teasdale's, a car dealership, in the early hours of the morning and returning at night. 'I must admit I left Kathy alone most of the time. We were starting to grow apart,' he conceded.

But as time passed, Kathy began to lose patience with her husband, and in 1995 she demanded that he see a counsellor, to help him come to terms with the loss of their children. 'Kathy gave me the ultimatum because I wouldn't even talk to her about it,' Craig admitted later. 'I refused, and she moved out of the house ... to a flat in Waratah. Before she left, she wrote me a six-page letter explaining her feelings.'

Kathy's handwritten letter was open, pragmatic, and painfully frank. It was also heart-rending, revealing that Kathy, in the depths of despair had privately – if only briefly – considered suicide.

It bore all the hallmarks of a strong and stoical woman, a mother who, despite the triple tragedy she had suffered, was determined to carry on with her life and make something of it. In it, she acknowledged the grief that her husband felt, but also alerted him to the reality that their relationship had suffered and was cracking at the seams.

She told Craig how close she had come to leaving him before Sarah was born, but also, how she thought that having

Sarah would solve the problems she was having. 'That was a mistake,' she confessed. 'Cruel fate' had intervened, and Sarah had died, 'and now I am left with all the feelings and thoughts I had before, but worse.'

Riven by grief, she wrote: 'I think this last one has broken me.'

Kathy told Craig she wanted her life to change, and set out two possible options: to try living on her own, or chillingly, to die. She ruled the latter out, crediting her survival instinct as being 'too high' to end her own life.

As Kathy wrote her letter to Craig, all of her insecurities flooded to the surface. She confessed that a few months before, she had seriously considered leaving Sarah with him and abandoning their marriage. She told him she felt she couldn't 'serve' him as a wife should. 'You think you've failed, so do I in a major way. I'm sorry is all I can say.'

Kathy's letter shocked her husband out of his misery, and together, they went to see a counsellor who offered care and support to mothers who had lost their babies.

'I loved my wife, and I desperately wanted her back in my life,' Craig said later.

Even so, Kathy carried through her announced separation and for several months between January and April 1995, she and Craig lived apart. 'We kept in touch, and we still loved each other,' Craig said later on, adding: 'She could see that I was doing something for myself, and I was so very proud of her for standing on her own two feet and being independent.'

Kathy started dieting and going to the gym. Eventually, Craig, who was missing having her at home, asked her to move back in with him. 'I had come to terms with the children, and I wanted to start our life over,' he said.

Craig was earning good money, and Kathy started a new job as a sales assistant at the electronics company Retravision. In late October, they bought a three-bedroom home with a swimming pool in the historic and picturesque riverside town of Singleton, on the northern edge of the Hunter Valley wine region. They made friends with their new neighbours and started to enjoy life again.

Even after suffering three terrible tragedies, Kathy still wanted a family of her own, and in early 1996, two and a half years after Sarah had died, she spoke to Craig about it. Craig for his part would only entertain the possibility of trying for another child if they received the best advice possible, and in early May, they were referred to a sleep physician, Dr Chris Seton from the Sleep Disorders Unit at Westmead Children's Hospital in Sydney, who was also a SIDS specialist. They travelled to Sydney, and had a long and detailed discussion with Dr Seton at his rooms.

Both, understandably, were extremely anxious about the risk of losing a fourth child to SIDS, and during the extensive consultation, Dr Seton spoke to them about SIDS prevention, and about the risk assessments that could be applied to any future children they had. His initial view was that the history given to him by Kathy and Craig was 'highly suggestive of familial clustering of obstructive apnoea'. Or in other words, that there might be an inherited basis for the fact that Kathy's three children had simply stopped breathing while asleep. He noted that Craig, along with his siblings, was a heavy snorer, and that Patrick and Sarah had also snored. Sarah in particular was a very loud snorer who had been observed to suffer episodes of apnoea and choking while asleep.

However, the message that Craig took away from the meeting with Dr Seton was that 'any child of ours would not necessarily have a greater risk of dying than any other child, and with his sleep study, if the baby had a problem, he would detect it and know how to deal with it'.

Against all the odds, there seemed to be grounds for hope that they could still have a family. But it wasn't easy. The marriage was rocky, and Kathy constantly blamed herself for what had occurred. Over the next year, her emotions seesawed, as she tried to reconcile the personal responsibility she felt as a grieving mother for her children dying on her watch, with the hopes she still harboured to have a child with Craig who would survive. And all the sadness, depression, fears and regrets spilled out in a private journal she kept.

In one entry, dated 11 September 1996, Kathy wrote that she couldn't stand it when Craig talked down to her, as if she were some sort of inferior being. She was already feeling depressed and inadequate for not having fallen pregnant, and she blamed herself for this, writing: 'I suppose I deserve never to have kids again.'

One month later, with the 'children thing' still not happening, she was despairing at having a fourth child and was thinking of giving up altogether. As before, she blamed herself, suggesting that 'nature, fate and the man upstairs' had decided she shouldn't get another chance, adding, poignantly, 'and rightly so, I suppose.' She talked about all her mistakes and 'terrible thinking' and how she would like to correct them, and added as an aside: 'Obviously, I'm my father's daughter.' What she meant by those five words, and why she wrote them, would later become the subject of the most intense argument.

At the same time, Kathy believed she was no longer getting so frustrated and losing her temper; she was feeling better able to go with the flow.

In early December, it finally happened – after taking two tests, she found out she was pregnant for a fourth time. Naturally enough, she was both happy and scared, and particularly glad because it meant that Craig would have what he wanted most – an heir to the Folbigg family name.

The entry she wrote in her journal on 4 December was filled with good intentions. But there was a sting in the tail: Kathy had already decided that if she felt overwhelmed by anger or jealousy, she would leave Craig and her baby. It would be the only way she could cope.

One month later, on New Year's Day 1997, Kathy felt confident that everything would go well. She had learned the lessons of the past. This time, if she needed help, she would ask for it and not try to do everything by herself. Her failure to ask for help before had been the main reason for her stress, and stress, she wrote, had made her do 'terrible' things.

In a touching tribute to her husband, Kathy told her journal she believed that as soon as the new child's first birthday came around, Craig would relax and become a father of 'great magnitude'.

But if Kathy felt happy and optimistic as the New Year began, it was a false dawn. One month later, in the early hours of the morning, she couldn't sleep, thinking of Sarah, Patrick and Caleb. She was starting to have doubts about having another baby, and she was haunted by guilt, and by the weight of responsibility she felt for what had happened to them, not to mention, her fear of it happening again. She was also haunted by the fear that she and Craig would split up if the baby died.

In the journal entry she wrote on 4 February, she berated herself, saying that it all boiled down to the fact that she had been a 'terrible' mother, and she wondered privately whether the decision to have a fourth child wasn't just a means of proving to herself that she could get it right – that she could do what other mothers did.

'What scares me most,' she wrote, 'will be when I'm alone with the baby. How do I overcome that? Defeat that?'

Again and again in her journals while she was pregnant, Kathy wrote that this time, with the added support of family, friends and doctors, everything would be fine – as if the one person she couldn't quite convince of this was herself.

She was gearing up for her 'trip down labour lane' and was starting to get excited. She told her journal that the baby would be an extension of the love she and Craig shared, and a symbol of their unity and strength.

Kathy remarked in a journal entry in June that with Sarah, Patrick and Caleb, she had never bothered to think about them in the future as school kids and teenagers, adding: 'Maybe because I knew they'd never get there.'

But with her fourth child-to-be, she felt more optimistic. She could see this child going to school and doing homework with Craig. Before, she wrote, she hadn't been ready for family life, but now, she was.

Towards the end of July, Kathy wrote an entry in her journal analysing her own reasons for wanting a fourth child; she realised that the thought that without a child, her own identity and existence would end with her, was too much. But a child would love her, need her, cherish her, and outlive her to keep her existence 'alive'.

The idea of this was heightened for Kathy by her perception that she had no past to draw on, and no blood relatives to remind her of who she was. With Caleb, Patrick and Sarah, she had felt as if she didn't deserve to be 'extended' and was condemning them to a life with her. Now, she felt differently. 'All is well & well it will go,' she wrote.

Eight days later, Kathy's growing impatience with her pregnancy burst through. She was desperate to give birth and be able to focus on the future. She was anxious and nervous, as she wrote about the way forward she saw for herself, as a loving wife and caring mother, 'something I truly wish to succeed in and be.'

On 7 August 1997, finally, Kathy gave birth to her fourth child, Laura Elizabeth Folbigg. For Craig, it was a moment of pure joy.

When Kathy felt strong enough to write in her journal five days afterwards, she recorded her mixed emotions: relief at the successful birth and apprehension too, worrying even now if her decision to have a fourth child had been right. 'But then I look at Craig & know I did the right thing.'

Little Laura embodied all of their hopes for the future.

7
'THE BIGGEST PARTY EVER!'

After suffering three infant deaths, it's hard to imagine the level of paranoia felt by Kathy and Craig as they left hospital with their precious newborn, Laura.

At home, she slept in a bassinet next to Kathy and Craig, and twelve days after she was born, she underwent an overnight sleep study at the new Children's Hospital at Westmead in western Sydney. The results revealed mild central apnoea of infancy, but no evidence of the more serious obstructive apnoea or bradycardia.

'Given the family history, this was a rather pleasing result, even though Laura's sleep-breathing is not entirely normal,' Dr Seton commented at the time. 'Most children with central apnoea mature and evolve out of it over a period of a few months without symptoms.'

However, he cautioned that there was the potential for the apnoea to get worse if Laura developed an upper respiratory tract infection, if she slept in the same bed as her parents, or if she was exposed to cigarette smoke. Craig had been a habitual smoker for years.

Two days after the sleep study, Laura was taken home with a monitoring device to record her breathing and heartbeat. It allowed her parents to download the cardiac and respiratory data by telephone to the hospital, and over the following months, Dr Seton and his colleagues kept a close eye on Laura's progress.

Dr Seton was optimistic that Laura would progress through her infancy without sleep-related problems and was hopeful that the measures being undertaken would minimise her risk of SIDS.

As an added precaution, Kathy and Craig were again instructed on how to carry out CPR, should the need ever arise.

In contrast to the apnoea blanket which had been provided for Sarah, the monitor provided this time was far more technical. 'It required actually sticking electrodes on her so that it was measuring breath and heartbeats all the time, and it was on her anytime she was asleep,' Kathy later explained. 'You would just unplug her and leave the electrodes on her during the day, and just plug her back in when she went to sleep. There was no question about that, it was on every time she slept, even if it was only for a fifteen-minute nap.'

The alarm itself was sensitive, and ear-piercing – so much so, that even Craig would often wake up when it went off at night. It came as a relief to Kathy to know that the alarm would alert him as soon as it alerted her, and that she wouldn't be left on her own to deal with a crisis. Sometimes it would wake Laura, but often – very surprisingly – she would sleep through it.

Shortly after returning from the sleep study, Kathy wrote an emotional entry in her journal, in which she admitted feeling scared that for the first time, her maternal instinct had kicked in; she 'actually' loved Laura and had bonded with her. It was coupled with the realisation that she 'never had it with the others.'

On 2 October, nearly two months after she was born, Laura underwent a further study, which revealed that her sleep-disordered breathing had improved slightly. There were occasional mixed episodes of apnoea and moments of shallow breathing, but Dr Seton's judgment was that 'the obstructive component of sleep-breathing is not severe'. He cautioned, however, that the apnoea monitoring at home had to continue and stressed that the data downloaded from the monitor would be carefully studied at the hospital.

'All other SIDS-protective factors should continue to be undertaken diligently,' he emphasised. 'Extra precaution, including serious consideration of hospitalisation, should be undertaken if Laura develops an upper respiratory tract infection.'

In November, Kathy's foster father, Neville, died from heart problems. Yet again, the feeling that she was being shunned and rejected by her foster family, and by her mother, Deidre, in particular, raised hurtful and distressing emotions for her. In her journal she complained that the family would probably not invite her to the cremation and, clearly stung by the thought, she lashed out, writing 'they can all get stuffed', and 'I give up & mum wins.'

In an echo of what she had written while pregnant with Laura, Kathy speculated that she no longer existed as far her foster family was concerned, but now she had her own family, with her own future heir apparent. 'That's enough. It's all I need,' she wrote.

* * *

The following day was Alex's fifth birthday, and Kathy went to the party hosted by Megan with mixed emotions. Sarah, had she still been alive, would also have been five years old.

'Megan's Alex is 5. Tough though Sarah would have been 5 as well. But past is past & Laura is future,' she wrote.

On New Year's Eve, friends came round to celebrate, but Kathy felt depressed and reluctant to join them. She was tired and wanted to be alone.

In her final journal entry for 1997, she looked forward to Laura joining the New Year's Eve celebrations the following year. She was a good-natured baby, and thank goodness, Kathy wrote, it had saved her from the fate of her siblings. 'I think she was warned,' she added.

To an outsider looking in, some of her entries might have seemed odd, her train of thought difficult to decipher. But her journals were private, written only for herself. None of them were meant to be read by anyone else, even though she suspected Craig occasionally did so, and only she knew what the words she wrote meant, and what she was thinking when she wrote them.

At the end of January, Kathy felt depressed and angry with herself, fearful and ashamed after she momentarily lost her temper with her daughter. In her journal she admitted she had 'lost it' with Laura and yelled at her, scaring her and leaving her in floods of tears. Her temper had almost got the better of her; she had nearly deliberately dropped her on the floor and left her – but stopped herself and instead, placed her on the floor and walked away, leaving her to cry.

Kathy was only gone for five minutes or so, but to her it felt like a lifetime. She vowed to ensure it would never happen again.

Even so, it was typical of her propensity to blame herself that she declared: 'I feel like the worst mother on earth.' In her heightened depressed mood, her worst fear was that Laura would leave her now, as Sarah had before her. She had been short-tempered with Sarah and even sometimes, she admitted, 'cruel' to her, and Sarah had left 'with a bit of help'. Years later, those last comments would come back to haunt her.

Laura's moaning and whinging drove her up the wall. But Kathy marvelled at the bond she felt with her, and told her journal that she couldn't wait until her baby would be old enough to tell her what she wanted.

For Craig and Kathy, the joy of welcoming Laura into the world couldn't completely heal the grief they had endured at losing her three siblings, and as Kathy wrote in her journal on the night of 1 February, her heart was breaking: 'Well, happy birthday Caleb. He would have been 9 today.'

Even more heartbreaking was Kathy's admission that she had no memory of Caleb any more without seeing a picture of him. All three of her children were becoming distant, unless Laura did something to spark a memory of them.

Two days after this, a third sleep study was undertaken. This time, the results were better than ever. 'Her sleep breathing has now normalised,' Dr Seton wrote. 'There is no evidence of upper airway obstruction in sleep. Sleep quality is excellent. Home apnoea monitoring should continue, but a further Sleep Study will not be required unless there is evidence of new or changing sleep breathing symptoms.'

The news could hardly be better, and yet at home, with Laura doing so well, Kathy was growing sick of the monitor alarm going off when nothing bad had happened. Craig was adamant that it had to remain active – Laura was still only six months old, and he wanted to ensure that it stayed connected, come hell or high water.

A compromise was reached. Kathy would turn the monitor off during Laura's daytime sleeps, when she was checking on her regularly, but they always had it on at night when they were all asleep.

In the meantime, Kathy was back at the gym and taking Laura with her. But at the end of March, things came to a head. This time Kathy wrote about Craig in her journal as if their relationship was terminal.

Depressingly, she had decided that having Laura 'didn't fix our problem'. She regretted not having stuck to her guns when they last split up, as their relationship by then had already run its course. Laura was the only thing keeping them together; they were in a hole as far as their relationship was concerned.

But at the same time, Kathy was determined to try and make their relationship work – for Laura's sake. She wanted Laura to have a stable home life with both parents and Kathy told her journal that she would have to suppress her negative feelings about Craig until Laura was a lot older.

Kathy's final entry in this journal at Easter time was more negative about herself than any before it had been. She confessed to feeling 'fat and ugly' and told herself she had to change her life if she was going to be a 'hot-looking' energetic mother for Laura, and a sexy wife for Craig.

But the strain of everything that had happened over the last few years was beginning to tell, and Kathy and Craig started sleeping in separate rooms. 'We didn't argue, we just seemed to grow apart, and we were both just living for Laura,' Craig admitted later.

Someone Kathy trusted implicitly to take care of Laura was Karren Hall, a friend who lived nearby at the Country Acres Caravan Park in Singleton. Karren had only known Kathy since 1994 – after Sarah had died – but when Laura was born, she offered to help, and even arranged to be trained in CPR, in order to be allowed to do so.

'I went and did a course on resuscitation for babies,' she said later. 'I took every precaution that I could think of. Because she wasn't gonna go on my watch.'

One day when Laura was approaching twelve months old, Karren took her home to babysit her while Kathy ran some errands. Laura fell asleep on her couch, and about twenty minutes later the phone rang.

'It was Kath, checking on Laura to make sure she'd behaved herself or was doing alright,' Karren said. Everything was fine, and the two kept talking, but when the phone conversation ended and Karren returned to the living room to check on Laura, she got the shock of her life.

'She was a funny colour, like it had drained,' she said. 'I actually got on the floor and bent over. I couldn't hear her breathing, couldn't feel her breathing. I went into panic mode. I put my arms under her and scooped her up and was about to put her on the floor to start CPR, and she took a big "in" and then a couple of breaths, and it was all good from there.

'But it was very scary. I believe she had stopped breathing. I did everything that I was trained to do to see whether she was breathing or not, and to me there was no breath, none at all.'

If Karren's judgment was correct, Laura may have suffered an ALTE – an apparent or acute life-threatening event – similar to the 'near-miss' event suffered by Patrick when he was four months old. If Karren hadn't been there, it might have proved to be fatal.

Fortunately, Laura was fine, and on 7 August 1998 Kathy and Craig and their friends and family put on an almighty celebration in a hall in Singleton to mark Laura's first birthday. She was a child who was adored by all, and it was an emotional occasion.

'When she reached her first birthday it was the biggest party you've ever seen in your life,' Kathy said later. 'It was just a humungous big party with all these friends, and better than you'd give an adult probably, but we were just so happy that she had reached one.'

After that, Kathy allowed herself to breathe and look to the future.

None of the other children had made it this far. It was a major milestone.

8

'I'VE HAD THREE GO ALREADY!'

Compared with her other three children, Laura was calm and well-behaved, but that didn't stop Kathy continuing to feel anxious and apprehensive. 'My paranoia was through the roof by the time I'd got to Laura,' she would say later.

She feared that if she failed as a mother, Laura would leave her, by dying, as the others had.

In 1989, when she had held Caleb in her arms for the very first time, Kathy thought that this was what she was on the planet for. 'I was the same with every one of them, always felt the same with every one of them. Probably just more desperately so, by the time Laura came around. If I was gonna do this, I was gonna do it full time. Because she was staying, whether God or anyone else liked it or not.

'By then, of course, so much trauma, so much sadness, and so much grief.'

But even with all the anxiety and paranoia, the danger period for Laura seemed to have passed with her first birthday. The nurse at the hospital told them that it was probably time to return the apnoea monitor to the hospital, as all the readings were fine. Even so, they were reluctant to do so. 'I didn't sleep too well while she was off the monitor ... and Craig actually slept lightly, which is the first time he's ever done that in years,' Kathy said later.

The monitor was packed away but brought back out again when Laura came down with flu. 'We put her back on it that night, just for that few days,' Kathy recalled. 'Then we packed it up again and we didn't have it back out again after that.' Eventually, Craig took the monitor down to Sydney and returned it to the hospital.

Laura's health, though, was up and down. One week after her first birthday, she was taken to a local doctor after suffering flu-like symptoms for the previous five days. She had been coughing, her throat was red, her sleep was disturbed and she was off her food. Her chest was clear and there were no signs of respiratory distress, but the doctor diagnosed a viral upper respiratory infection.

Her GP saw her on several occasions over a period of seven months. In January 1999, she had a rash, followed by a fever and a sore throat. In early February, a medical review by her GP showed that Laura was well, and her throat and ears were clear of infection.

Kathy admitted that after Laura's first birthday and the return of the monitor, 'we, unfortunately I suppose, got a bit complacent, thinking she's heading for her second birthday, everything is hunky dory and fine'.

Part of this for Kathy was the joy in knowing that she had bonded with Laura in a way that she hadn't felt able to do with her other three children. Laura was no longer a baby; she was learning to walk and talk, and 'she would actually figure things out and come and ask you what she wants. She was getting out of the baby bit that was so frightening to us and into more of the toddler child sort of thing,' Kathy explained later. 'So we relaxed.'

In early February 1999, Kathy started working part time back at Retravision in Singleton, and a friend took care of Laura when she was working. But all was not well in Craig and Kathy's relationship. They were still sleeping apart, and one day when he was at home, sleeping on the lounge, she approached him.

'Kathy woke me up and told me not to sleep on the lounge,' Craig said later. He told her that he was going outside for a cigarette and she gave him a letter. She said, 'Read this while you're out there.'

Kathy's letter was, if anything, even more confronting for Craig than her previous outpouring had been. It carried the threat of ending their relationship, once and for all. Kathy wrote that the problems that had previously surfaced only occasionally were now a 'recurring nightmare'. She was no longer happy living with Craig. Laura was the only thing keeping her there.

For the first time, Kathy laid out a plan for the future where she and Craig would live apart. Laura wouldn't suffer as long as both her parents loved and cherished her.

Kathy's letter gave a blunt assessment of what was needed now. She wanted to leave with Laura, offering Craig full access. Optimistically, she wrote that under this arrangement, they could still be friends, and life for Laura wouldn't be all that different. Craig could still see her every day; and they could still do things together as a family. The fact that her parents were no longer living together would be 'just a minor detail'.

Underneath, Kathy signed her name with the words: 'Write or talk!' alongside.

After reading the letter, Craig went into their bedroom, and they talked it through. Craig told Kathy he wouldn't allow her to leave 'because every time you have ever left me, you have devastated me, and if you leave this time, I will not only be devastated by losing you, but I would have lost Laura as well. I couldn't live without either of you.'

Craig and Kathy spoke at length, promising to support each other and to try to be more considerate of each other's needs and feelings. Craig said he would try to get home earlier, to help take care of Laura. 'We embraced each other, and I was confident that we could work it out,' Craig said later.

'Finally, you talked to me!' Kathy told him, and together, they agreed to try to make things work.

Laura meanwhile was becoming too big for her cot and so Kathy and Craig set up a single bed in Laura's bedroom. Kathy made it up with two cotton sheets, a *Wiggles* quilt and a pillow with a *Wiggles* pillow cover. She put a brown woollen 'teddy bear' rug and a matching cushion on the bed.

The bedroom had a pink carpet and a small *Bananas in Pyjamas* rug. In one corner was a pile of soft toys on top of a child-size chair, and in the other corner, an air cooler with two cushions carefully placed at its base in case Laura stumbled against it.

There were soft toys hanging from the ceiling, and a big teddy bear sat on top of a small, brown patterned chest of drawers, alongside an audio monitor with a night light from BabyCo, and an array of nappies, baby wipes, talcum powder, cleansing lotion, chest rub and liquid Panadol. It was, to all intents and purposes, a typical toddler's bedroom.

On Sunday, 28 February, Craig filmed Laura playing around the family pool, and on the morning of Monday, 1 March 1999, Craig woke Laura up at about 6.30 am. She had a runny nose and some congestion in her chest and had been given medication prescribed by a local Singleton doctor. Craig gave her a bottle of milk and she drank it.

Laura started to cry, and Craig and Kathy had an argument. She wanted him out of the house, not hanging around with Laura and unsettling her. 'I remember having words with Craig. Stating that she doesn't behave like this when he's not around. Telling him to go & get ready for work.' Voices were raised, and Laura looked frightened, Kathy later admitted.

'Craig & I rarely argued with loud voices & never in front of her. I remember Craig looking at me and saying I looked like I would like to punch someone. I interpreted that he was suggesting I'd hurt Laura. I said if I punched anyone it would be him – never her. We calmed down. I think I said I'd see him later at work.'

Craig went to work and Kathy showered and dressed while Laura watched her favourite video, *Dumbo*. When Craig had arrived at work, Kathy called him and apologised for getting angry. He invited them over to the office for morning tea.

Kathy left with Laura for the gym between 8.30 am and 8.45 am. She had a class to attend at 9 am. Laura had a cold and a cough, but otherwise was her usual self. She was wearing a T-shirt, singlet, bike shorts and her *Teletubbies* sandals. The class finished at 10.30 am.

Kathy enjoyed having coffee with 'the ladies' at the gym after they trained, but by this time she had stopped doing so, because Laura was so active; 'I was chasing her too much. So that morning I said, "No, I won't worry about the coffee, I'll take her home and we'll start our day." So, we went home that morning after the class.'

On the way, they stopped off at Teasdale's, to see Craig. Kathy said she had 'decided to see Craig, apologise, and show him everything was okay'. Even with a runny nose, Laura was well enough to play in the office for half an hour, until Kathy took her home for her morning nap. As they left, Craig gave them both a kiss goodbye and told them he would come home to see them at lunchtime.

As she often did, Laura fell asleep in the car, and when they got home, Kathy lifted her out of her seat and carried her into the house. She took Laura's shoes off and put her into her bed on her left side, facing out into the bedroom with her back facing the wall. Kathy would always do this, conscious of the flow of air around her.

Kathy put the blue and brown throw rug, with teddy bears on it, over her, pulled her old cot mattress out from under the bed, in case she fell out of bed, and once she was comfortable, left the bedroom with the door half-closed so that, if Laura stirred, she wouldn't just get up and wander out.

Kathy went out of the back of the house with the baby-listening monitor, put it on a bench on the verandah and walked into the garden to check on the dogs.

When she walked back towards the house she heard Laura give a cough on the monitor but didn't go to check on her straight away. Instead, she fixed up the dog's bed and cleaned up the verandah. Ten or fifteen minutes elapsed before she walked back into Laura's bedroom to see how she was.

A couple of minutes later, as lights flashed on the console in front of her, an operator at the New South Wales Ambulance control centre picked up a call.

> Ambulance Emergency.
> Um, my baby's not breathing!

The mother's voice was panicked, almost hysterical.

> Okay, and how old is your baby?
> Twenty months old. Can you just hold a minute? I'm trying to do CPR!
> Twenty months old?
> I'm not getting any heartbeat or anything!

The woman was frantic.

> Okay, do you know why this is?
> I've had three SIDS deaths already!
> Pardon?
> I've had three go already!
> And your name?
> It's Kathy, Kathy.

Immediately, at 12.12 pm, an ambulance sped out of Singleton Ambulance Station, arriving two minutes later at Kathy's home.

Minutes before, Kathy had walked in from the verandah to check on Laura; she had heard her cough on the portable monitor but hadn't thought it serious enough to check on her immediately – something, she would later say, she profoundly regretted.

'When I opened the door, I noticed she was on her back ... I rushed over to check, only because I worry when she's on her back. I always worried if she was, and I was thinking that all I needed to do, is to roll her back over – I always did that too.

'I looked at her and she was pale; her lips were slightly blue, but not too bad, and she was cool to touch but not cold, like one of the others. I immediately scooped her up after calling her name and trying to get a response of some kind.

'I ran out to the breakfast bar and placed her there; we were taught that if CPR was needed, it was to be done on a firm surface. I rang the ambulance while doing breathing CPR and I checked her heartbeat. There was none and I immediately started heart massage.'

It was disturbingly reminiscent of Karren Hall's experience some months earlier, when she too had found Laura apparently not breathing, with the colour drained from her face. Karren too had scooped her up and was about to start CPR, when Laura drew in a big breath.

Kathy was hoping for the same reaction – but it never came. At first, she didn't panic. 'Being a lot bigger than the others, she was heavy to pick up, but I didn't think about it, it was just: pick her up and race out to the breakfast bar and go from there.'

The breakfast bar was in the dining room, opposite Laura's highchair. There was a phone on the wall at one end of the bar, which Kathy used to call the ambulance as she tried to resuscitate Laura.

'I laid her on her back, tilted her head back, started the breaths,' she later explained.

When the two ambulance officers arrived at 12.14 pm, Kathy was still trying to revive Laura. The more senior officer, Brian Wadsworth, saw her crying as she did so. 'I went straight up to the child, checked the vital signs and found that the child was not breathing and had no pulse. I tilted the child's head slightly ensuring that the airway was clear. I then continued CPR for a period.'

A second ambulance officer, Harold Picton, came into the house, and took over, noting that Kathy, who was sitting on a chair, was screaming and crying. Laura was dressed in floral tights and a small top, and her body was warm to the touch. Her lips and face were bluish. Brian Wadsworth administered three doses of adrenaline into Laura's right elbow, but neither of the ambulance officers could detect a pulse or any breathing.

Kathy was asked what happened and she replied: 'I heard her coughing in the bedroom and when I checked her five minutes later, I found her not breathing.' She added that Laura had been suffering from a runny nose and a cough for a couple of days.

A third ambulance officer arrived, and together, at 12.29 pm, they stretchered Laura to the ambulance, where a fourth dose of adrenaline was administered. She was driven to Singleton Hospital, and shortly afterwards, pronounced deceased.

At around lunchtime, as Craig described it later, he was talking to his nephew on the phone, when a colleague at Teasdale's ran into his office and told him to go to the hospital, because there was something wrong with Laura. He raced there and was taken to see Kathy in a waiting room.

'I said: "What's wrong? Where's Laura?"'

'Kathy said: "Why didn't you come home? I rang you!"'

'I said, "I didn't get any phone call."'

'She said, "I tried, I tried everything I could."'

Craig ran into the room next door where Laura was laid on her back on a bed. 'Hospital staff looked as though they were packing up,' he said later. 'I yelled at them: "You can't stop! This is my fourth baby!"'

Craig went back to Kathy, who was crying uncontrollably and being comforted by nursing staff.

At 1.20 pm, two detectives from Singleton police station arrived at the hospital.

A social worker took the detectives to meet Kathy, who told them what had happened. Craig formally identified Laura's body, and shortly afterwards, a call was made to a senior constable from the Coroner's Support Section at Glebe mortuary in Sydney, telling him to expect the delivery of Laura's body for an autopsy.

At 3.30 pm, Detective Senior Constable Bernie Ryan, one of the two detectives who had spoken to Kathy and Craig, drove to their home in Millard Close, where he spoke with a crime scene detective, Glen Ward.

Together, the officers inspected Kathy's home. Detective Senior Constable Ward took forty-one photographs, showing Laura's bedroom in detail, together with the breakfast bar where

Kathy had tried to revive her, her white *Teletubbies* sandals and a red plastic drinks bottle which were on the lounge in the living room, and Laura's yellow T-shirt which had been cut open by the ambulance officers and dropped on the floor next to the breakfast bar, as they administered CPR.

Detective Ward also photographed a small blood stain on the breakfast bar, and a close-up of Laura's yellow pillowcase on her bed, showing four small stains close together.

The detailed examination of the house was a clear indication that the detectives were treating 8 Millard Close as a potential crime scene.

In an extensive statement which he would make later, Detective Ward described what he found.

'About 3.55 pm that afternoon while at the home I had a telephone conversation with Dr Allan Cala, a forensic pathologist at Glebe, regarding the inquiry,' he wrote.

The detective noted that Kathy's home was clean and tidy, 'and in some areas I noticed child safety precautions had been taken'. These included:

a. a listening device in the child's bedroom allowing the parents to monitor its sleeping from the living room,
b. simple hooks and eyes on the bathroom and laundry doors,
c. cushions placed over the legs of an air cooler in the child's room in case of a stumble or fall, and
d. childproof locks on the door of the bathroom vanity.

The house 'appeared to be a healthy environment with furniture and fixtures modified for child safety'.

The detective noted the small dark stains on Laura's pillowcase, and later collected the pillow, blanket, quilt and sheets from the bed for scientific analysis. At the breakfast bar, he collected a swab of the blood stain there to be analysed.

A local court registrar, Ron Woodrow, was informed that Laura had died, and he located the previous coroner's files documenting the deaths of Caleb, Patrick and Sarah, so that they could be viewed by Dr Cala and the police investigators.

Laura's body was placed in a body bag tagged with the number, 391361, and driven by Government contractors 210 kilometres south to Sydney's Glebe mortuary, where Dr Allan Cala prepared to conduct an autopsy.

For Kathy and Craig, there were agonising calls to make to other members of the family, including Kathy's foster sister Lea and her husband Ted, whose birthday it was that day.

'Laura was special in that she lived longer; we had more time with her. She was more of a person. She wasn't just a baby. And she was adored by everyone,' Ted recalled sometime later. 'So, when she died, I think it hit everybody harder because she'd been around for so long that everybody really got to know her. She was a beautiful little kid, and suddenly, she's gone.'

'We finally went home later that day and our lives were turned upside down again,' Craig lamented. 'People were around us trying to help and be there for us, and I just didn't know what to do. Once again, I was overcome with grief.'

Kathy spent the night crying uncontrollably. Craig packed up Laura's toys and Kathy helped him put them in her room. They were together in grief, but inconsolable.

9

'FOUR IS FUCKING MURDER!'

Joe Lavin is a tough, old-school copper who used to run investigations for coronial inquests at the New South Wales state coroner's offices in Sydney. By 1999, he had served almost twenty years as a police officer, crime-scene examiner and forensic investigator, and his duties had included assisting with the aftermath of the disastrous landslide at the ski resort of Thredbo in 1987, in which eighteen people died. Joe has a vivid recollection of Monday, 1 March, the day he received a phone call from the Singleton detective, Bernie Ryan.

Detective Ryan asked the senior constable to speak to the coroner in Glebe and to Professor Hilton, to give them the name 'Folbigg' and tell them that this was 'number four'.

John Hilton was the pathologist who had carried out Sarah's autopsy, ascribing her death to SIDS (Sudden Infant Death Syndrome) and he had his offices above the mortuary. 'I briefly informed the coroner, and I then went into Professor Hilton's office,' Joe Lavin says.

Professor Hilton was a memorable character in his own right, a straight-talking Scotsman who had found his way to Australia, where he was regarded as one of the very best in the business.

As Joe Lavin relates the story: 'I just told him I received a phone call and the investigators up at Singleton have asked me to come in and tell you the name Folbigg and number four. His reaction was, essentially: "One is tragic, two is unusual, three is suspicious", and if I could just use the Prof's accent, he says: "Four is fucking murder!"

'And I was quite stunned, it started to tick with me then what this was all about, that this is the fourth infant death relating to this particular family, the Folbigg family.'

If this story is true, Professor Hilton was echoing the prevailing mantra of the time – Meadow's Law – which, as we've seen, referred to a statement made by a British paediatrician, Professor Roy Meadow, in a book he had written on child abuse, that: '"One sudden infant death is a tragedy, two is suspicious and three is murder until proved otherwise" is a crude aphorism but a sensible working rule for anyone encountering these tragedies.'

Crude it may have been, but from 1989, when his book was published, support for the theory grew and it underpinned a number of criminal cases in which mothers who had suffered multiple infant deaths in their families from natural causes were falsely accused and convicted of killing their children.

In the same year that Dr Meadow published his theory, two American medical examiners, Dr Vincent JM DiMaio, and his father Dr Dominick DiMaio, published a textbook, *Forensic Pathology*, in which they wrote: 'It is the authors' opinion that while a second SIDS death from a mother is improbable, it is possible and she should be given the benefit of the doubt. A third case, in our opinion, is not possible and is a case of homicide.'

The DiMaios took as an example the notorious case of a woman called Waneta Hoyt, who under extreme pressure in a police interview, confessed to killing five of her biological children by smothering them – and then recanted her confession. Their deaths had originally been attributed to SIDS. Shockingly, Dr Vincent DiMaio, in a letter to the American medical journal *Pediatrics*, theorised that in cases like this: 'The perpetrator is virtually always the mother and she will continue this killing unless stopped or until she runs out of children.'

It was against this backdrop that Kathy and Craig's fourth child Laura arrived at Glebe mortuary on the day she died. The job of carrying out the autopsy fell to the duty pathologist, Dr Allan Cala.

Professor Hilton, in his capacity as Director of the Institute of Forensic Medicine at Glebe, was present when Dr Cala conducted the autopsy. Both men were aware that Laura's three siblings had died, and both held suspicions that, with four deaths having occurred in the same family, foul play might have been a factor in Laura's death.

Dr Cala was told the basic facts of Laura's medical condition before she died: she had been diagnosed with central apnoea but with no evidence of obstructive apnoea, and no significant sleep abnormalities had been detected while she was being monitored. She had, however, recently been unwell with cold- and flu-type symptoms.

The one-page interim autopsy report signed by Dr Cala gave the cause of death as 'undetermined' and was dated 1 March 1999. This was the first of Kathy's four children for whom a pathologist had recorded the cause of death as being undetermined.

Years later, in a rare interview, Dr Cala explained to the Australian Broadcasting Corporation (ABC) that one reason he wrote 'undetermined' was because of Laura's age. She was nearly twenty months old when she died, and: 'that's just far too old for that death to be called sudden infant death syndrome'.

In the same ABC program, *Australian Story*, Detective Inspector Bernie Ryan, as he was then, recalled a conversation with Dr Cala in which the pathologist sensationally remarked: 'Well, I can't say to you one hundred per cent that Laura wasn't suffocated.'

However, suspicion isn't proof, and Dr Cala himself admitted that: 'I suspected one thing, but medically, I couldn't prove it.'

In his final autopsy report from December 1999, Dr Cala said he had found no significant external injuries on Laura, and no facial injuries or injuries to her mouth.

There was, however, one highly significant finding. Dr Cala discovered that Laura was suffering from myocarditis – an inflammation of the heart muscle – before her death. The condition can be fatal.

'Histological examination of tissues showed an inflammatory infiltrate in the heart, consistent with myocarditis, of probable viral origin,' he reported. 'This accords with the history of cold/'flu-like illness for several days prior to the death of the child.'

He added: 'Although there was an inflammatory infiltrate in the heart consistent with myocarditis, this may represent an incidental finding.' Despite finding myocarditis, Dr Cala asserted that in Laura's case, it hadn't caused her death.

The day after Laura died, a conference took place at the state coroner's office, involving the state coroner himself, Derrick Hand, a couple of the sergeants assisting him, Professor Hilton and Joe Lavin. The homicide squad was also represented. According to Joe Lavin, 'The conference was quite extensive, and it covered not only Laura's deaths, but raised the issue of the three previous deaths.'

Joe Lavin is adamant that it was Professor Hilton's concern about this being the fourth death in the one family which rang 'alarm bells' for himself, and for the Singleton detectives. But surprisingly, the homicide squad made it clear that it didn't want to get involved. Joe Lavin's impression was that the squad's detectives had shuffled the case into the 'too hard' basket, preferring to leave it to the local detectives to resolve.

The man leading the investigation in Singleton was Bernie Ryan – an ambitious thirty-one-year-old detective who had no experience with major crime investigations, but who wasn't going to shy away from the challenge posed by the case. His fellow detective Dave Frith was a solid thirty-two-year-old copper who worked side by side with Detective Ryan through the lengthy investigation.

'We were two very junior police, in the grand scheme of the police service,' Detective Sergeant Frith revealed on the ABC's *Australian Story*. 'We didn't have a lot – one car and a couple of computers. That's about it, for resources. Bernie requested the assistance of Homicide. Due to the circumstantial nature of the brief, it wasn't given a high priority. If the matter was to progress, it would have had to be done by Bernie and whoever could help him.'

Another version of the events which immediately followed Laura's death comes from Robin Napper, a former British police officer who at the time was seconded to the New South Wales Police Force, to help the force enact DNA legislation in Australia for the first time. Mr Napper's view from the outset was that an independent team should be brought in to investigate the deaths, but this didn't happen.

Robin Napper told me that Bernie Ryan 'walked into this and was dropped into a case like the Bermuda Triangle.' Speaking from his own experience, he told me how confronting cases involving child deaths can be for a police officer. The case, Mr Napper recalled, had come up at a weekly meeting of the leading homicide detectives in New South Wales, in what was known as the Crime Agencies, headed by the legendary copper Clive Small, who had himself been the lead investigator of the infamous 'backpacker murders' – the murders carried out by Ivan Milat.

The homicide detectives decided to let Bernie Ryan take charge of the investigation, but to offer advice in the background if called on to do so.

To begin with, there was little to implicate Kathy or Craig in the deaths of any of their children. On 9 March, Dr Christopher Marley, a GP who had treated Patrick and Sarah, provided an Expert Certificate saying: 'I saw no sign of neglect on either child. Mrs Folbigg impressed me as a caring and concerned parent, as did her husband Craig.'

Three days later, the detectives received a statement from Dr Ian Wilkinson, who had treated Patrick, saying: 'I think it is fair to say that no particular cause for the deaths of these children was ever established, despite quite a lot of work-up from various laboratories. I have no explanation for why these children have died.' However, he added: 'It is certainly extraordinarily unlikely that this can all be blamed on "cot death", and indeed the latest child was well past the age one would expect this to happen.'

In reality, only two of the deaths had been ascribed to SIDS: Caleb's and Sarah's.

Kathy and Craig, meanwhile, were battling their own overwhelming grief. Kathy took Craig to see their family doctor, who prescribed an anti-depressant for her husband, and she would later tell Tracy Chapman that: 'When Laura died, I just didn't feel anything anymore … So I was just one foot in front of the other, doing what I was supposed to do.'

For her, it was agonising to wrap her head around the idea that: 'I'm not going to be this mother, I'm not going to have this family, it's all just going to get denied. I immediately just blamed myself, went, "Oh my God, I've got complacent."'

Kathy went back to the gym on the Monday following Laura's death, to be with her girlfriends there who were supporting her, and Craig went back to work two days later.

But unsurprisingly, the marriage was falling apart. Craig only wanted to talk about Laura, while Kathy wanted to be on her own. She tired of seeing the sadness in his eyes and 'photographs of things that will never be'. Craig said she told him: 'All I want is to be alone and only be responsible for how I feel and what I do. I don't want to have to prop you up because it's hard enough to prop myself up.'

Given all the grief, sadness, stress, arguments and difficulties that Kathy and Craig had endured in the previous ten years, it is hard to imagine how their bond, at this point, could have remained strong. A week later, Kathy left their home and moved into a flat a few minutes away by car.

Craig went to visit her one evening in the first week she was there. 'I was hurt and I desperately wanted her back. I love this woman, she is my wife,' he told the police. 'I spoke with her, hoping that she would use the time in the flat for her grief, without carrying me. I said: "Are you ever coming back?"

'She said: "No."
'I said: "Never?"
'She said: "That's right."
'I said: "You are still my wife."

'She said: "Only on paper."'

It was a brutal rebuff, and in May, when Craig gave Kathy a Mother's Day card at her flat, the reception he received was no better. 'I handed her the card and she said, "What did you give me that for?"' he later recalled.

'I said: "You are the mother of my children."'

'She said: "You know how I feel about Mother's Day."'

'I said: "You can't hide from Mother's Days for the rest of your life."'

'She said: "I can try."'

'I said: "The kids might be dead, but you are always a mother."'

'She said: "You always wallow in self-pity. The sooner you realise she's dead, the better you will be."'

That one, unhappy encounter summed up the emotional chasm which had opened up between them, and their own completely different ways of dealing with their grief and terrible loss.

When Kathy moved out, Craig remained at their home in Millard Close, and while he was there, he found the journal that Kathy had kept between June 1996 and June 1997 – two months before Laura was born – and, without asking her if he could do so, started reading it.

'I found some entries which concerned me,' he said later.

Then, in an act which some would regard as a rank betrayal of his wife and her privacy, he handed the journal over to Bernie Ryan, claiming that he felt 'an obligation and duty' to his children to do so.

Craig's boss, Evan Teasdale, told the police that one morning after this, Craig approached him at work, looking grim. He told him: 'I found a diary which was in a box at home, the stuff that Kathy didn't take with her. There's stuff in the diary that I can't explain, and it indicates that Kathy may have killed the children.'

Speaking out years later on the ABC's *Australian Story*, Detectives Frith and Ryan described the moment that Craig came forward with his wife's private journal. That one act, they said, provided the key breakthrough in their investigation.

'The big turning point in the case was when we received a phone call from Craig,' Detective Frith explained. 'He wanted to have a talk about things, and he unloaded on us all the things that had been on his mind over the years.'

One evening in May, five days after his Mother's Day rebuff, Craig was sitting at home in Millard Close with his boss, drinking beer, when they heard a knock at the door; it was Bernie Ryan and Dave Frith. As the two detectives came in to speak to Craig, Evan Teasdale excused himself and left.

In a formal statement later, Detective Ryan said Craig told them that he suspected that Kathy might have killed their children.

It was an astounding accusation, and the two detectives listened intently as Craig laid out six reasons for his suspicions. He told them to begin with that Kathy had always found motherhood to be a stressful experience, and she lost her temper on a regular basis.

Secondly, on the night before Sarah died, Kathy became agitated when she wouldn't go to sleep, carried Sarah up to Craig, and 'threw' her onto his lap.

Thirdly, at 1 am on the morning when Sarah died, he woke up and saw that Kathy and Sarah were not in their beds, and the door to the bedroom was closed, with a light on in the other part of the house. Craig told the detectives that he went back to sleep and about half an hour later, was awoken by Kathy standing in the doorway. The light was on, and Sarah was 'apparently deceased' in her bed.

Fourthly, he had found a diary written by Kathy which contained entries relating to his children's deaths which he found 'disturbing'.

The fifth observation made by Craig was that on the morning Laura died, he and Kathy had an argument after she had become 'stressed and agitated' with Laura's behaviour. Craig told the detectives that Kathy's behaviour frightened Laura, who was scared of going near her mother.

The final reason he gave the two detectives for suspecting that his wife might have killed their children was that one day after Laura's death, he had overheard Kathy speaking to herself, using three different voices.

The two detectives knew that Kathy had left Craig and were aware of the emotional turmoil he was going through when he came forward. They suspected that he might be out for revenge and asked him to consult his family before giving them a formal statement. After doing so, Craig was interviewed by Detective Ryan and handed over the diary kept by Kathy in 1989, when Caleb was born, and the journal covering the year from June 1996 to June 1997.

Craig's police interview later in May lasted all day, and Detective Ryan asked him to return the following day to finish his statement. But Craig told him he had work commitments and would come back another time.

Four days later, he did so and — to Bernie Ryan's astonishment — retracted the allegations he had made. In a remarkable about-face, Craig said he had been motivated by spite in what he had said four days previously: 'Time has rolled on, and my wife hasn't come back to me. I have seen her out in Singleton, and she appears to be enjoying herself. I am deeply hurt, and I want her back. I believe because of this, I contacted Detective Ryan and told him some things that were not true,' he confessed.

'I told him that on the night Sarah died, Kathy and Sarah were not in the room when I woke up at 1 am. I also said that after Laura died, I heard Kathy talking to herself, using a different accent. I must admit that I was hurt at the time I said these things to Detective Ryan, and also, I was naturally suspicious about the deaths of my children.'

He added: 'I love my wife and still do. I would never seriously think she has hurt my children but of course everybody around me are saying that it is suspicious. I suppose I told Detective Ryan those things out of spite and because I was hurt that Kathy wouldn't come back to me. Even so, everything that is recorded in this statement is the truth, honest to God.'

What Detective Ryan didn't know at the time was that the evening before he said this, Craig had left home to watch the flat in Singleton where Kathy was staying, because he knew she had a date that night. He waited in his car and when Kathy and her friend returned, watched them embrace and disappear into the flat she was staying in. He would later describe how he walked over to the flat and saw Kathy and her friend undressing each other in the loungeroom, 'so I sat down on the step and started to cry'.

Feeling jealous and enraged, he banged on the door, and when Kathy answered, he challenged her, asking her: 'Why did my daughter have to die for you to achieve all this?' Kathy slammed the door in his face, and he drove home.

Later that night, Craig explained, Kathy drove round to see him, and she asked him: 'How could you think that of me? I was their mother, I loved them, you know I loved them.'

Craig said: 'It hurt ... Here was this woman who'd spent so many years with me, who had given birth to these children for me, and I had done this, I had broken her heart. I, dead set, I'd have necked myself if I could've right there and then, that's how bad I felt.'

Years later, in relating this story, Craig told Detective Ryan that his wife 'always has had this "you beaut" unique ability to appear to be a broken sparrow, and it just reaches right into the depths of your soul'.

When Craig walked back into the police station to retract the accusations he had made, it was after he and Kathy had stayed up most of the night, talking.

He ended his statement with a resounding endorsement of his wife: 'I know that having four children die is not common, but nobody knows my wife like I do. I have been with her for fourteen years and we have been literally to hell and back. I have seen how she loved our children and how she dealt with their deaths in her own way ...

'Having watched Kathy as a mother and saw the joy these children gave her, then to watch that disappear, I don't and can't believe that Kathy killed my children.'

Many detectives at this point might have thrown in the towel and decided that if Laura's father had admitted lying to them, he should be charged with obstructing a police investigation and suffer the consequences. With no confession from either parent or any forensic evidence to incriminate either of them, the entire investigation could have been shelved. The homicide squad had already run a mile from the case.

But not Bernie Ryan. Armed with Dr Cala's strong suspicions about how the children had died, he was determined not to let the matter drop. But the challenge ahead of him was huge.

As Detective Frith later put it colloquially when he spoke to the ABC: 'The common view was, yeah, it looks suspicious, yeah, we think she did it, but basically, you'll never prove it.'

10

'OBVIOUSLY, I'M MY FATHER'S DAUGHTER'

The row that Craig and Kathy had on the night in May before he retracted his allegations would prove to be the catalyst for the two of them getting back together.

But one month later, just after her thirty-second birthday, Kathy hit a low point. Tossing and turning in bed, she was close to despair, trying to understand everything that had happened to her in her life, and why she had even been born.

At 4am on 19 June 1999, in a new entry in a journal, she described herself as being 'unwanted at birth', with a father who had taken her mother from her and ruined her life through the act of murdering her.

In the last few days, she wrote, 'my heart has been breaking, soul torn apart'.

In the midst of her despair, her thoughts were dark. She knew she was deeply depressed, and felt tempted 'not to bother' anymore, to let herself slip away 'anywhere but here and present time'.

Surprisingly perhaps, given how far apart she and Craig had grown, Kathy wrote that the only thing stopping her was Craig's 'undying love' and adoration, something, she wrote, she would never understand. And in her state of constant, chronic self-blame, she had trouble justifying to herself that she deserved his love.

In a touching tribute to Craig, she professed her love for him, writing that he had shown her what love is. His happiness, wellbeing and security depended on her and she believed it had prevented her from dying inside – although with Laura gone, that had happened anyway, to a great extent.

'I just want to cry all day and night,' she wrote.

Kathy had vowed not to write her feelings down ever again, but it seemed to help her process and release them.

She knew Craig would read what she had written, and she reassured him that she wasn't leaving him or slipping away. She just felt confused and was tired of being sad the whole time.

The only comfort she felt now, was that, wherever they were now, her children were carefree and always loved. It was something she had to believe to preserve her sanity.

Detective Ryan and Detective Frith now had a problem. If 'Meadow's Law' was to be believed, one of the parents and – if the DiMaios were right, almost certainly Kathy – had killed at least one, and maybe all, of her children. But where was the evidence?

After pointing the finger at his wife, Craig was now telling the detectives that he couldn't believe she had harmed them in any way. Dr Cala couldn't prove it. And, when they took statements from Kathy's neighbours, the evidence they gave was tentative at best. One neighbour who had lost a boy of her own to SIDS thought the way Kathy behaved after Laura died was suspicious.

'She doesn't appear that affected by the death of Laura. I don't know how other people cope with grief, but I know when I lost my baby, I was overcome by grief and I couldn't go anywhere,' she told the police.

Another neighbour complained that after Laura died, 'I saw that Craig was crying and appeared devastated. Kath did not have a tear in her eyes, and she appeared calm.'

This though, hardly amounted to evidence of foul play. Yes, Kathy had returned to the gym soon after Laura died to get the support of her female friends, but Craig was equally culpable; even overcome by grief as he undoubtedly was, he returned to work soon afterwards.

Maybe sensing that the investigation was on its last legs, Detective Ryan applied for a telephone intercept to be placed on Kathy and Craig's phone line at home.

To this day, it's unclear what justification he put forward for doing so, and why permission was granted, given that no charges had been laid, and no hard evidence had been produced to implicate either parent in harming any of their children.

But permission was granted, and the following day, a warrant under section 46 of the *Telecommunications (Interception) Act 1979* was forwarded to Telstra — Australia's main telecommunications provider — asking the company to help set up an intercept, to enable the police to listen to phone calls to and from the Folbigg home. Technical assistance was given by the Australian Federal Police.

One week later, in a bare-faced invasion of their privacy, a warrant was approved by a judge for listening devices to be planted in the couple's bedroom and loungeroom, and a listening post was established to monitor and record their conversations. The devices were activated at 11 pm the next night, and for the next three weeks whatever they said at home was recorded and monitored.

The phone recordings started automatically, whenever Kathy or Craig lifted the handset at home, and whenever their number was dialled. The code name given to the operation to intercept the phone calls was 'JETTY', and the overall police investigation was code-named 'Open Bay'.

One evening, police officers listened in as Kathy and Craig had a conversation in their loungeroom. They heard Kathy tell Craig she had decided that if he wanted to read what she was writing in her diary, he could.

The next morning, Detective Ryan and another detective, Detective Senior Constable Marita Engdahl, drove to Millard Close and knocked on the door. Detective Ryan told Kathy that the investigation had reached a stage where he now wished to interview her about the deaths of all four children. He asked her if she was prepared to be interviewed and she agreed. She would later tell Tracy Chapman that in doing so, she wanted to be helpful.

Kathy drove herself to Singleton police station and called Craig on the way, telling him to come and join her. The detective told them both that Kathy wasn't under arrest, but that he wished to interview her alone, as Craig was a 'witness in the matter'. He asked Kathy if she wished to call someone to be present with her during the interview and she said no, clearly believing that the interview would be short and straightforward.

There is no record of Detective Ryan advising her to bring a solicitor to the interview, but at the outset, he cautioned her, telling her that she wasn't obliged to answer any questions unless she wished to do so, but warning her that anything she said or did would be recorded and might be used in evidence.

What Kathy could not possibly have expected, was the time it took for the interview to be completed. It began just after 9.25 am on 23 July, and, with a break for lunch, finished at about 5.40 pm – more than eight hours later.

During the first part of the interview, Kathy told her own story, and the story of her children, volunteering as much helpful detail as she could. But after lunch, the tone of the interview changed, and for the next four hours, Kathy was interrogated about the circumstances surrounding each of the children's deaths, and – to her amazement – about several of the entries she had written in her journal which Craig had handed over to Bernie Ryan.

Kathy explained that she used to write in journals as a 'vent or a release', and to write her thoughts down rather than talk to Craig, but that she had stopped doing so after discovering him reading one of her journals, which she regarded as an invasion of her privacy.

She told the two detectives that on Mother's Day that year, she had got rid of all her diaries, three in total, and hadn't written in one since.

Detective Ryan focused his interrogation on Sarah's life and death. It was by far the longest part of the interview, encompassing a total of 283 questions.

He asked Kathy to comment on the allegation that Craig had made – and later retracted – that when he woke up at one o'clock on the morning Sarah died, he saw that Kathy wasn't in bed and neither was Sarah. The door to the bedroom was closed and a light was on somewhere else in the house. 'Now what can you tell me about that?' he challenged her.

'That is incorrect,' she replied. 'Sarah never left the bedroom; she was in the bedroom the whole time.'

Detective Ryan pressed Kathy further on the allegation – even though Craig had told him later that it wasn't true. 'Do you understand the significance of that statement that Craig made to me at your family home in May this year?' he asked.

'Yep, but that's not how it was,' she replied.

It was only then that Detective Ryan admitted: 'And to be fair to you, when I took a statement off Craig he did retract that statement and said that you were out of the room when he woke up, but Sarah was in bed.'

When the interview turned to the entries in the 1996/97 journal, Kathy said Craig had told her he had handed it over to the police. 'I wasn't happy about it, but he said there was a few passages in it that he didn't understand himself, so he asked me some questions and I answered them.'

Detective Ryan asked Kathy what she meant by the phrase 'lose control like last times' in an entry from June 1997, where she had written:

> I'll have help & support this time. When I think I'm going to loose control like last times, I'll just hand baby over to someone else.

Kathy replied: 'The frustration that I felt with Sarah every now and then, the frustration that I feel with Patrick. They were never frustrations that was detrimental to the kids in any way, it was usually always directed at myself or at Craig ... Instead of trying to handle everything myself, let other people sort of do it for me.'

There were other journal entries that Detective Ryan wanted Kathy to explain. In one of them, from October 1996, Kathy bemoaned the fact that she still wasn't pregnant; her conclusion was that nature, fate and 'the man upstairs' had decided to deny her the chance of giving birth to a fourth child. And, she surmised, that was rightly so. As she consistently had in her journals, Kathy again blamed herself, writing that she wanted to correct all her 'mistakes and terrible thinking'.

Detective Ryan asked her: 'What were your mistakes and terrible thinking?'

'Just the frustrations that I might have felt with Pat,' she replied, 'and the occasional battles of will that I would have had with Sarah. To me, looking back at that time, I thought that was a terrible way of thinking. I kept telling myself that that shouldn't have happened.'

Then he asked her: 'What do you mean by, "Obviously I'm my father's daughter"?'

'My natural father is just a total big loser to turn around and to do what he did, stuffin' up his own life, stuffin' up my life, stuffin' up anybody they come in contact with,' Kathy replied. 'To me, that's just a loser in general. So I was thinkin' along the lines of am I a loser? Is it just not meant for me to, I was very sort of down on myself in certain areas but not in others back then, so.'

'Tell me about your dad,' Detective Ryan continued.

'I found more information out just recently which doesn't help his case any in my eyes, as far as I'm concerned,' Kathy replied. 'He killed my mother by stabbin' her twenty-odd times. This is supposed to have been over who had me when and where and why. And my natural family was responsible for hidin' me all over the place 'cause he turned out to be not a very nice sort of man.

'I just found out recently that he was actually one of Lenny McPherson's major hit-men sort of thing, he was his right-hand lieutenant man, used to go and do debt collectin' and all that sort of thing ... I was thinking maybe I was a loser of some kind that sort of was destined to have some sort of tragic life of some kind, but it is a passing thought. I sort of didn't, I tried not to let it dwell or anything. But that was more of a recrimination of him rather than me in general.'

The detective asked Kathy, bluntly: 'Did you ever feel as though you hated the children?'

'Never, no,' she replied. 'I've never, never hated my children. How can you hate a child?'

Not content with her answers so far, Detective Ryan moved on to the entry written on New Year's Day 1997, in which Kathy, with a baby on the way, looked forward excitedly to the year ahead. She felt confident, now, that everything would go well.

Unlike before, she said she would ask for help if she needed to and wouldn't try to do everything on her own. Cryptically, she wrote: 'I know that that was the main reason for all my stress before & stress made me do terrible things.'

What had she meant by the phrase: 'Stress made me do terrible things'?

'Yeah, as in have an angry thought here or there,' Kathy answered. 'I don't think I've met a parent that doesn't have an angry thought every now and again if their child's arguing with them or something's not going quite right or it's just not happening, as in, well, take Sarah, for example, when she wouldn't go to sleep, sure the battle of wills would kick in, the frustration would kick in and yes I would have an angry thought, but it was never to harm her, it was always, why wasn't Craig here to help me, you know? Or something along those lines, yeah. So I sort of decided that stress must have been the trigger for all that.'

Detective Ryan moved on to an entry just one month later in which Kathy's mood seemed to have changed dramatically. In contrast to the excitement she had felt on New Year's Day, she was now thinking about Caleb, Patrick and Sarah, and questioning whether she was doing the right thing by having a fourth child. 'My guilt of how responsible I feel for them all, haunts me,' she wrote. And her fear that it would happen again.

'Do you seriously think that you are responsible for your children's death?' the detective asked her.

'I regarded it, and I still sometimes do now ... that it was a failure of mine somewhere along the lines if I couldn't keep my children alive and with me,' Kathy replied.

'How have you failed?' Detective Ryan asked.

'Didn't do something, didn't walk in the room two minutes earlier, didn't check two seconds earlier, I didn't do something that would have meant when I walked in the room that they were alive and well, instead of when I've walked in the room they weren't,' she responded.

'"My fear of it happening again, haunts me." What's "it"?'

'Death,' Kathy replied.

In the same diary entry, Kathy asked herself a rhetorical question: 'What sort of mother am I, have I been – a terrible one ...'

'Why do you say you were a terrible mother?' the detective asked.

'Because they weren't there with me, no other reason. I look at other mothers who can be popping out five, six, seven, eight of them, probably having even more stress and trouble than I have ever had in my lifetime with that many of them, but they were all still there.'

By this time, Kathy was tiring, both mentally and emotionally, but the questions kept on coming. Question 732 from Detective Ryan was: 'Are you all right to continue?'

'Yeah,' she replied, clearly worn out.

Towards the end of the interview, Detective Ryan asked Kathy: 'How can you explain the deaths of your four children?'

'I can't,' she replied. 'I have had ministers stand there and tell me that God only takes the best and, you know, along the lines of, your child was one of the best so he decided to take ... I don't agree with that ... that makes it sound like every other child that's on the planet wasn't one of the good ones, that's just, you know, unacceptable. So, I'm not religious. I don't think of it like that.'

Detective Ryan asked her: 'Can you close your eyes and see the faces of all four of your children?'

'I honestly tell you now I can see Laura's clearly; Sarah's, Patrick's and Caleb's take photographs for me to remember what they looked like,' she replied.

'How do you feel for them?'

'That they are somewhere peaceful, happy.'

'Do you really believe that?'

'I don't know, I don't know, I prefer to believe that. That's probably what it is.'

Then, after seven hours of interrogation, came the kicker: 'Do you think Craig is responsible for the deaths of your children?'

'No!' she replied, barely whispering.

'Do you know what sort of person would kill four children?'

'I have no comprehension and I don't even want to think about it.' Again, she was barely whispering.

'Are you responsible for the death of Caleb?'

'No.' At this point, she was crying, dabbing her eyes and clearly, simply stunned.

'Are you responsible for the death of Patrick?'

'No, no.'

'Are you responsible for the death of Sarah?'

'No.'

'And are you responsible for the death of Laura?'

'No!' she exclaimed, with added force.

But the detective wasn't done. There was a fifteen second pause as she quietly wept, before he asked her again, 'Kathy, did you kill Caleb?'

'No!' she responded, with a visceral yell.

'Did you kill Patrick?'

'No,' again emphatic. Kathy couldn't believe she was even being asked the question.

'Did you try to kill Patrick on that near-miss episode?'

'No.'
'Did you kill Sarah?'
'No.'
'And did you kill Laura?'
Kathy answered wearily: 'No.'

It was only many years later, talking to Tracy Chapman, that Kathy spoke about this moment publicly. 'It wasn't until he was asking those questions that I sort of finally semi-clicked what was going on. It was just so shocking to me, and it was a dawning realisation that people have been saying things, and people are alleging things, you know?' she told her friend.

As Detective Ryan wrapped up the interview, another officer entered the room and asked her: 'Have you any complaints about the manner in which you have been interviewed?'

'No,' she replied, exhausted.

11

'ALL NIGHT I'VE BEEN THINKING, MAYBE I KILLED THE KIDS'

Immediately after the police interview finished, Detective Ryan told Kathy that they were going to search her home in Millard Close, and the flat where she had been living in Andrew Street. He told her they were looking for other diaries she had written, and she volunteered that she had just started a new diary which was up at the house.

At Andrew Street, as Detective Ryan formally cautioned Kathy, the conversation was filmed by another officer. There, they found the 'May Gibbs' diary in which Kathy had recorded Caleb's progress during his short life, in a yellow milk crate, and they also took a handwritten letter, five pages long and the Mother's Day card that Craig had given Kathy. In a concertina file inside the pantry, they found a four-page typed record of the interview that the police had conducted with Kathy's father, Thomas Britton, after arresting him for the murder of her mother, Kathleen Donovan, in December 1968.

Forty-five minutes later, they went to Millard Close, where Craig was. Detective Ryan cautioned them both, and Kathy told him that there was a diary there that she had bought the day before. She opened a bedroom wardrobe, retrieved it and gave it to one of the officers. Again, the search was filmed.

Shortly afterwards one of the other officers found a second diary in a crocheted carry bag, which was wrapped in clothes and placed in a blue plastic container in the bedroom wardrobe.

Kathy remarked that she hadn't known it was there – she thought it had gone.

It had been a long and demanding day for Kathy, and later that evening the police listened in as she and Craig went over the day's events and discussed the eight-hour interview that Kathy had endured, without the benefit of a lawyer – or anyone indeed – to help her through the ordeal.

By now it was crystal clear to both of them that Detective Ryan believed that Kathy had killed her children.

Kathy homed in on the lines of questioning he had adopted, including focusing on the stress and frustrations she had sometimes felt while looking after the children. 'Talking about Patrick seemed to make me cry,' she told Craig. 'I tried to explain everything we did, how I looked after him, the whole lot. We were trying so hard to keep him with us, because when I said that I burst into tears … then it all got turned around along the lines that caring for Patrick was all too much for me, you know?'

Kathy told Craig her theory that the detectives believed she was suffering from Munchausen Syndrome by Proxy, a psychiatric disorder that, in layman's terms, involves a parent inventing a sickness in their child, to attract attention. Coincidentally, the disorder was first defined by Professor Roy Meadow.

In the intercepted call, Kathy told Craig: 'Obviously, I'd get pregnant for the attention, have children for the attention, and kill 'em for the attention. From what I can gather that must be where they're aiming.'

Three days later, the police listened in on another conversation in the couple's loungeroom. It was first thing in the morning, and Craig asked Kathy how she was feeling; her response, according to the police transcript, was inaudible, as was much of the remaining conversation. Most probably, she said she was stressed.

Craig appeared worried; something was bugging him. When he told her what it was, it hit Kathy like a shock of cold water, and the detectives listening in must have been stunned.

Craig: 'Yeah I'm really stressed out too. You know, all night I've been thinking, maybe I killed the kids.'
Kathy: 'Why?'
Craig: 'Why can't they think that?'
Kathy: 'The problem was, I found them all.'
Craig: 'Yeah.'

Some of Kathy's responses at this point, according to the police transcript, were inaudible, or couldn't be transcribed.

Craig: 'Every time we've had a kid ... that's, ah, driven a wedge between us and the best solution for me to get your attention and ... back is ... the kids. And how do I do it? You're asleep, I get up, I kill Caleb ...
Kathy: '...'
Craig: 'Hold on a minute, hold on a minute, hold on a minute, can you hear me out? Alright, so I get up and I kill Caleb, because the next person to find him would be you, alright? Sarah, you're out of the room, I wake up, I admit that I wake up at one o'clock, I kill her in her sleep while you're out of the room.'
Kathy: '...'
Craig: 'Doesn't take long to kill 'em. Patrick, when he was three months old, I go into his room, I try to kill him, but ... I didn't do a good enough job ... but Patrick died epileptic ... during the day while you were nursing, cause you battled so hard to keep him. And Laura, Laura is ... relationship problems ... I came up while youse home, you were outside. I came in the front door; you have no idea I'm here ... Who had anything to gain out of them not being around? Me ...'
Kathy: '...'
Craig: '...'
Kathy: '... conversations ... ridiculous.'
Craig: 'It's not ridiculous. It's as feasible as what they're trying [to] say about you. And in this whole relationship and

this whole house the only person that was on the ... was me, the only person that had anything to gain out [of] them children not being with us at any given time was me, so what did I gain? You ... I could come in that door, you'd be watching a video, I could come in that door and and move around in this house without ... you wouldn't have known I was here.'

A further passage of conversation at this point was recorded by the police as being inaudible. Craig, presumably, was acknowledging that what he had said up to that point wasn't fact – it was entirely hypothetical. And, that he would never, ever have harmed the children.

> Craig: 'Well, you know why; because I was so in love with them.'
> Kathy: 'Yeah.'
> Craig: 'So were you. Alls I'm trying to show you is, the futility of the bullshit he's going on.'
> Kathy: 'No, all you're doing is, I'm already worried about you, by what's going [to] happen through all this. Now you're just making me scared even more.'
> Craig: 'For me.'
> Kathy: 'Yes.'
> Craig: 'What, what, mentally?'
> Kathy: 'Yeah. What it will do to you and what it's gradually doing to me ...'

There is no record of how the police reacted to this conversation when they first listened to it – but it must have sounded chilling, and unsettling.

Here was Craig – who had already retracted his original allegation that Kathy had killed the children – suggesting it was just as plausible that he could have killed Caleb, Sarah and Laura, and tried to kill Patrick, as it was that Kathy might have done so. He was saying, frighteningly, that it 'doesn't take long to kill 'em', giving a detailed explanation of how he could have done so, and in addition, what his motive could have been – to repair his relationship with Kathy which had broken down repeatedly while the children were alive.

Equally clear, however, is that Kathy was having none of it – it was nonsense, as far as she was concerned, and it disturbed her to hear him talk like this. She was worried about his state of mind and she slapped him down.

> Kathy: 'I don't ever want to hear you talking about, you might have done it, again.'
> Craig: 'Why, 'cause you've wondered whether I did?'
> Kathy: 'Of course, the same as you wondered whether I did. A quick fleeing moment and then it's, shake your head, don't be so stupid!'
> Craig: 'Because of the situations that I've just posed, the scenarios I've just posed are pretty feasible and … oh shit, did he get up and do this?'
> Kathy: I just don't want to hear you mention it again, it's bad enough he's going for one of us; I'm not having him going after you.'

Craig for his part was plainly furious with Detective Ryan.

> Craig: 'I don't think he knows how to give up. It's just a sick theory of what he's put together on you, yeah, and it's just as untrue … But they're not willing to see that, all they [want] to see is bad shit.'

That wasn't all. In the same conversation, Craig referred to one occasion when Detective Ryan had visited him at Teasdale's and pulled him aside – ostensibly, to persuade him that, sometimes, mothers do kill their children. He referred to it as 'the conversation that set me on my spew of thoughts … Bernie Ryan put that shit in my head. Nobody else, everybody else I've ever spoken to saw you for exactly what you were.'

By the time this conversation was recorded, three days after Kathy's interview, she and Craig had seen a solicitor, and in a telephone conversation from home with a friend later the same day, which was also secretly recorded, Craig referred to this. He said that their solicitor had told them that the police were trying to intimidate them.

'They've just got this bee in their bonnet that she's a mother and she must have done it,' he said, adding that in his view, Detective Ryan was a 'gung-ho, young detective that's out to make a name for himself'. His friend agreed: 'That's what Kathy said, he's out for a promotion.'

The local solicitor who Kathy and Craig had approached to represent them was Brian Doyle, who would later talk to this writer about the first time he met them. 'They came into the office. And when you have a couple who you were told the police were investigating for the murder of four children, you don't know what to expect. And I was surprised when this very, very nice young couple came in and sat down.' Mr Doyle had done prosecutions before going into private practice, and by a twist of fate had worked with the first Director of Public Prosecutions in New South Wales, Reginald Blanch QC, who as a judge would later play a pivotal role in Kathy's story.

Neither of the two struck him as being in any way dishonest, and Kathy and Craig's position was 'that they'd unfortunately lost four children, that they were heartbroken by that experience and that they themselves, although the police had suggested they were responsible, had nothing to do with it'.

When the police were secretly recording the couple, Craig told Kathy he knew she was innocent. Detective Ryan was the villain.

> I don't want him going after you for something you didn't do. You and I know, I know you didn't do it, like you know I didn't do it.

Craig wrapped up the conversation with a startling personal confession:

> I really only wanted to propose all that to you, to show you that you're not a wicked person either. I can be a wicked person. I can be a deviate person, that's how I sell motor cars. I use whatever I can to my advantage, to sell a motor car, whether it's my children's lives or my children's deaths. When Laura was alive, I used the fact that she was alive and part of my life as an advantage to sell a motor car. Laura died; I used that as an advantage to sell a motor car.

It was a surprisingly honest self-appraisal from the second-hand car salesman.

12

'WITH THREE, YOU YELL "MURDER!"'

In the late 1990s, the pervasive influence of Meadow's Law had spread through the ranks of forensic pathology. From October 1999, Detective Ryan began to gather statements from doctors and medical experts – almost all of whom subscribed to Meadow's mantra, either overtly, or by inference.

One of the first statements Detective Ryan received was from Dr Ian Wilkinson, who had treated Patrick, in which he said: 'I would not have issued a death certificate if Patrick's death had been preceded by the death of his siblings.'

Shortly afterwards, the detective received an email from Dr Janice Ophoven, a paediatric forensic pathologist from St Paul, Minnesota, who coincidentally had re-examined the medical evidence in the Waneta Hoyt case. Detective Ryan was enthusiastic about having her onboard, writing in the police running sheet that Dr Ophoven's CV 'indicates that she will be a valuable witness in this matter'.

That same day, he asked Rozalinda Garbutt, a police psychologist, to prepare a report on the case.

Ms Garbutt wrote: 'If natural causes are eliminated, then in my opinion Kathleen Folbigg became angry and frustrated with her children's crying and need for constant attention to a point where it overwhelmed her, and she lost control and consciously ended the lives of each child.'

This conclusion was certainly helpful to the lines of inquiry being undertaken by Detective Ryan, and it was reached with the help of an early brief of evidence supplied to her by the detectives, together with letters written by Kathy and Craig, transcripts of their police interviews, and Kathy's diaries.

Ms Garbutt was an enthusiastic adherent of Meadow's Law, writing that: 'Accidental death through Sudden Infant Death Syndrome or natural causes is believable for one child within a family, concerning for two and suspicious when three or four children die.'

She quoted Dr Linda Norton, a Dallas-based pathologist who had lobbied for the unfortunate Waneta Hoyt to be charged with killing her children: 'There are some who say one infant death is SIDS, two leaves a big question mark and with three, you yell "Murder"!'

If Garbutt's opinion buttressed the detectives' suspicions, they were left hanging when, at the end of November, the results of scientific tests on the stain on Laura's pillowcase were revealed. A preliminary screening showed the stain was indeed blood. Only much later would further laboratory tests confirm that the blood was human, but that it hadn't come from Laura or Kathy. It had come from a male – though probably not from Craig.

Even so, in early December, Dr Susan Beal, a paediatrician from Adelaide, became the second expert in the case to nail her colours firmly to the mast of Meadow's Law, telling Detective Ryan: 'I have no hesitation in saying I believe that all four children were murdered by their mother.'

Dr Beal was seen as a bona fide expert. She had studied SIDS for over thirty years and had interviewed the families of more than 500 infants who had died suddenly and unexpectedly.

She thoroughly endorsed Dr Meadow. 'I would agree with the pathologist who said the first unexplained death in a family may be called SIDS, the second should be labelled undetermined; and the third is murder until proven otherwise,' she wrote in the Expert Certificate she submitted to the police investigation. And for the record: 'As far as I am aware there has never been three or more deaths from SIDS in the one family anywhere in the world, although some families, later proven to have murdered their infants, had infants who were originally classified as SIDS.'

On the surface, this definitive statement stood completely at odds with an article which Dr Beal had co-authored eleven years earlier, in which one family was recorded as having suffered three infant deaths from SIDS. But it didn't deflect her from declaring that Kathy had murdered her children.

In mid-December, Dr Allan Cala delivered his final autopsy report, in which he reiterated his initial view, that Laura's cause of death was 'undetermined'. But his conclusion went much further than that.

'The possibility of multiple homicides in this family has not been excluded,' he wrote. 'If homicidal acts have been committed, it is most likely these acts have been in the form of deliberate smothering. Smothering, whether deliberately or accidentally inflicted, may leave no trace. There are no specific postmortem findings for smothering. It is usually performed by one person, in the absence of any witnesses. It is relatively easy for an adult to smother an infant or small child with a hand, pillow, soft toy or other similar object.'

Dr Cala had found no physical evidence of Laura being a victim of homicide, but he had found forensic evidence of myocarditis. Despite this, he went on to theorise that if Laura was killed, it was likely by smothering.

As he later told the ABC's *Australian Story*: 'I suspected one thing, but medically I couldn't prove it.'

By now, though, Detective Ryan was on a roll, and in June 2000, six months after Dr Cala delivered his report, he was given the funds to travel overseas to consult with two experts. In his luggage were slides containing tissue samples from Kathy's four children. He gave some of the slides to Dr Ophoven, when he met her in Minnesota, and after that he travelled on to the UK where, at the Swallow Hotel in Bristol, he gave the remaining slides to a British paediatrician, Professor Peter Berry, who had been recommended to him by the British police officer seconded to the New South Wales force, Robin Napper.

Both experts were also handed transcripts of the intercepted conversations recorded by the police, along with some of

Kathy's diary entries, even though the diaries and their meaning lay well outside their respective areas of expertise.

In early September, Dr Ophoven submitted an Expert Certificate, in which she concluded that 'these four children were all the victims of homicidal assaults that resulted in their suffocations'. She added: 'In small infants, this typically does not result in any external signs or physical evidence.'

In what would prove to be an enormously controversial statement, Dr Ophoven wrote that: 'None of the deaths in this case can be attributed to SIDS. It is well recognized that the SIDS process is not a hereditary problem and the statistical likelihood that 4 children could die from SIDS is in excess of 1 in a trillion.'

In a clear nod to Dr Meadow and the DiMaios, she added: 'Forensic standards of practice would not allow for consideration of a second diagnosis of SIDS after a second sudden death and by the time a third child has died, the death must be investigated as a homicide.'

In her opinion, Caleb's cause of death was 'Undetermined'. But the cause of death for Patrick, Sarah and Laura was 'Suffocation' and in all four cases, the manner of their death was 'Homicide'.

Two days after Christmas, Detective Ryan received Professor Berry's report.

In considering how Caleb had died, Professor Berry commented that Kathy's own observation of blood-stained froth around Caleb's nose and mouth when she found him not breathing 'is a common finding in sudden infant deaths and accidental or deliberate suffocation'.

The professor had read her diary entry on the day Caleb died: 'Finally Asleep!!' – with two exclamation marks after it – and, without offering any further evidence for his opinion, suggested that, 'The mother's diary entry is, on the face of it, extremely worrying.'

He also noted the finding of haemosiderin, signifying a previous haemorrhage in Caleb's lungs, and wrote: 'Faced with a similar case today, I would not give the cause of death as SIDS because of the finding of haemosiderin in the lungs. That and the diary entry would lead me to suspect suffocation, and I would recommend a full police investigation.'

This must have come as music to Detective Ryan's ears.

Professor Berry also speculated that Patrick's acute life-threatening event, which resulted in brain damage, was concerning, 'because the window of opportunity to find a child in extremis and affect resuscitation is very short, probably a matter of only a few minutes. This raises the question that the person who finds the baby may have been present when the collapse occurred and may have been its cause. Such "acute life-threatening events" are not part of the usual natural history of SIDS.'

He acknowledged, however, that: 'Taking this case in isolation I would have given the cause of death as "not ascertained", ascribing it to brain damage following an unexplained collapse.'

With Sarah, Professor Berry again turned to the extraneous evidence, saying that: 'It is of concern that Craig's account indicates considerable tension in Kathy on the evening that Sarah died. Nevertheless, in these circumstances and after careful investigation I would probably give the cause of death in isolation as SIDS, but with misgivings.'

The professor's most interesting finding related to Laura, and the myocarditis found at her autopsy. His comments showed him grappling – struggling even – with the obvious forensic evidence, but also with the allegation that Laura may have been smothered.

'It is generally agreed that even quite minor inflammation can result in abnormal heart rhythms and sudden death,' he wrote. 'In Laura's case the infiltrate in the heart was quite extensive, and most pathologists would have accepted it as the cause of death, although I was unable to convince myself of actual damage to heart muscle cells.

'However,' he added, 'it is recognised that an inflammatory infiltrate in the heart muscle is also quite commonly found in those who die of other causes, for example in road traffic accidents. It has been described as an incidental finding in suffocation …

'The finding of an inflammatory infiltrate in the heart does not necessarily mean it was responsible for death. Nevertheless, taken in isolation I would have ascribed this death to myocarditis recognising that although the infiltrate was quite extensive, I could not see actual damage to heart muscle.'

It was only in considering all four deaths together that Professor Berry endorsed Detective Ryan's view that Kathy had killed her children.

'The sudden and unexpected death of three children in the same family without evidence of a natural cause is extraordinary,' he wrote. 'I am unable to rule out that Caleb, Patrick, Sarah, and possibly Laura Folbigg were suffocated by the person who found them lifeless, and I believe that it is probable that this was the case.'

The reports provided by Dr Cala, Dr Ophoven, Dr Beal and Professor Berry added considerable weight to the view that Kathy had murdered her children, but they provided no proof, and in early 2001, a local prosecutor in Newcastle, Greg Coles, was tasked with reading an early brief of evidence and deciding whether Kathy should be charged with murdering her children.

Remarkably – and no doubt, to the detectives' dismay – he decided against doing so. In a letter to Detective Ryan in February 2001, he advised that, after carefully considering the brief, 'the matter should be referred to the State Coroner, in order for a full inquest to be held'.

Mr Coles clearly believed that there was not enough evidence to charge Kathy with four homicides, but Detective Ryan thought otherwise. He met with the Deputy State Coroner for New South Wales, Jan Stevenson, at the coroner's court in Glebe, and in early April, Ms Stevenson telephoned Detective Ryan and advised him that Kathy should be charged with murdering her children.

This was a decision that would normally be made by a coroner only following an inquest, and after all the available evidence had been given by those most closely associated with the events – including in this case, most crucially, Kathy and Craig. But the deputy state coroner didn't believe this was necessary. On 6 April, Detectives Ryan and Frith attended a meeting at Westmead Coroners Court with Ms Stevenson and Crown Prosecutor David Frearson. Together, they agreed that there was now sufficient evidence to charge Kathy with murder.

There was one remaining weak link in the detectives' case, however. Craig was still on the record as supporting his wife. He had given the police an apparently damning version of the night Sarah died in his first police interview, and then retracted it four days later. It didn't help the prosecution's case one bit that he had done so, and in fact it weakened it considerably. Ideally, they needed Craig as a prosecution witness.

With this in mind, on 19 April 2001, the two detectives arrested Craig at the car yard, Teasdale's, and threatened to charge him with hindering their investigation into the children's deaths. He knew then that they meant business.

Craig agreed to be interviewed without a solicitor but with Evan Teasdale there to support him. The interview at Singleton police station was filmed, but the film of the interview has never been released.

In the interview, Detective Ryan reminded Craig that he had previously told the detectives that he had suspicions that Kathy had killed their children. 'It didn't add up,' Craig replied, in an effort perhaps to fit in with the detectives' agenda. 'How could I kiss a perfectly gorgeous little baby goodbye and half an hour later be confronted with that child dead? It didn't add up. And it frightened me.'

Detective Ryan quizzed Craig again about the night that Sarah died, asking him pointedly: 'Craig, what is the truth?'

Craig didn't sound confident. 'I'm fairly sure when I woke up that morning, that Sarah wasn't in the bed,' he said, directly contradicting what he had said on the day he retracted his previous statement. 'Mate, she wasn't in that bed. Her mother had her out there.'

Detective Ryan tried to nail him down: 'So what you're telling me today, Craig, if Sarah wasn't in the bed, and Kathy was up to her at one o'clock outside, tending to her in the other parts of the house, that would put Kathy with the baby, with your daughter, half an hour before she was discovered dead?'

'Correct,' Craig replied.

Then he changed his story again. It was no longer 1 o'clock in the morning when he woke – it was ten past one. 'I can see the clock as, as clear as I can see the room now,' he declared.

By this point, Craig was giving the detectives what they wanted to hear. And his motive for implicating Kathy in Sarah's death may have been that their relationship had finally ended the year before, when on her thirty-third birthday in June 2000, things came to a head.

Craig said Kathy told him she no longer loved him and didn't want to spend the rest of her life with him, and four days later, they had a violent argument which ended with Kathy slamming a door in his face and Craig shoving his foot through the door.

Craig admitted that at the height of their argument, he threatened her, saying: '"If you keep on going, you'll end up like your mother," and with that she smacked me in the face, and I just broke down and cried then, I sat on the lounge crying, because I didn't believe that I could be pushed to that sort of anger level.'

The next morning, Kathy left.

In his police interview, Craig became emotional, telling Detective Ryan that in the eighteen months since retracting the allegation that Kathy had killed her children, he had lived with 'the shame of what I've done ... I've lived with the shame of coming and changing that story ... I've felt that I couldn't protect those children in life and, and certainly didn't protect them in death.'

He told the detectives that there was one thing he had done 'that's made me just slightly prouder. I've organised to lay my children to rest at All Saints Church. I'll protect 'em in their death. I'll protect them ... with a resting place, so that ... she will never get them.' Craig was referring here to All Saints Cemetery in Parramatta, in Sydney's western suburbs, where a plaque was placed in memory of the children.

By the end of the interview, Detective Ryan knew he had what he needed to take the case to court. No charge was laid against Craig for hindering the police investigation, and instead, half an hour afterwards, Detective Ryan and Detective Frith went to the flat where Kathy was living with her new boyfriend.

Standing at the front door, Detective Ryan told her: 'Kathy, you are under arrest for murdering your four children. Do you understand that?'

'Yes,' she replied.

Kathy was taken to Singleton police station, formally charged and kept in a police cell overnight. Understandably, given what had happened previously, she declined to be interviewed again. As if the nightmare of all four of her children dying suddenly and unexpectedly wasn't enough, she was now being accused of murdering them all and was facing the prospect of her husband appearing in court to testify against her.

And there was the ghastly prospect of being tried, convicted and sent to prison for life, for crimes that, she insisted, she didn't commit.

13

'I COULDN'T LEAVE THE LADY IN THE LURCH'

The fact that Craig was prepared to have Kathy back in his life when he harboured strong suspicions that she had killed their children never sat well with Megan Donegan.

'Kathy and Craig split up not long after Laura died and while they were split up, Craig handed the diaries in to the police,' she says.

'They then reconciled. And they turned up on my doorstep at 8 am on Christmas morning 1999. And Craig was full of plans for the future. They weren't going to try and have any more of their own children. They weren't going to adopt. He wanted to foster, so that they could foster a child who was similar to Kathy. To give back to someone like Kathy. But they weren't going to do that for a little while. They were going to travel and get to know each other again.

'That's why it was so shocking when she told me that she'd been charged later. But what kind of person, if they thought that's what their wife was capable of, would go back to them? That's always concerned me, what his motive was in that, in going back to Kathy or in handing in the diaries that he thought were so bad, that he actually went and gave them to the police.'

Be that as it may, for Kathy, things were looking very dark. She was now in police custody, and the same day the detectives ferried her to Muswellbrook Court – an hour and a half north-west of Newcastle – to ask the court to deny her bail.

Brian Doyle, her solicitor, was appearing in court at Belmont, just south of Newcastle, which made it impossible for him to travel to represent her. The police knew he was Kathy's legal representative, and he wondered if they had taken her to Muswellbrook deliberately, to make it harder for him to do so.

Instead, a young local lawyer represented Kathy, as she sat, dressed in a T-shirt and denim shorts, listening as she was formally charged with murdering all four of her children. She didn't enter a plea.

The police prosecutor, Sergeant Dave Barron, told the court that Craig's evidence, together with extracts from Kathy's diaries, and the reports supplied by British and American experts, would play a part in the prosecution. The police case was strong, he suggested, and a study of Kathy's diaries showed that they contained partial admissions of guilt. 'All deaths were caused by smothering, and all deaths are homicides,' he alleged. Bail was duly refused.

The following Monday, Mr Doyle appeared for Kathy at Maitland Court, where he took instructions from her in one of the cells and was handed a lengthy 'statement of facts' prepared by the police.

The statement concerned him greatly. He knew it would be available to the media, who could pick out the most sensational allegations contained in the documents. 'It didn't make pretty reading,' he said. 'Some of it was in fairly lurid terms. It had references to all these supposed experts from overseas who were giving opinions about the possibility of children dying from SIDS.

'One of them was referring to a theory by Dr Meadow from England, who said: "One death, unfortunate, two, something else, and three – that's murder." That was pretty dramatic stuff and of course as I expected, that's the kind of stuff that was reported. And once it was in the media, people could have access to it at any time in the future. I tried to have that kept out – unsuccessfully.'

Brian Doyle was long enough in the tooth to know how these things work. The police produce a statement of facts that – on the surface at least – is damning, the press report it, and before you know it, the accused person is found guilty, in the court of public opinion at least.

And his fears were realised. Under headlines such as: 'Odds of Baby Deaths "Astronomical"' and '"Chance of One in a Million"', the papers reported how, as Kathy sat in the dock in her prison greens, police prosecutor Sergeant Daniel Maher tendered the report from Dr Ophoven in which she claimed that the odds of four unexplained infant deaths occurring in the one family, were 'one in a trillion'.

Sergeant Maher suggested that if all four children died from natural causes, 'it would mean this was the only case ever occurring in the world', adding: 'that is just not likely'.

The police statement also referred to the fact that Thomas Britton had murdered Kathy's mother, and Sergeant Maher quoted the entry she had made in her diary: 'Obviously, I am my father's daughter,' as further evidence suggesting that she had killed her children.

Kathy's new boyfriend, Tony Lambkin, a Singleton builder, was in court as Brian Doyle asked for bail on Kathy's behalf and Sergeant Maher opposed it. Mr Doyle explained that Kathy and Tony Lambkin had started a relationship eight months before and were living together when Kathy was arrested. 'He asked her to marry him, but she hasn't been able to say yes, because of this being over her head for two years,' Mr Doyle told the magistrate.

That too was welcome fodder for the press. 'Accused Mother Cannot Say "I Do"' ran one headline.

Brian Doyle argued that the police case was actually weak, that the deaths of her children were coincidental, and there was no direct evidence linking her to their deaths. In addition, he argued, all four children had been ill at some point in their lifetime. He pointed out that the medical experts had reached their conclusions only after reading Kathy's diaries.

Mr Doyle assured the court that Kathy would abide by her bail conditions because of her close relationship with Mr Lambkin, her ties to Singleton, and her wish to continue working as a waitress in the job she had held for the previous two years.

Even so, bail was refused. As Kathy was led to the prison van, she spoke one word to the waiting media: 'Innocent!'

By now, armed with the dramatic statement of facts, the media was well and truly on the case. Brian Doyle believes that even at this very early stage in the criminal proceedings, the publication of Dr Ophoven's opinion and the details of Kathleen Donovan's brutal murder by Kathy's father were extremely damaging.

But three and a half weeks later, it was Detective Ryan's turn to come away from court empty-handed when his efforts to keep Kathy behind bars failed, and she was granted bail at last.

Kathy, speaking via a video link from the maximum security Mulawa Correctional Centre in western Sydney, told the New South Wales Supreme Court that if granted bail, she would go home to her flat and continue living with Tony Lambkin, with whom she had a stable relationship, adding: 'He wishes me to be his wife.'

Mr Lambkin stepped up and posted a surety of $4000 for Kathy, confirming that she would stay with him and wouldn't abscond. And, the court heard, Kathy could continue her waitressing job at a local hotel while she prepared her defence for the trial.

Detective Ryan didn't want Kathy to be freed. He was anxious to ensure that Craig wouldn't change his evidence for a third time, telling the court he had 'grave concerns' that Kathy, if released on bail, 'will attempt to manipulate her estranged husband into changing his evidence in relation to this matter'. He stressed that Craig was 'crucial to the Crown case'.

But his warning fell on deaf ears. Following her one-month long incarceration, bail was granted. Kathy smiled briefly as Justice Robert Hulme delivered his decision, saying that in his opinion, she posed no danger to the community and was unlikely to flee before her trial took place. She was also entitled to prepare her defence properly for the trial.

Outside court, a throng of newspaper reporters and TV crews were assembled. Brian Doyle remembers it well. 'I walked out of the court and the media were waiting and they asked me a number of questions which I wouldn't answer. But I did say to them that: "You, the people of the media, have been responsible for one woman to have already been convicted of the murder of her child. Would you please leave my client alone?"

'And I was referring, of course, to Lindy Chamberlain, and they were aware of that.' After that – at least for a time, she was left alone.

Kathy was released from Mulawa the same night. Her trial was expected to take place the following year, but excruciatingly, it would take another two years for her case to come to court.

Meanwhile, the police continued to gather evidence to support the prosecution case. Craig had already agreed to give evidence at the trial, and Detective Ryan had delivered a substantial brief of evidence to the Office of the Director of Public Prosecutions in April 2001, eleven days after Kathy was arrested and charged. But there was more work to do.

In June 2001, Dr Cala wrote a letter to Detective Ryan, answering several questions raised by the detective in relation to Laura's death.

To begin with, Detective Ryan wanted to know if tests had been carried out at Laura's postmortem for the presence of haemosiderin. Dr Cala told him that it had, with a negative result. He added that while the presence of haemosiderin was regarded by some pathologists as a marker for deliberate smothering, this was a view that had not been widely accepted by forensic pathologists.

Dr Cala also addressed Laura's myocarditis once again. He described it as being 'light in amount and patchy in distribution'. However, he conceded: 'If I had examined the body of Laura Folbigg in isolation, without the knowledge I had at the time of previous infant deaths in the family, I might have given the cause of death as myocarditis.'

Although Dr Cala had not performed autopsies on Caleb, Patrick or Sarah, the conclusion he reached was that: 'I remain very suspicious that all four Folbigg children may have died as a result of deliberate smothering.'

In November 2001, armed with Dr Ophoven's Expert Certificate and Professor Berry's report, Detective Ryan went to meet Professor Peter Herdson, an experienced consultant forensic pathologist, at his office in Canberra, following several phone conversations beforehand. Detective Ryan left him with 128 slides taken from the children's postmortem examinations, and five large dossiers of material relating to the case.

After examining all the material, Professor Herdson wrote in his report that in the case of Caleb, 'the findings taken in isolation leave the cause of death undetermined, but apparently consistent with Sudden Infant Death Syndrome'.

The professor rejected the notion that Patrick's death was due to SIDS, suggesting that it was more accurate to describe the cause of death as 'undetermined'.

He agreed with Professor Hilton that his findings at Sarah's postmortem, taken in isolation, could be diagnosed as SIDS. And he concurred with Dr Cala that the cause of Laura's death was undetermined, and that Laura's myocarditis was 'probably incidental' to her actual cause of death. He pointed out, as others had, that her age when she died was 'significantly older' than the usual age range for SIDS.

'Considering these four infant deaths together,' he wrote, 'I would draw attention to the comments of other Pathologists (and in agreement with my own experience) that the first unexplained death of an infant in a family may be attributed to Sudden Infant Death Syndrome, the second should be labelled undetermined, and the third should be considered homicide until proven otherwise.'

He added: 'I am unaware that there have ever been three or more thoroughly investigated infant deaths in one family from Sudden Infant Death Syndrome.'

Based on all the material he had read: 'In my opinion all four infants probably died from intentional suffocation'.

As with the other medical experts, this came straight from the playbook of Dr Meadow.

Four months later, in May 2002, a committal hearing took place before a local Newcastle magistrate, Alan Railton. Nine volumes of evidence, making up the police brief, were tendered, including Dr Cala's autopsy report, and the reports submitted by Professors Berry and Herdson and Dr Ophoven.

Mr Railton acknowledged that the prosecution case was circumstantial but added that 'at this stage there is not before the court any hypothesis which would entitle the court not to proceed'. Greg Coles, the Newcastle-based prosecutor who the year before had declined to recommend that Kathy be charged, was now telling the court that all four children could not have died of natural causes.

But the committal did deliver a minor victory to Brian Doyle, who persuaded Mr Railton to issue an order suppressing any reporting of the diary entries, transcripts from the listening device recordings, and medical expert opinions. In doing so, the magistrate picked up Mr Doyle's point that in the famous case of Lindy Chamberlain, the intense media attention had helped to damage her cause. 'We have seen the terrible injustice that can flow from the public attention in respect to Lindy Chamberlain and it would be a tragedy if it happened in this case,' he said, adding that the evidence was 'very emotive because babies are involved'.

In a sign of how favourably Brian Doyle regarded Kathy, he had agreed to act for her unpaid, and at her committal hearing he made it clear that he for one was not accepting the prosecution's view of the diaries. 'In preparation for the matter, of course, I read the diaries,' he said later.

'I read everything, chapter and verse. I spent a lot of time on it. I was acting for Kathy, from the day she was arrested, I was acting pro bono, for her. I couldn't leave the lady in the lurch and she had no income.'

In any event, legal aid was granted to Kathy, but only on the basis that she would be represented by the Public Defender, instructed by the Public Solicitor.

At the committal hearing, Mr Doyle was the first to argue that the diary entries pinpointed by the police could be viewed in two entirely different ways. Rather than being admissions of guilt to killing her children, he said, 'They could be the view of a mother tortured in the face of other children having died, and blaming her own motherly inadequacies for their deaths, and not her own actions.'

The scene was set for a mighty battle at Kathy's trial.

PART 2

14

THE TRIAL

On April Fool's Day 2003, four years and one month after her fourth child Laura had died, Kathleen Folbigg walked through the doors of the dour New South Wales Supreme Court in the Sydney suburb of Darlinghurst, accompanied by her legal team.

It was day one of her trial. Her heart was in her throat; inwardly, she recoiled in disbelief at what was happening.

The court stands close to the old Darlinghurst Gaol, where more than seventy men and women were hanged between 1841 and 1907, and the mood that day matched the dark history of murder trials gone by.

As Kathy entered the dock and the trial began, five charges were read out to the jury: four, that Kathy murdered her children, and the fifth, that she maliciously inflicted 'grievous bodily harm' on Patrick, causing his ALTE, or 'near-miss', episode.

To all five charges, Kathy pleaded 'not guilty'.

The case against her was led by Mark Tedeschi, then the Senior Crown Prosecutor for New South Wales. Mr Tedeschi, a slender, fiercely intelligent, highly experienced counsel, was a formidable presence in court. He had an undoubted gift for strategising questionable cases and presenting the evidence in ways that left juries believing they had no option but to convict.

Peter Zahra, the moustachioed Senior Public Defender arguing Kathy's case, had a very different style. Where Mr Tedeschi had a flair for the dramatic, Mr Zahra was much more cautious and stolid in the presentation of his arguments. When it came to attracting and holding the jury's attention, there was really no contest.

Mr Tedeschi, in his opening address to the jury, made his own task crystal clear. 'At the end of this trial, at the end of all of the evidence, it will be necessary for me, as the Crown Prosecutor, to be able to say to you: The Crown has proven each of those charges beyond a reasonable doubt.'

Mr Zahra cautioned the jury to understand: 'It is not for the accused to prove that the children died of natural causes. It is extremely important ... to always keep that in mind.'

The trial was overseen by the grey-haired Justice Graham Barr, a judge of considerable repute who was himself a former Crown prosecutor and who would go on to sit in judgment at several other headline-grabbing trials.

The fact that Kathy had even been charged, let alone sent for trial, was enough to cause shudders of disbelief among her closest friends and allies.

Years later, Tracy Chapman told me, 'I was watching television one night and I'll never forget the moment that I found Kathy was being charged with the murder of her children, and I just sat there, just looking at the screen, going, "There's no way. There's no way." It was just surreal; I still can't even put it into words because it floored me really.'

Kathy's close friend Megan Donegan had given a statement to her legal team, who wanted her to appear as a character witness in Kathy's defence. 'I've always thought that if I'd got my side of the story out to the jury, maybe it would have had a different outcome,' she would tell me later.

But although she was desperate to give evidence on Kathy's behalf, Megan was heavily pregnant, and suffering from high blood pressure, and her doctor wouldn't allow her to travel to Sydney. Tracy, for her part, had fallen out of touch with Kathy, who was facing the enormous ordeal of her trial on her own and hadn't thought to ask her wider circle of friends to be there to support her.

Looking back on it later, Tracy told me, 'This is typical Kath. If she'd reached out when she bloody should have, and thought to ring, we'd all have been there. Megan couldn't, but everybody else. We all weren't talking the way we should have, that's what's upset me the most.'

Like Megan, Tracy had a cast-iron excuse for not being at the trial; she too was undergoing a difficult, complicated pregnancy. Even so, she felt wracked with guilt that she hadn't been present when her best friend needed her most.

Kathy, for the most part, attended court in a state of stunned disbelief, disconnected from the drama around her, and accompanied on most days by a kindly Salvation Army Major who made it her business to be there for her, talk to her, support and protect her throughout the proceedings.

A few months before, Joyce Harmer and her husband Hilton had been invited by Kathy's lawyers to help look after her during the trial. It was an inspired choice; they were warm, caring, sympathetic and above all, non-judgmental.

Joyce, in the very best tradition of the Salvos, had devoted her life to helping those in need, and supporting men and women accused of heinous crimes, as they appeared in court to be tried. Kathy fell squarely into that category.

At a moment in time when she was being portrayed as that most evil of women, a baby-killer, the Harmers shielded Kathy from the worst of the media. Some of the most enduring images of the trial would be the sight of the two women, heads held high, dressed in matching blue jackets, walking arm in arm as the Salvation Army Major guided Kathy to and from the proceedings.

Adding to Kathy's distress was the fact that two of her closest former allies had turned against her and agreed to appear as witnesses for the prosecution: her foster sister Lea Bown, and her husband Craig.

Kathy felt deeply betrayed.

Where Kathy cut a lonely figure, Craig, by contrast, was surrounded and supported by his own family members, with his long-term girlfriend Helen Pearce by his side. Craig and Helen were engaged to be married, but Kathy and Craig hadn't yet obtained a divorce and so Craig was asked to confirm in court that he did indeed wish to give evidence against his wife.

In his opening address to the jury, Mark Tedeschi suggested that Kathy deliberately smothered her children, but not necessarily in order to kill them. The prosecution team was aware of a case in the United States in which, it was reported, a babysitter had confessed to killing two babies accidentally, four years apart, after using suffocation as a means of pacifying infants and sending them to sleep, in scores of other cases.

Mr Tedeschi put forward three possible scenarios. 'We say that at the time she either intended to kill them or she deliberately intended to render them unconscious to, in effect, put them to sleep, or she restricted their breathing by smothering them knowing that they may well die. And any one of those three would be sufficient to prove the mental aspect of murder.'

The subtext lying behind the second scenario was the suggestion that Kathy might have habitually used partial suffocation as a means of pacifying her children and getting them to sleep. And this indeed was the theory held by Detective Ryan who, the following year, told the ABC's *Australian Story* program that Kathy had 'suffocated the children to render them unconscious', adding, 'Once Caleb died, she must have known that the technique was not only dangerous, but deadly. But she continued to do it.'

In reality, there was absolutely no evidence that Kathy had done so, and common sense dictated that if any mother had smothered their firstborn by mistake, they would be highly unlikely to risk doing so a second time, let alone, with a third and fourth child.

Mr Tedeschi proposed a range of possible motives Kathy might have had to kill her children.

'She had a very low threshold for stress, and she was also deeply resentful at the intrusions that her children made on her own life and, in particular, on her sleep, her ability to go to the gym, and her ability to socialise, including going out dancing,' he alleged.

'She was constantly tired, resentful against her husband, Craig, for not providing her with what she considered to be adequate help, and she was ... we say, constantly preoccupied, to an exaggerated degree, with her weight gain due, in part, to the fact that she couldn't get to the gym as much as she liked because of her children.

'The Crown case is that she either intended to kill them during a flash of anger, resentment and hatred against her children, or, alternatively, that she deliberately sought to render them unconscious in an attempt to put them to sleep, either so that she could get to sleep herself or that she could have some time to herself.'

Here, the prosecution was trying to have it both ways, because either Kathy was a mother who grew frustrated with her children not going to sleep, and who attempted to get them to do so by rendering them unconscious; or she resented and hated them and killed them in flashes of anger. Which one was it? The prosecution was taking an each-way bet.

Arguably, the implication of either scenario was that Kathy was mentally deranged – because why would a sane mother keep on smothering her children to try to get them to sleep, when it resulted in them dying in front of her? And if she hated them so much that she wanted to kill them, why, if she was sane, would she have three more children after the first one had died?

Paradoxically, the jurors were told that Kathy was actually a loving, caring mother while the children were alive. Craig himself had told the police that she was a good mother ninety-nine per cent of the time. The family GP praised the parents. And Jan Bull, a fitness leader at Kathy's gym, who saw her interacting with Laura, told the jury: 'I thought she was a good mother. I thought she was a caring mother. The little girl was always dressed well. They seemed to have a really good bond. The little girl was outgoing, which usually comes from a child that is secure and happy.'

To go from that evidence to an allegation that she smothered each of her children in turn, in order to have more time to go to the gym and socialise, or just to get more sleep, was quite a stretch. But this was the argument put forward by the prosecution.

'Kathleen Folbigg did not kill or injure her children to get attention for herself or in a state of profound depression. The Crown says she killed them because she couldn't stand their crying and the demands that they made on her life,' Mr Tedeschi asserted.

The Senior Crown Prosecutor painted a picture of a woman whose frustration with her children drove her to extreme lengths. 'Whilst all parents sometimes feel frustration, exasperation and anger with their children her feelings ran deeper to intense anger, hatred and resentment to the extent of prompting her to kill her children.'

The prosecution started with one big advantage: the defence had failed in repeated attempts to have the four deaths tried separately. It was accepted that had they succeeded in doing so, Kathy would have been found not guilty, because when considered separately, plausible natural causes of death existed for each of her children: SIDS for Caleb and Sarah, epilepsy for Patrick, and myocarditis for Laura.

It was only when all four deaths were considered together that the prosecution stood a chance of obtaining convictions for murder.

Mr Tedeschi used his considerable prosecutorial skills to cast a dark shadow over what was an entirely circumstantial case. There was no positive forensic evidence to suggest that any of the children had been smothered, but neither was there any evidence to prove that her children had died from natural causes. Unfortunately for Kathy, because smothering can leave no discernible forensic signs, it allowed Mr Tedeschi to argue that smothering was in fact the most probable cause of death in all four cases.

Mr Tedeschi put forward three main planks of evidence. One of them was the medical evidence, and here, the experts who subscribed to Meadow's Law were confident in saying that they had never come across other cases of families where three or more infants had died from natural causes.

That evidence on its own would prove to be devastating, but it was also untrue and misleading; there *had* been other cases of families with multiple children who had died from natural causes, but the jury wasn't told this.

Secondly, there was 'coincidence' evidence, which in reality was an attempt by the prosecution to demonstrate that the four deaths were not coincidences; there were marked similarities in how each death had occurred.

Mr Tedeschi suggested that there were ten similarities between the four cases:

(1) They all occurred suddenly;
(2) They all occurred unexpectedly;
(3) They all occurred at home;
(4) They all occurred during the child's sleep period;
(5) They all occurred when the child was in a bed, cot or bassinet;
(6) They all occurred when Kathy was the only adult at home or awake, giving her the opportunity to have done them harm (Craig was a particularly heavy sleeper);
(7) They were all discovered dead or moribund by her;
(8) They were all discovered dead or moribund by Kathy during what she claimed was a normal check on the well-being of the children in the course of their sleep period (three of them on her way from the toilet);
(9) They were all discovered dead or moribund by Kathy at around or shortly after death when they were still warm to the touch (two of them still had a heartbeat, so these were found by her very shortly – literally minutes – after they had stopped breathing); and
(10) In relation to four of the five events, Kathy failed to render any assistance at all to them after discovering

them dead or moribund, to the extent that she did not even lift them up out of their beds.

Mr Tedeschi told the jury: 'Those ten similarities on their own are incapable of being explained, except by the one common feature, that is this accused. This accused is common to all of these deaths and the ALTE [Patrick's 'near-miss' episode], and that is because she was responsible for all of them. That is why she raised the alarm so soon after it had happened.'

But several of the similarities he listed were easily challenged. Kathy was the children's primary carer, getting up in the night repeatedly to care for them, and Craig was a heavy sleeper, and so arguably, it was unremarkable that it was she who had found each child moribund or lifeless.

It was also accepted in the medical literature that most children who die from SIDS do so while asleep in their cots or beds; and any sudden unexpected death, whether natural or not, is by definition both sudden and unexpected. And differing evidence was given as to whether the children were warm or cold to the touch after death.

In four of the five incidents, Craig administered CPR, but in the fifth, Kathy, who by then was fully trained to do so, didn't hesitate to give Laura CPR – in fact, she lifted her from her bed and carried her to the breakfast bar, in order to do so more effectively.

The third major plank of the prosecution's case was the diaries. Most of what the prosecution considered to be the most incriminating entries were in the journal written following Sarah's death and when Kathy fell pregnant with Laura, and in the journal she wrote after Laura was born.

Mr Tedeschi told the jury: 'The Crown case is that these diaries contain entries which show her involvement in the deaths of her children, her attempts to deal with the guilt about her involvement in their deaths, her belief that she has grown and matured and learned from what happened to the others and that it will not happen again with Laura, her belief that she is now able to be a proper good mother to this child, despite what has happened to the others, her belief that the dark moods which overtook her with the others will not happen again with this child.

'Then, later on,' he continued, 'her frustrations with parenthood, when Laura was a little older. You will see right throughout both diaries her continuing preoccupation with her weight, with tiredness, with a battle of wills, particularly with Sarah, but also, to some degree, with Laura, her frustrations that she didn't get more assistance from Craig, her belief that if she ever gets into the dark moods again that this time she will know better and she will just hand over the baby to Craig or someone else so that the same thing will not happen, and the like.

'Basically the Crown case is that from these diaries you will be able to ascertain that Kathleen Folbigg genuinely believed that she had changed, that she had grown, that she would no longer place herself in a position where she would kill one of her babies.'

Mr Tedeschi read out nearly forty extracts from Kathy's journals in support of the proposition that 'there were times when she could not abide or cope with the demands of parenthood. She eventually resolved her frustrations, her resentment and her flashes of anger by killing her children. The Crown case is that she was totally obsessed by her own needs, wants and desires.'

To anyone who knew Kathy well and supported her, this was an absurd proposition, but, frighteningly for her, it would be supported in court by two witnesses, who in the past had been among her strongest advocates: Lea and Craig.

15

'HONEST TO GOD'

If hell hath no fury like a woman scorned, then Craig, initially spurned and eventually abandoned by his wife after Laura died, would prove to be the male equivalent and the most potent witness for the prosecution at her trial. Whether the evidence he gave was motivated by spite and by a desire for revenge, we will never know, but there can be no doubt that it affected the jury profoundly in their deliberations.

Here was a man who, tragically, had lost all four of his children in sudden and unexpected ways, who, following every death, had been consumed with grief, and who from the outset was desperate for answers to how and why they had died.

In the end, it was one man – Detective Bernie Ryan – who offered him the certainty he craved. And the detective did so – according to Craig's own account – by exploiting his emotions after Kathy had left him.

When the police investigation began in March 1999, Kathy and Craig separated, and then shortly afterwards, reconciled. In an intercepted phone call in July, when the two of them were back together, Craig told a friend that the police were trying to build a picture of a woman who wanted to 'keep doin' runners from the relationship, and offin' the kids was her way out, you know, which is ridiculous'.

Craig had already given the police the diary he had found, which caused him so much concern, but in this later conversation, he insisted that if he had had even an 'inkling' that Kathy had killed her children, he wouldn't still be with her.

'I think you would have killed her,' his friend on the phone suggested. 'You would've shot her or fuckin' knifed her or somethin'. A long time ago.'

'Correct,' Craig replied.

This ran completely counter to the suspicions he had voiced when Kathy left him, that she had killed their children.

He told another friend that Bernie Ryan was a 'gung-ho' young detective who was out to make a name for himself. Detective Ryan, he said, had 'come and planted some bullshit in me head when I was at me lowest point there when Kath had left me'.

In conversation with his sister Kaz, Craig accused Detective Ryan of having 'planted horrible things in my head'. He described how the detective had approached him at Teasdale's, the car dealership where he worked, when he and Kathy were apart, and told him that Kathy was out enjoying herself, playing on his distress about Kathy leaving him. Craig told Kaz:

'I mean, he started that. Come and saw me at the car yard. "S'pose you feel pretty bad", you know. "I mean, she's cleaned ya out and she's goin' out with her girlfriends and goin' to the gym and you're all alone and got, haven't your kid and your wife's walked out on ya and, you know? Isn't it all pretty convenient for her?" And all that sort of shit.'

In another intercepted conversation, he remarked with a laugh: 'I think what also narks him too is anybody sittin' there waxin' lyrical about how good a mother she was when they saw her as a mother. You know what I mean? 'Cause that's like he don't wanna hear that.'

When Craig gave evidence at Kathy's trial nearly four years later, he said he didn't recall making this remark, claiming that it didn't represent his state of mind at the time.

'Well, were you lying to this female?' Mr Zahra asked.

> I'd say I was.
> Lying and laughing at the same time?
> I'd say I was.

'You see, Mr Folbigg, it is now becoming increasingly difficult to tell when you lie and when you don't,' Mr Zahra remarked, sardonically.

Between Laura's death in March 1999 and the trial four years later, Craig had done a complete about-face; now, apparently, he believed that Detective Ryan was right. In the interim, as the police investigation progressed and Craig and Kathy separated for a final time, he took onboard the 'shit' that Detective Ryan had told him.

Craig told the court that: 'Detective Ryan was explaining to me that mothers do kill their children. I couldn't understand that, and I couldn't accept that, but Detective Ryan told me that I really needed to open my eyes, that it wasn't just always drug addict mothers, housing commission women, and those type of people that killed their children. That loving, caring mothers did it as well.'

The challenge for the jury was to try to decide when Craig was lying, and when he was telling the truth. In one exchange with Mr Zahra, referring to the day when he retracted his earlier allegations against Kathy, the jury's conundrum took on an almost farcical dimension – except that it wasn't funny.

> And that was a lie?
> The part about I'd been down there and told some lies was a lie.

Given how inconsistent his accounts had been, and how critical the question of his credibility had become, it was surprising – shocking even – that Craig, at the prosecution's request, was given an indemnity during the trial by Justice Barr against being charged for perjury, following his assertion that he lied in the statement where he supported his wife and told the police that this was 'the truth, honest to God'.

This he said was now not the truth, but he had a ready excuse, telling Mr Zahra: 'I didn't have a Bible at the police station. I didn't actually put my hand on a Bible.'

> So, it was okay to use the expression 'honest to God' because that was not on a Bible?
>
> That's correct.

The question left hanging by this admission, and by the fact that he changed his story after being arrested for hindering the investigation, is whether undue pressure was placed on Craig to give evidence in court against Kathy. As Peter Zahra suggested at the trial: 'He in fact suggests that he has been manipulated by Detective Ryan.'

Mr Tedeschi asked Craig about the day the police arrested him.

> How did that make you feel?
>
> Very frightened.
>
> What were you frightened of?
>
> My name being associated as a criminal. Possible jail. I didn't know what the charge carried; only that it was serious.
>
> Did that cause any change in your attitude?
>
> Yes.
>
> What sort of a change?
>
> I told the truth.
>
> Did you tell the truth to Detective Ryan in that recorded interview?
>
> As best I could.

At the heart of the evidence given by Craig were the negative observations he made about Kathy's mothering skills. This was rich, considering how little help he himself gave her at home, but the lurid accounts he gave of her moods and actions formed a central pillar in the prosecution's case that she was the kind of woman who was capable of snapping and killing her children on impulse.

Craig spoke about a number of incidents which, he said, had occurred on the weekend before Laura died, and which he had described for the first time in a statement given to the police in December 2002 – more than three years after the events and just four months before the trial. This followed an earlier conference Craig had had with Mr Tedeschi in October 2002.

Kathy's counsel Peter Zahra put it to Craig that 'in that statement concerning this weekend you are not telling the truth?'

> That's not the case.
> That you refer to some things that have occurred, but that you fabricate evidence in order to paint a very dark picture of your wife's mood on this weekend?
> That's not the case.
> That you have taken what are otherwise normal domestic situations and have made them look sinister?
> That's not the case.

When Craig told the jury about the morning Laura died, it cast Kathy in a far worse light than the account he had given in his statement to the police, soon after her death, and even, in his later interview with the police. In that interview in 2001, he had said that Kathy was a good mother ninety-nine per cent of the time.

At the trial, Mr Tedeschi asked him about the day that Laura died, when he had an argument with Kathy over the fact that Laura was agitated and upset.

Craig told the court that he wasn't in the room at the time, but as he had previously, he heard Kathy 'growl'. It alarmed him, and he walked down the hall to find Laura in her high chair, with both of her hands pinned on the deck of the high chair by Kathy, who was trying to feed her her breakfast cereal.

Mr Tedeschi asked Craig if Kathy was 'force-feeding' Laura, and Craig replied that she was. He said that Laura was 'whinging' and twisting her head, and that he told Kathy: 'She's a bloody baby,' and not to bother trying to make her have breakfast if she didn't want to.

Craig said that, after this, Kathy grabbed her daughter, pulled her out of the high chair, and 'plonked her' on the ground, telling her to 'go to your fucking father'. As Laura started to cross the floor towards him, he heard a 'guttural growl' and a scream from Kathy.

Mr Tedeschi asked Craig what that sounded like, and Craig repeated the sound he said she had previously made: 'Oh, grrh …' He said Kathy screamed that she couldn't handle Laura when she was like this, and that as this was happening, Laura fell to the ground crying, and he scooped her up and made a quick exit with her, down to the bedroom.

Craig's account was far more dramatic than the earlier accounts he had given to the police, and the jury couldn't have failed to be left with the impression that Kathy had an uncontrollable angry streak, which at times led her to be physically rough with her children. But at Laura's autopsy, Dr Cala had found no evidence of any physical harm being deliberately inflicted on her.

The description of Kathy growling whenever she was upset or stressed with the children became a rolling metaphor through Craig's evidence at the trial. It began with the description given by Craig of the difficulties which, he said, Kathy had when Patrick was diagnosed with epilepsy.

Mark Tedeschi asked him to tell the court how Kathy 'coped with all of that'.

'Not very well,' he replied. Craig explained that Kathy would lose her temper 'a bit' with him and with Patrick, and would sometimes show her frustration by going 'grr, grr, grr …' in a cranky way, 'like a growl'.

After this, the word 'growl' was repeated more than fifty times during the trial, either by counsel, the judge or by Craig.

Mr Tedeschi reminded Craig of his earlier evidence that before Sarah died, Kathy's 'growling' was happening on a daily basis. It was the 'same deal' in the months before Laura died, Craig asserted. Mr Tedeschi asked him if it was happening on an 'almost daily basis' during those months.

'Daily,' he replied.

Craig's account of Kathy being physically rough with the children was backed up by her foster sister Lea when she gave evidence.

In 1999, after Laura died, Lea gave a statement to the police in which she said: 'I also have seen Kathy become angry with Laura. On one occasion Laura wouldn't go to sleep and another time when she was feeding her, Kathy got a bit angry and short-tempered with Laura. It probably was because she was tired herself.'

Lea was referring to the Christmas of 1998, when Kathy, Craig and Laura came to stay with her and her husband Ted at their home in Melbourne.

However, by the time she gave evidence at the trial, Lea had added a very damaging detail to her account, under questioning from Mark Tedeschi.

> Kathy lost her temper with Laura when she was trying to feed her in the highchair.
> What did she do, what happened?
> Laura didn't really want to eat her meal and Kathy got angry with her and put the food down on, because the high chair was close to the table so she put the food down on the dining room table and got Laura out, pulled Laura out by the arm.
> Can you describe to us how she pulled her out?
> She has got her by the arm that way and yanked her out.
> Just by a single arm?
> Yes.

Under cross-examination, Lea conceded that she had only mentioned this to the police for the first time in 2003, just before the trial – and more than four years after the event. And, she also conceded, she had only ever seen Kathy lose her temper with Laura twice.

But, by the time Mr Tedeschi gave his closing address to the jury, Lea's original statement that 'Kathy got a bit angry and short-tempered with Laura', and then, in evidence, that she had 'got her by the arm that way and yanked her out', had been embellished even further, and quite dramatically by the Senior Crown Prosecutor, who told the jury that these flashes of temper were characteristic of a pattern of behaviour: 'What was the accused's reaction? The accused's reaction was, "You're going to do it my way if it's the last thing I do", and she started to growl and get angry and yank her out of the highchair.'

The motif of Kathy growling constantly was a potent one. And in his summing up, Justice Barr cautioned the jury about it, pointing out that: 'Mr Zahra says to you, well, why would the accused agree to have a fourth child if she was so concerned about the others, if she was unable to cope with the others, if she was growling all the time? You would think, if that were true that she would not have another child because by that time surely, she would understand that she could not handle a child. Yet she was happy at having the child.'

In his evidence Craig admitted to having lied repeatedly. Even so, he bristled at the line of questioning taken by Peter Zahra, when he challenged Craig's credibility. At one point, Mr Zahra asked him to look at the statement he had made in May 1999, in which he retracted his earlier allegation that Kathy had killed their children.

'Do you recognise that statement?' Mr Zahra asked him.

'Yes,' Craig replied. 'I have one in the bottom of my budgie cage.'

It was a smart-arse comment, and in his re-examination of Craig, Mr Tedeschi sought to clarify it.

> Did you literally keep your statement in the bottom of your budgie cage?
> No, I still have that statement.
> So, why did you say that?
> Basically because that's about what it means to me, that statement. It's only good enough to be on the bottom of the budgie cage.
> Why was it good enough to be at the bottom of your budgie cage in your view?
> Because it was all lies.

Mr Zahra wanted to know why Craig had turned against his wife.

'That was the motivation for you to go to the police, wasn't it?' he asked. 'Revenge, because your wife had left you?'

> No. I was devastated my wife had left me. I had no thoughts of revenge against her whatsoever.
> You weren't motivated at any time to get back at your wife at that time?
> No.
> Never?
> Never.

But Mr Zahra reminded the jury of what Craig told Kathy about retracting his allegations against her, when he spoke to her after her interview with Detective Ryan in July 1999. The conversation was intercepted by the police:

> I said I went there because I was so full of hate and spite and anxiety and grief and anguish over the fact that not only had I lost my daughter, I'd lost my wife, you know ... I was so frustrated, I was hurting, so I thought I'll fucking fix this ...

I'll fuck your life. You fucked mine. I'll fuck yours. I will go and tell some fucking horrible thing about you that the police think you did it anyway.

The question the jury had to answer was this: at the trial, was revenge his motive, or did he genuinely believe by then that Kathy had murdered their children?

16

THE VERDICT

Kathy's trial lasted nearly a month, and every day, Joyce Harmer sat in the public gallery, in Kathy's eyeline, so that she could look over at her whenever she wished to do so.

The mental strain Kathy had suffered was immense. 'I felt like I was just hanging on to a cliff by one finger,' she would later tell Tracy Chapman. And it was clear from the photos and camera footage of her going to and from court that she wasn't coping with the pressure. She felt disconnected from reality.

But if Joyce was Kathy's armour against unwelcome media on the outside, nothing could protect her from the prosecution's onslaught inside Court Number Two, and as the apparently damning evidence grew, Kathy's stoic demeanour began to crumble.

On day ten of the trial, the video filmed by Craig of Laura playing in and around the family pool was shown to Dr Cala who was in the witness box. As the film played, and Laura's happy voice rang out around the courtroom, Kathy bowed her head and sobbed.

Matthew Benns, a prominent tabloid journalist who sat through much of the trial, told this author: 'To me, sitting in that courtroom, one of the pivotal moments was when we were shown a home video of Laura, the day before she died, in her floaties, swimming around in the pool, and it was absolutely heartbreaking to think that that little girl was dead twenty-four hours later.'

He was echoing the question that every member of the jury would have asked themselves when they watched the video:

how could an apparently healthy little girl have suddenly died, so soon after enjoying an afternoon playing by the pool?

To make matters worse for Kathy, the idea that Laura could not possibly have died so soon after seeming so well was backed by the prosecution's main medical witness, Dr Cala, whose opinion, nevertheless, appeared to be based less on clinical expertise, and more on a layman's surmise that she looked pretty healthy at the time.

'I think that Laura Folbigg appeared to me in quite normal health on that video, and that was about twenty-three hours roughly before she died,' he told the court. 'Given that she appears in quite good health, I think it is quite unlikely that she has died as a result of the effects of myocarditis.'

'What do you say to the possibility that she died of myocarditis?' Mr Tedeschi asked him.

'I think, it's known that myocarditis can cause sudden death, usually by a cardiac rhythm disturbance, and I can't say that didn't happen with Laura Folbigg but I think it's, in all likelihood, very unlikely.'

'Is it a reasonable possibility in your opinion that she died from myocarditis?'

'I don't believe it is.'

Professor Roger Byard, an internationally recognised SIDS expert, appeared for the defence, to rebut what Dr Cala had said, in what the team regarded as a 'major coup'.

'Professor Roger Byard is quite probably the most well respected worldwide expert in this field,' Kathy's solicitor Peter Krisenthal noted some months earlier. 'He is in charge of the Forensic Science Centre in Adelaide [and] has published extensively worldwide.'

But he nearly didn't appear for the defence. In a letter to New South Wales Legal Aid, Peter Krisenthal revealed that to begin with, Professor Byard was not prepared to get involved, because he had previously come to Sydney on another court matter and had been put up at the 'Koala Motor Inn'. He agreed to appear at Kathy's trial only after Mr Krisenthal assured him that he would be lodged in more comfortable accommodation. But the constraints of the budget imposed on Kathy's defence by Legal Aid were no joking matter. Mr Krisenthal felt obliged to stress that the benefit of having Professor Byard contribute to the defence case had already been 'immeasurably greater' than the accommodation costs that would be incurred as a result.

In court, in response to Dr Cala's evidence, Professor Byard was asked whether you could make a diagnosis of health by watching a video: 'What the video shows is that apparent normal little girl, but it doesn't tell me whether she has a fever or tell me whether she is off colour, or doesn't tell me anything much,' he said.

'Even if she was normal that doesn't prevent her dying from myocarditis. There is a report in the literature of a young girl who, I think she played basketball for an hour, swam forty metres in a pool and dropped dead from myocarditis.'

Professor Byard addressed all four deaths in his evidence to the court, saying that in Caleb's case he had found no proof of suffocation, and the presence of haemosiderin in the baby's lungs did not indicate that he had been smothered. 'We are not dealing with a bullet hole or stab wound,' he told the court. 'We are dealing with findings that are not absolute.' Professor Byard pointed out that in a study he himself had conducted, he had found haemosiderin in 'something like twenty per cent of SIDS babies' lungs.' Moreover, in his view there was no proof that Patrick's 'near-miss' episode or his death were caused by suffocation. In Sarah's case, there was also no proof of suffocation.

And in Laura's case: 'Laura had an established inflammation of the heart, myocarditis. It was of moderate myocarditis. It was the sort of inflammation that I have seen in a number of cases of sudden death in children.'

On day seventeen of the trial, another video was shown to the court – the film of Kathy's interview with Detective Bernie Ryan. At the point where Detective Ryan asked Kathy if she was responsible for the death of Caleb, Kathy, sitting watching in the dock, uttered a cry, and a few moments later, at the point in the film where Detective Ryan asked her if she had killed Laura, Kathy stood up and staggered out of the dock, trembling. As she wandered towards the public gallery, Justice Barr barked an order: 'Stop the tape!' and Joyce Harmer rushed to Kathy's aid.

After Justice Barr ordered Kathy to re-enter the dock, the trial was paused and Kathy was taken to nearby St Vincent's Hospital. Peter Zahra explained to the judge that Kathy hadn't tried to flee the court; her solicitor had asked her to step out of the dock when he saw her collapsing. Outside court, she was photographed looking pale and extremely unwell.

By now it was clear that she was in no fit state to give evidence on her own behalf. She could never have withstood days of brutal cross-examination by Mr Tedeschi, and she stayed silent throughout the trial.

Only once did the mood lift just a little for Kathy. But even that was tinged with a dark irony. Megan Donegan recalls the moment.

'She was talking to me after the close of the trial one day, she was walking down the street and she said, "I wish I could laugh." And I said, "That's a really odd statement to make." And she said, "There's a cameraman walking backwards in front of me, and he's just fallen into a garbage bin! But if I laugh, they'll take a photo of me laughing leaving the courthouse, so I can't laugh."'

It was a sign of how acutely aware Kathy was of the potential for trial by media: if she was photographed laughing, that would be interpreted as the laughter of a callous, unfeeling murderess. But if — as she did — she held her emotions in check — that too meant, as it had in Lindy Chamberlain's case — that she was a callous, unfeeling killer, incapable of grief or remorse for the terrible deeds she had done.

At 1.15 pm on Tuesday, 20 May, after listening to twenty-nine days of evidence, the jury retired to consider their verdict. It had been a sensational trial, given blanket coverage in the media, and the challenge for the twelve men and women was to decide, based on an entirely circumstantial case, with no proof of foul play, whether Kathy had murdered Caleb, Patrick, Sarah and Laura, and whether she had inflicted grievous bodily harm on Patrick when he nearly died.

The trial's medical experts had told the jury that they had never heard of a family where three or more children had died from natural causes. This could only mean that if all four of Kathy's children died from natural causes, her case had entered the medical history books – it was unique and unprecedented.

In his closing address, Mr Tedeschi speculated about what Peter Zahra's closing argument would be: 'I think that essentially he will say that the Crown must prove that these children did not die from natural causes; the Crown can't prove, in relation to each individual child, that they didn't die from four incidental findings, therefore the Crown had failed to prove its case beyond the reasonable doubt.

'Caleb may have died from a floppy larynx or SIDS,' he acknowledged. 'Patrick may have had an ALTE, which was a first epileptic attack or encephalitis. His death may have been caused by an epileptic attack, an epileptic seizure. Sarah may have had a displaced uvula or SIDS. Laura may have died of myocarditis.'

And then, the zinger.

'Well, yes, ladies and gentlemen,' he declaimed. 'I can't disprove any of that, but one day some piglets might be born from a sow, and the piglets might come out of the sow with wings on their back, and the next morning Farmer Joe might look out the kitchen window and see these piglets flying out of his farm. I can't disprove that either. I can't disprove that one day some piglets might be born with wings and that they might fly.

'Is that a reasonable doubt? No. Is the hypothesis that the defence advances a reasonable doubt? No. Why not? Because if you look at what they are suggesting, not in isolation, but in totality: there has never ever been before in the history of medicine that our experts have been able to find any case like this. It is preposterous. It is not a reasonable doubt. It is a fantasy, and of course the Crown does not have to disprove a fanciful idea.'

By any measure, this was an audacious rhetorical flourish, designed perhaps to echo the mantra that could not be named at the trial — Meadow's Law — in the most flamboyant fashion. Four infants in the same family dying separately, from different natural causes was literally unheard of, he was saying.

But it was also patently untrue. There had been prior cases recorded of multiple infants in families dying from natural causes, and tragically, in the years to come there would be more. The fact that the medical experts hadn't heard of them didn't mean that they hadn't happened. The fact that the jury was not told about them was disastrous.

Following Justice Barr's summing up, the jury members left the courtroom to deliberate.

In the absence of the jury, both Mark Tedeschi and Peter Zahra paid tribute to the two Salvation Army Majors who had stood by Kathy's side and supported her throughout: Joyce Harmer and her husband Hilton.

The court was packed to the rafters with reporters hanging on every word spoken by Justice Barr, and desperate to hear the verdicts when the jury returned.

All afternoon, the jury debated behind closed doors, and the next day, returned to deliberate further.

Outside court, Craig's brother Michael asked a *Daily Telegraph* reporter to invite the media to bid for the family's private photos of Kathy and the children.

As Matthew Benns would later report, Michael said Craig felt entitled to a cut of the profits to be made from Kathy's story. Hearing this, even the most hard-bitten journalists covering the case recoiled — it just didn't seem right to be auctioning off the family's photos of the children who had died. But Craig it was who, in a conversation secretly recorded by the police, had admitted to using the fact that his children had died as a way of drumming up sympathy and selling more cars.

And, in fairness to Craig, TV's commercial channels were stalking the Folbigg family, offering tens of thousands of dollars for exclusive interviews. As Matthew Benns later wrote in his book *When the Bough Breaks*: 'It was a scramble for cash over four dead babies and no one was coming out of it in a good light.'

Later that day, Craig himself set the record straight, denying that he had any intention of selling the photos. Later still, as the evening drew in, a selection of images was made available, and Michael announced that his brother had given permission for the media to use them, 'to put human faces to this tragedy'. Craig hadn't been paid a cent to do so, he insisted. 'These are his beautiful children.'

As journalists and onlookers readied themselves outside the court, the suspense ratcheted up, and just before four o'clock the next day, they were called back into court, and the jury filed back in and took their seats. Had they reached a verdict, or would they be sent home for the night, to return again the following day?

The answer came almost immediately, as the jury foreperson announced that they had reached their verdicts on all five charges.

They had taken less than six hours to do so, which, considering the complexity of the evidence, was astonishing. Just before they entered the courtroom, Justice Barr called for silence, warning that: 'Anyone who interrupts the business of the Court will be removed.'

Kathy's heart was pounding. Standing in the dock, looking ashen-faced, stressed and exhausted, she could see Joyce Harmer – her only visible beacon of hope in the courtroom.

At 4.03 pm, and as the packed court held its breath, the jury foreperson was asked: 'Have you reached your verdicts?'

'Yes,' she replied.

The clerk of the court read out the first question: 'Do you find the accused Kathleen Megan Folbigg guilty or not guilty of the murder of Caleb Gibson Folbigg?'

The court held its breath.

'Not guilty' came the reply.

There was an audible gasp from the packed gallery. Craig and his family looked shell-shocked.

'When they said, "Not guilty," on the first one, I thought, "Thank God. If they found me not guilty of one, they've got to find me not guilty of the other three,"' Kathy later told Tracy, when, for the first time, she spoke about the moment the verdicts were handed down.

But there was a sting in the tail. The judge's associate asked the foreperson: 'Do you find the accused Kathleen Megan Folbigg guilty or not guilty of the manslaughter of Caleb Gibson Folbigg?'

'Guilty,' she replied.

When Kathy took herself back to that moment, she told Tracy: 'The first one I thought I had a little ray of hope, because the first one came back not guilty. I thought, "Oh, gosh, okay, this might work" and then it all just crashed after that.'

> Do you find the accused Kathleen Megan Folbigg guilty or not guilty of maliciously inflicting grievous bodily harm with intent to do grievous bodily harm to Patrick Allan Folbigg?
> Guilty.
> Do you find the accused Kathleen Megan Folbigg guilty or not guilty of the murder of Patrick Allan Folbigg?
> Guilty.
> Do you find the accused Kathleen Megan Folbigg guilty or not guilty of the murder of Sarah Kathleen Folbigg?
> Guilty.
> Do you find the accused Kathleen Megan Folbigg guilty or not guilty of the murder of Laura Elizabeth Folbigg?
> Guilty.

In a moment described by Matthew Benns as 'absolutely awful to watch,' Kathy crumpled in the dock, tears streaming down her face.

'I might have had every wall up trying to protect me, but there was nothing that could protect you from that,' she told Tracy, in conversations that were recorded for the ABC's

Australian Story. 'It's just like they'd got this big, giant sledgehammer and just gone smash.' Kathy recalled how devastating that moment was, and in her panic, as she looked around the courtroom, she saw no one who could tell her it was going to be okay.

Kathy's foster mother, Deidre, and her foster sister, Lea, were certainly not offering any support. They were sitting with Craig and his side of the family, and Lea let out a shout when the verdicts were handed down. It was a bitter pill to swallow for Kathy.

Four minutes after the verdicts were read out, it was all over. The jury was discharged, and Mr Tedeschi told Justice Barr that the certificate protecting Craig from being prosecuted for the lies he had told the police had been prepared for the judge's approval.

A date was set for sentencing, and the judge – in a brief act of mercy to the convicted killer, said that: 'If the accused wishes to be assisted by Major Harmer, she may be assisted,' adding: 'There is no more to be done today then. The accused may be taken down and is remanded in custody for sentence on Thursday, 26 June 2003.'

Tracy asked Kathy later if she remembered how she'd felt in that moment, knowing what was about to happen. Kathy told her that she remembered her tears flowing, and she'd remained silent while on the inside she was screaming her lungs out, going, 'No, this isn't right!' She remembered her legs giving way, as the courtroom staff half-carried her down the stairs and into the cells.

What Kathy didn't see or hear was her husband, Craig, stepping outside the court and, his voice breaking, making a brief, tearful statement to the waiting media: 'My most humble thanks go to twelve people who I have never formally met who today share the honour of having set four beautiful souls free to rest in peace.'

17

BEHIND BARS

As the media scrum crushed towards Craig and his family, following the verdicts, Kathy was escorted from the courthouse into in a locked prison van and driven to Mulawa Correctional Centre to begin her long-term incarceration. It was where, years earlier, Lindy Chamberlain had been held after being wrongfully convicted of murdering her baby Azaria.

In moments of terrible trauma, people remember the oddest details. For Kathy, who'd just felt numb as she was being driven to prison, it was the recollection of someone sitting in front of her asking how she felt about everything. She remembers looking at them, thinking, 'You're an idiot.' Then, as she described it to Tracy, someone told her it could be worse; she could be in a jail with a dirt floor and cockroaches running around. Remarks like those didn't help.

Kathy, when she arrived at Mulawa, posed a unique problem to the prison authorities. It had been a long time since they had had custody of a female prisoner who had been convicted of such heinous crimes, and so comprehensively vilified in the media. Everyone in the prison knew who she was, and the other inmates were out to get her.

Kathy recalled the prison authorities not knowing where to put her in order to keep her safe, so they left her in a concrete cell for a couple of days. As Kathy later told Tracy, 'I just did nothing but cry.'

Kathy was too upset to eat and scared of what might be in her food. Because of the horror of what she was judged to have done, and the prospect of being given a very long sentence, she would have been deemed a suicide risk. Her food was served on paper plates with no cutlery, and she later told Tracy that she wasn't going to eat it with her fingers: 'I'm not an animal and a beast.'

Her other fear was that her food would be tampered with. When she'd first walked into the prison, she was met with a hail of abuse from other inmates who'd recognised her from TV reports of her trial. The women threatened to kill her. Kathy's food, when it arrived, was uncovered, so she didn't touch it. The first few weeks were 'horrendous', and for the whole of the first year, she would later recall, she never had a proper conversation with anyone else.

Kathy was entering prison as a baby-killer, and that made her the lowest of the low – a 'rock spider' in criminal parlance, who deserved to die.

Five months after her trial, in October 2003, Justice Barr handed down his sentence. To Kathy herself, and to the media who reported it, it came as a shock. She received a sentence of forty years' jail – an extraordinarily harsh term, even for someone convicted of such heinous crimes, and the logic behind it seemed impenetrable. Justice Barr and three psychiatrists who examined Kathy struggled to find a cogent reason why she might have killed her children. Justice Barr himself acknowledged that the events for which she had been put on trial 'at first seem to defy explanation'.

He noted, 'Almost all mothers who kill their children do so because they suffer from some kind of psychotic illness. The evidence is unanimous that the offender is not psychotic.'

Forensic psychiatrist Dr Michael Giuffrida went to see Kathy five times. Despite by now being locked away behind bars, she never once admitted to harming any of her children. On the contrary, she continued to protest her innocence.

Dr Giuffrida, who was bound to examine Kathy from the standpoint that she had killed her children, said he believed that what happened to her in her first three years of life was that 'she suffered a profound and probably irreversible impairment of her capacity to develop any meaningful emotional bonding or attachment and that this impairment contributed in some part at least to her total inability to relate, care for and protect her own children.'

Justice Barr thought that the evidence about her early life enabled some understanding of what her adult state of mind was and 'suggests a reason why she killed her children'. What exactly that reason was, however, remained unclear.

He concluded that Caleb's manslaughter was carried out 'in the heat of uncontrollable anger by a young and inexperienced woman of prior good character'. And, that she intended to kill Patrick, Sarah and Laura.

He surmised that the stresses she experienced in looking after her children 'were greater than those which would operate on an ordinary person because she was psychologically damaged and barely coping. Her condition, which I think she did not fully understand, left her unable to ask for any systematic help or remove the danger she recognised by walking away from her child. She could confide in nobody. She told only her diary.'

Justice Barr suggested that the 'attacks' on her children were not premeditated 'but took place when she was pushed beyond her capacity to manage.' However, her attempts to get help, 'including what I think was a genuine attempt to perform cardio-pulmonary resuscitation on Laura, were genuine and made out of an immediate regret of what she had done. Her anger cooled as fast as it had arisen.'

The real issue in sentencing Kathy, it was suggested, was whether her 'dysfunctional childhood provides any significant mitigation of her criminality.' And, he concluded, 'I think that it does.'

Justice Barr went even further than this, acknowledging that Kathy 'was not by inclination a cruel mother. She did not systematically abuse her children. She generally looked after them well, fed and clothed them and had them appropriately attended to by medical practitioners. Her condition and her anxiety about it left her unable to shrug off the irritations of unwell, wilful and disobedient children. She was not fully equipped to cope.'

Given the significance of these mitigating circumstances, a sentence of forty years, which allowed no real prospect of rehabilitation, seemed to her legal team to be manifestly unreasonable. Immediately after the sentence was handed down, Kathy's solicitor, Peter Krisenthal, told the waiting media, 'Mrs Folbigg has asked me to say that she is innocent of these offences.

'She did not kill her children or harm them in any way. She has instructed me to immediately lodge an appeal against her conviction and sentence.'

That appeal took place in February 2005, where the three judges upheld the conviction but reduced her sentence to thirty years, with a non-parole period of twenty-five years. This meant that the earliest she would be released would be in 2028.

In his appeal judgment, Justice Brian Sully said he regarded the forty-year sentence as being 'crushing' and commented that, as matters stood, Kathy could not be paroled until she was sixty-six years old. He added, 'She might well not be paroled until she is even older; and if political reaction to media pressure and to meretricious polling operates at that future time as it tends to operate now, she might well not be released until she is aged seventy-six or thereabouts. That is, it seems to me, a life sentence by a different name.'

For Kathy, the length of the sentence handed down was, in one sense, irrelevant; what she had to do was to try and survive, one minute, one hour and one day at a time.

The shock and horror she felt was compounded by the merciless headlines that followed her conviction. Kathy Folbigg's name would now go down in infamy as Australia's worst female serial killer and – in the words she herself wrote in a letter, she was now 'The Most Hated Woman in Australia'.

Not only had Kathy lost her freedom, she had also lost the man she hoped to marry – Tony Lambkin. Mr Lambkin gave journalist Eamonn Duff an exclusive interview which was published in the *Sun-Herald*. The story revealed that the couple had been hoping to marry and have children.

'People had been asking me, "What are you going to do if the jury finds her not guilty, Tony?" I said, "The first thing I'm going to do is get down on one knee and propose". And then I'm going to tell her, "Kathy, I'd be honoured if you would have my children",' he told the newspaper.

It was a bitter-sweet moment for Kathy and a bitter one for Mr Lambkin, who remained convinced, even after the jury's verdict, that Kathy was innocent. He was head over heels in love with her, and kept asking himself why Kathy would continue to have kids if she didn't want them or if she had realised she wasn't cut out for motherhood. 'It just doesn't make sense,' he told Eamonn Duff. 'She loved children and I know she wanted more.'

Eamonn Duff described to me the media frenzy surrounding Kathy's conviction. 'It was huge news nationally. There were also TV current affairs reporters swirling around Singleton, trying to find Tony, armed with cheque books, so it felt like a real success to finally secure his story which we splashed across the front page that Sunday.

'I recall, very clearly, Tony being completely shellshocked by the verdict. He was extremely emotional and convinced that, somehow, it was all a huge mistake, and they'd got it wrong.

'As he said in the story: "I knew in my heart then, and I still believe today, Kathy didn't do it".'

Not content with securing one exclusive, Eamonn Duff went on to secure another major scoop – the first and only significant interview with Craig Folbigg.

'Fast forward to August 2006 and I actually became the first journalist to ever sit down with Craig Folbigg. Tony and Craig … two men with hugely contrasting opinions of the woman they once loved,' he told me.

'Craig had remarried in 2004 and I was tipped off by a source that he'd recently become a father again. A beautiful story.

'That interview also took considerable time to get over the line but eventually, he welcomed me into his family home. As you can imagine, the *SMH* photo desk was understandably desperate for pictures of him and his new son Connor – but Craig was determined, pictorially at least, to keep him firmly out of the spotlight.

'It was hugely touching, however, to personally witness this man cradling his eleven-month-old baby after everything he'd endured. In that interview, he also opened up for the first time publicly about losing his four "angels".'

Eamonn Duff told me, 'Aside from the fact that Craig lost four children in such a tragic way, I think what needs to be remembered about him is the fact that, at no stage, did he ever look to cash in and tell his own personal story, despite the enormous amounts of money being thrown his way.

'All too often we see the key individuals in major national news stories do sit-down Sunday night television specials for fees that roll into six figures. Yet despite the enormous pain, hurt and anger he undoubtedly felt towards Kathleen, especially at that moment when the verdict was delivered, he chose not to unload it all in public.

'When I met him, he was at pains to point out how much the major networks had offered following the conclusion of the trial. For a second-hand-car salesman, we're talking life-changing money.

'To this day, I'm the only person he's ever sat down with from the mainstream media and, as per *Sydney Morning Herald* policy, he didn't receive a single penny for his story.

'Anecdotally, after we'd finished up talking and taking photos, the only thing he requested from me, in passing, was a twelve-month subscription to the *SMH*'s Sunday newspaper (*The Sun-Herald*), then worth less than two hundred and fifty dollars.'

The *Sun-Herald* story was headlined: 'Craig Folbigg's Joy in New Life, Wife and Baby', and quoted Craig referring to himself as 'the luckiest man alive'. He told Eamonn Duff: 'Not a day passes when I don't think of my four other little angels. I see their faces always. They are with me everywhere I go and I will love them forever.

'Caleb would have been 17 now. Imagine how much fun life would have been for him today. He would no doubt be chasing girls, like all boys that age. Perhaps the girls might even have chased him.

'One thing's for sure though, he would have had the whole world at his feet – all four of them would have.'

Craig described how he had married his long-time partner Helen Pearce in 2004 and returned to his old job as a car salesman in Singleton. He had journeyed from despair to hope and had a simple message for others: 'Things do get better.'

But for Kathy, that wasn't the case.

Some of the stories zeroed in on her journals. 'Diary of Death: Why I Killed My Four Babies' screamed one headline. Other stories homed in on her father Thomas Britton, and the fact that one short sentence she had written in her journal had only just been released for publication: 'Obviously, I am my father's daughter.'

'Born to Kill' was how one newspaper reported this; 'Sins of Father Handed Down' read another. A swarm of similar stories were published around Australia, and across the world.

Her father's criminal associations were highlighted in many of the reports. 'Kathleen Folbigg is the daughter of an underworld henchman who worked for mafia boss Robert Trimbole,' read one report. 'Thomas Britton acted as a stand-over man for the late crime boss, allegedly "breaking legs" and "roughing up" associates who failed to pay their debts,' the *Central Coast Herald* proclaimed.

The idea that Kathy was 'born to kill' was a common theme. Thomas Britton had murdered Kathy's mother, ergo, she had inherited a killer gene. 'Is there such a thing as a natural born killer?' the *Courier-Mail* in Brisbane asked. 'Can we blame our genes for a propensity to violence?' And warming to the theme:

'She could never evade the reality of her genetic and environmental imprints. The daughter of a murderer, she was born to kill.'

The article declared: 'Our genes are inescapable. Did Folbigg's biodata, the 33,000 genes that constitute a human being, influence her homicidal propensity?

'Had she inherited, unwittingly and tragically, a blueprint for violence from her father and for maternal recklessness from her mother?

'If yes, it raises another argument over whether she could be held legally responsible, given that she was "born that way".'

It was heady stuff, and it helped to sell papers, but it was also utter nonsense, as at no point in the trial had anyone suggested that Kathy had inherited a homicidal streak from her dad, and had they done so, they would have been given very short shrift.

What had happened was that as the trial got underway, a highly charged argument took place in front of Justice Graham Barr – but with the jury absent – about the significance of the entry that Kathy had written in her journal on Monday, 14 October 1996. In part, the entry read:

> Obviously, I'm my father's daughter. But I think losing my
> temper stage & being frustrated with everything has passed.
> I now just let things happen & go with the flow. An attitude
> I should have had with all my children if given the chance.
> I'll have it with the next one.

Mr Tedeschi ascribed a deadly meaning to what she had written, and how she had explained it to Detective Ryan in her police interview. With the jury absent, he told Justice Barr: 'Here, in this interview, she really provides a link between that entry in her diary and the fact of her father in a fit of temper having killed her mother.'

'What she meant by "I'm my father's daughter" was that she considered that she might have been the same kind of person as her father in terms of losing her temper to the extent of forming an intention to kill.'

Peter Zahra, unsurprisingly, disagreed. He told the judge that if the diary entry was admitted into evidence, the 'prejudice is of the most extreme order and the danger is that the jury might draw inferences that the accused is also a person of generally violent disposition in a domestic relationship'.

Kathy's own explanation of what this infamous comment meant has never wavered.

Tracy Chapman, who grew closer and closer to Kathy over the years, commented: 'She didn't mean, "I am my father's daughter", as in "I've been killing my children." She didn't mean that at all. When she talks about it, she's like, "I meant I'm a loser like my dad." She was wracked with guilt that she couldn't be a good mother. She always had this self-doubt in her head about the fact that she was partially to blame. Not saying she actually killed these children, but what was she not doing right that this kept happening?

'So when she said, "I am my father's daughter", she meant, "God, I'm such a loser. I can't keep my children alive; I can't keep my husband happy. You know, I can't keep my weight down. I'm a loser", and I think that she actually really had quite low self-esteem.'

After hearing from both Peter Zahra and Mark Tedeschi, Justice Barr ruled this one journal entry inadmissible as evidence in the trial. And that might have been the end of the matter, except for the fact that just two days later, when Craig was asked in front of the jury about finding Kathy's journal and telling her about it, he mentioned the reference to her father. Mr Tedeschi asked him, 'What did you tell her about the diary?'

> I told her that I had found her diary. Had some pretty horrible things written in it, and that I gave it to Bernie [Ryan].
> Did she say anything to you about that?

She said things like 'What's written in it?' And I said – well, I remember a couple of excerpts, and I said, 'Oh, there was that thing about being your father's daughter.'

Whether deliberately or not, Craig had spilled the beans about the one entry which had been explicitly ruled inadmissible, and because of that, it was open to Peter Zahra to ask for the jury to be discharged, and a new jury empanelled – but that didn't happen. The defence simply let it slip by, and in the event, that was a fatal mistake.

What no one knew at the time was that, following Craig's reference to 'my father's daughter', one of the jurors went away and carried out an internet search to find out who Kathy's father was. The jurors were expressly forbidden to carry out any research outside the courtroom while the trial was in progress, but the juror then told the other members of the jury about Thomas Britton, and his murderous history.

Four years after the trial, the fact that a juror had done this formed one ground of Kathy's second appeal to the Court of Criminal Appeal. There, Kathy's lawyers argued that the trial 'miscarried by reason of a juror or jurors obtaining information from the internet, which revealed that the appellant's father had killed her mother'.

There was no disputing the fact that, during the trial, several of the jurors had become aware – when they shouldn't have – that Thomas Britton had murdered Kathy's mother when she was a young child. On the surface at least, this provided an unanswerable argument for a retrial, but the judges disagreed.

The appeal was dismissed, after the Crown's counsel put forward the surprising assertion that the knowledge of what Thomas Britton had done would have prompted sympathy for Kathy in the jury room. To anyone who had read the welter of lurid publicity about Kathy and her father following her conviction, the argument didn't sound credible.

In the media, there was universal agreement that Kathy's reference to being her father's daughter was a tacit admission that, just as he had murdered her mother, so too she had murdered her children.

In my view, the judges' conclusion that such a clear case of jury misconduct 'did not give rise to a miscarriage of justice' was eyebrow-raising at least, and the decision by Kathy's defence to allow Craig's remark in the trial to slip by was most unfortunate.

When Kathy started to try to process what had happened, following her trial, it was Lea's betrayal, as she saw it, and her mother, Deidre's, belief that she was guilty, that hit her harder than anything else – harder maybe even than the verdicts themselves.

By this time, Deidre hadn't seen or spoken to her daughter for eight years. She was seventy-five years old. It took several more years for Kathy, with Tracy Chapman's help, to contact her.

'I remember having a lot of conversations with Kathy,' Tracy told me later, 'saying, "Your mum's getting older. We need to just be brave and talk to her, because this is just nonsense. You've got to be able to explain properly what happened. She's your mother. You love her." You know? "And I think this is just ridiculous."

'And little by little, after two phone calls, she softened,' Tracy told me. 'And then she actually opened up and said that she loved her daughter, and how could she actually reconcile with her daughter? You know, will her daughter forgive her?'

Kathy and Deidre talked for three or four years after that, until Deidre passed away. Kathy wrote a loving, heartfelt letter, thanking Deidre for teaching her good manners, respect and sound moral values, to be placed in her mother's casket with a red rose.

Lea's perceived betrayal hit Kathy even harder. Kathy's sister had always been someone she adored and respected, and growing up, someone she could always turn to for help and advice as she faced the challenges of her teenage years. So, as Kathy told Tracy, when Lea stepped into the witness box at her trial to give evidence against her, Lea's 'nastiness' and the look on her face were 'destroying'.

Speaking from prison years later, Kathy told Tracy that, to begin with, Lea had stood by her, declaring angrily that the police investigation was a 'witch hunt'. So when Lea turned against her, Kathy felt blindsided. She told Tracy that although she would always love Lea, she would never understand why her sister had done it, nor trust her again.

From prison, Kathy wrote a letter to Lea. Many convicts who profess their innocence at trial end up later, in prison, confessing to the crimes for which they have been found guilty.

Kathy isn't one of them. Before, during and after the trial, she always insisted that she never harmed her children in any way. And in her letter to Lea, she vehemently denied it, accusing her sister of choosing only to see the worst in her. In strong language, Kathy wrote that she would not be 'forced' to take responsibility 'for something I have not done,' adding, defiantly, that this was the last time she would declare: 'I did not kill my children.'

She told Lea that Craig's 'vengeance' for her decision to leave him had begun the process which had ended with her behind bars. It had taken four years, she wrote, for the police and prosecution to come up with a case that was entirely circumstantial.

She asked her sister to try to imagine her life being ripped to pieces, her character assassinated, her every word and deed questioned, and as a result, 'becoming the most HATED woman alive.'

This, she told Lea, was what she lived with every day. She cried every night at the thought that there were people who believed she was capable of killing her children. She cried when she learned her own sister was one of those people.

The tone of her letter was angrier than many of her journal entries, and she protested that it was a sad day when a woman could be put away for being a normal mother who had described her feelings, anxieties and frustrations in 'bloody books'.

She delivered a bitter reprimand to her sister, telling Lea that she knew Kathy wasn't capable of such 'disgusting' acts of violence towards her children. And in a remarkable show of faith in the future, she told Lea that she endured all of this, knowing that 'vindication will one day be mine.'

As Kathy faced up to her own family's betrayal, and the open, dangerous hostility of other inmates, her friends rallied round and started to visit her in prison. And, notably, so did Joyce Harmer, who came regularly.

One year after the trial, Kathy wrote a poetic, heartfelt, almost biblical tribute to the woman who came to be known as an 'angel in the court'. It was published in Anne Henderson's book, which carried the same title.

'Joyce guided me, protected me and never once hesitated. The foremost impression came when the media behaved as they usually do. When the scent of blood is in the water. And who is walking proudly, head held high and parting the sea as she walks through? Quite the sight – five feet nothing and the appearance of a lovely little lady who wouldn't hurt a fly.

'Her kindness of heart and soul is never-ending, and no-one seems beyond her reach. She reminded me of a pilgrim with strong messages but a soft style.'

18

THE CHAMPION BRIDGE PLAYER

When Kathy crumpled in the dock after hearing the jury's verdicts, and later the same year, was sentenced to forty years in prison, I, like many, felt both fascinated and horrified. At the time I was working for *Four Corners*, the ABC's flagship investigative current affairs program, which has a long and honourable history of holding those in power to account.

One of the people who helped me with my research for several stories was a quietly spoken amateur sleuth called Peter Gill. Peter is a bit of a maverick. After graduating with a science degree and working in various laboratories, he reverted to his first love – bridge – and as a professional bridge player he has won more than fifty national championships, representing Australia on its national team multiple times. Regarded by many as the best bridge player in Australia, he is blessed with the high-level analytical brain needed to win, coupled with razor-sharp attention to detail and, when you talk to him, an almost compulsive tendency to dart from detail to detail, as he discusses his latest pet theory or a particular criminal case. 'Do you get it?' he will often ask after making a point.

Peter and I would often meet up in the old canteen at the ABC to have a chat, and the conversation would turn inexorably to Peter's bugbear – the life and times of Mark Tedeschi, and the men and women he had helped to put behind bars.

Sometime earlier, Peter had sent me a 4800-word email laying out his, frankly, disorganised thoughts on the multiple cases Mr Tedeschi had prosecuted. He called it his 'hobby'.

'Sorry that my attachments are unedited, a bit of a mess,' he wrote. 'As you can see, this hobby has snowballed and almost got out of control. But I love it.'

From our earliest encounters, Peter suggested that several of the cases prosecuted by Mr Tedeschi were worth a second look. And he wasn't alone in this. His fellow bridge players were part of his team. 'Are we all (about ten of us, my friends and I) deluding ourselves?' he wrote to me. 'The evidence is overwhelming that we are not. If lawyers allow it, there may be two or three *Four Corners* stories in amongst all our material.'

Peter was right. There were at least two. Following a lengthy investigation, in 2011, I reported a story for *Four Corners* about a famous Sydney case, which in a blaze of publicity, Mr Tedeschi had prosecuted.

This was the case of Gordon Wood. Tall, handsome, with classically chiselled features, Wood was found guilty in 2008 of murdering his glamorous girlfriend Caroline Byrne by propelling her over a cliff at The Gap – then a notorious suicide spot – in Sydney's Eastern Suburbs.

At the trial, Mr Tedeschi had called his star witness, Associate Professor Rod Cross, to the stand, to theorise that Gordon Wood had lifted his girlfriend up in the dead of night and propelled her – like a spear or javelin – from a rocky ledge, over the cliff.

It was an entertaining theory, with no convincing evidence to back it up.

During filming for my *Four Corners* report, I interviewed Professor Cross, asking him what his academic specialty – plasma physics – had to do with biomechanics, the scientific discipline required to buttress his eccentric theory.

'Nothing,' he replied.

I asked him: 'What are your formal qualifications in biomechanics?' He replied: 'I don't have any formal qualifications in biomechanics, so in that respect I'm self-taught.'

If nothing else, this demonstrated how dangerous it is for prosecutors to rely on expert witnesses who are not in fact experts in the relevant field.

Our program went to air following Gordon Wood's appeal court hearing, but before the panel of judges had reached their verdict. In February 2012, they quashed his conviction and ordered his release from prison. He had already served three and a half years of a minimum thirteen-year sentence.

The three judges were unanimous in acquitting Wood. Justice Stephen Rothman declared: 'There was no direct evidence linking the accused to the death of Ms Byrne.'

Bottom line, the forensic evidence for murder was non-existent. And despite the jury's verdict in 2008, the judges' opinion in the Court of Criminal Appeal was that the prosecution had failed to prove its case beyond reasonable doubt.

Five years after Gordon Wood's acquittal, Peter Gill and I sat having coffee again in the ABC canteen, when we started discussing another of Mr Tedeschi's cases – the conviction of Kathleen Folbigg.

I knew very little about Kathy then, but what I did know, and discussed with Peter, was that her case and Gordon Wood's had a common factor – Mark Tedeschi. That on its own was encouragement enough for me to look closely at her case.

There were other similarities. As Peter pointed out, both cases were entirely circumstantial. In the Folbigg case, there was no direct forensic evidence linking her with the act of smothering any of her children, just as later, no forensic evidence could be produced to link Gordon Wood with the body of Caroline Byrne.

And, as with Gordon Wood and the infamous spear throw, the fundamental prosecution argument in the Folbigg trial was based on a deeply flawed, discredited premise – Meadow's Law – that when three or more infants in a family die, it must be murder unless proved otherwise.

Peter steered me towards a 1997 book called *The Death of Innocents: A True Story of Murder, Medicine and High Stake Science*. It was about the Waneta Hoyt case.

'There is today a maxim in forensic pathology,' the book's publicity declared. 'One unexplained infant death in a family is SIDS. Two is very suspicious. Three is homicide.'

Peter pointed out something else. In June 2003, one month after he had led the successful prosecution of Kathy Folbigg, Mr Tedeschi had written an online review of *The Death of Innocents*: 'I am a Crown Prosecutor (i.e. District Attorney) in Australia, and this is the best, the very best, true crime book that I have ever read. I couldn't put it down. I was so upset when I had finished it.'

Here, in his brief review, was, in my view, a clear indication that Mr Tedeschi might have subscribed to Meadow's Law, and so in 2017, working with colleagues at the ABC's *Australian Story* program, I set about re-examining Kathy Folbigg's case. I wanted to explore the evidence suggesting that in every case there was positive forensic evidence to suggest that Kathy's children had died – not by her hand – but from natural causes.

But first, there was much more digging to be done.

19

MOTHERS IN THE DOCK

At Ayers Rock (Uluru) in 1980, a young couple were on a camping holiday when something unimaginably dreadful occurred. A dingo, lurking nearby, crept into the camp, entered a tent, grabbed a small bundle in its mouth, and raced away.

The bundle between the dingo's teeth was a small baby, Azaria Chamberlain, and Azaria's mother Lindy would later be accused of murdering her child. Her story, brought to life in a Hollywood movie starring Meryl Streep, became known around the world as the most notorious miscarriage of justice in Australian criminal history.

But she was far from being the only mother who had suffered a terrible miscarriage of justice.

In the 1990s and early 2000s, several women who had infants die suddenly and in unexplained circumstances were accused, and in several cases were convicted of murdering them. In England the cases included those of Sally Clark and Angela Cannings. There were other cases in Australia – including most notably, the case of Carol Matthey, whose impending trial was effectively stopped from going ahead by a judge in Victoria.

Of all these miscarriages of justice, Sally Clark's was the most significant, because her acquittal took place before Kathy came to trial.

Sally Clark was an English solicitor and a police commander's daughter, and in 1999 she was convicted of killing her two infant children, Christopher and Harry. Like Kathy, she had always protested her innocence, and following her conviction, her father managed to have her case referred to a body that didn't exist in Australia then, and to this day, still doesn't – the Criminal Cases Review Commission.

The Commission learned that microbiological tests had been carried out by a pathologist, showing that Sally Clark's second child, Harry, had a bacterial infection which could have killed him, but this hadn't been disclosed to the prosecution or to the defence and, consequently, hadn't been considered at her trial – a shocking omission.

The Commission referred the case to the English Court of Appeal, which also reviewed the evidence given at her trial by Professor Roy Meadow. He had testified that the odds against two children dying of SIDS in a single family like Sally Clark's was 1 in 73 million – something that might happen once in a hundred years.

In order to calculate the odds, Professor Meadow had told the jury at her trial that the risk of a family like hers suffering a single death from SIDS was 1 in 8543, taking into account her age, the fact that she and her husband were wage earners and the fact that they didn't smoke. The chance of two infants dying from SIDS, he argued, was 8543 multiplied by 8543 – roughly, 73 million. To illustrate how unlikely this was, he said it was the equivalent of betting and winning on an 80 to 1 outsider in the Grand National four years running.

On the day Sally Clark walked free in January 2003, Lord Justice Kay emphasised that the two cases relating to the deaths of Sally's two children 'should not have been heard together', and that the statistic of 1 in 73 million 'is clearly inadmissible in law, could not have failed to mislead the jury, and should never have been allowed in evidence'.

Lord Kay and his fellow appeal court judges ruled in a fuller judgment handed down on 11 April – ten days into Kathy's trial – that: 'Putting the evidence of 1 in 73 million before the jury with its related statistic that it was equivalent of a single occurrence of two such deaths in the same family once in a century, was tantamount to saying that without consideration of the rest of the evidence one could be just about sure that this was a case of murder.'

The significance of this for Kathy could hardly have been greater. The English Court of Appeal had ruled that the cases of the two children's deaths should not have been heard together. At Kathy's trial, all four of her children's deaths were heard together, and at her earlier committal, Dr Janice Ophoven had gone even further than Professor Meadow, suggesting, fantastically, that the chances of Kathy's four children all dying from natural causes was one in a trillion.

And there were more cases of mothers being wrongfully convicted.

In 2002, the year before Kathy went on trial, Angela Cannings, an English shop assistant and mother of four, was jailed for life for murdering her two boys by smothering them. Professor Meadow gave evidence for the prosecution in this case as well.

Ms Cannings appealed successfully in 2004 and was set free, after the court heard evidence of other infant deaths from natural causes – as well as other life-threatening events – in her extended family.

Lord Justice Igor Judge, heading the bench of three Court of Appeal judges, sounded a strong warning to those who would assume that two or three unexplained deaths of infants in a family are necessarily suspicious. 'We recognise that the occurrence of three sudden and unexpected infant deaths in the same family is very rare, or very rare indeed, and therefore demands an investigation into their causes,' he ruled.

'Nevertheless, the fact that such deaths have occurred does not identify, let alone prescribe, the deliberate infliction of harm as the cause of death. Throughout the process great care must be taken not to allow the rarity of these sad events, standing on their own, to be subsumed into an assumption or virtual assumption that the dead infants were deliberately killed, or consciously or unconsciously to regard the inability of the defendant to produce some convincing explanation for these deaths as providing a measure of support for the Prosecution's case.'

Here was a specific warning to other courts not to demand that a mother who had lost her children provide a convincing explanation for their deaths. But it came too late for Kathy, who by now was locked away behind bars.

As if to hammer home the point in Angela Cannings' case, Lord Justice Judge concluded by saying that: 'In expressing ourselves in this way we recognise that justice may not be done in a small number of cases where in truth a mother has deliberately killed her baby without leaving any identifiable evidence of the crime. That is an undesirable result, which however avoids a worse one.

'If murder cannot be proved, the conviction cannot be safe. In a criminal case, it is simply not enough to be able to establish even a high probability of guilt. Unless we are sure of guilt the dreadful possibility always remains that a mother, already brutally scarred by the unexplained death or deaths of her babies, may find herself in prison for life for killing them when she should not be there at all. In our community, and in any civilised community, that is abhorrent.'

Most remarkable of all, however, was the Australian case of Carol Matthey, who lived in Victoria. The mother of five was charged in 2005 with murdering four of her children. Two boys and two girls passed away; her fourth child Shania was the eldest, dying in April 2003 when Kathy was on trial in the New South Wales Supreme Court. She denied harming any of them.

The deaths had occurred over a period of four and a half years, and all four autopsies were carried out at the Victorian Institute of Forensic Evidence in Melbourne, which was headed by a highly respected forensic pathologist, Professor Stephen Cordner.

None of the pathologists who carried out the autopsies, independently of each other, found any positive support for the conclusion that any of the children had been deliberately killed.

Even so, Victoria Police, just as Detective Bernie Ryan had done, decided to approach the American pathologist Dr Janice Ophoven, whose finding in Kathy's case, as we have seen, involved statistical speculation.

Justice John Coldrey, who oversaw a preliminary hearing into Carol Matthey's case, made a point of emphasising that the use of statistical evidence – of the kind used by Dr Ophoven at Kathy's committal hearing – had been 'expressly disapproved' in Sally Clark's case.

In Carol Matthey's case, Dr Ophoven said: 'It is my opinion to a reasonable degree of medical certainty that Jacob, Shania and Joshua were the victims of homicidal assault, most consistent with intentional suffocation.'

Her report included the comment that: 'There is no known entity that is consistent with the facts present to explain these deaths except the homicidal act of another person.'

But Professor Cordner countered: 'I obviously accept that homicide is a possibility. I simply do not accept that a pathologist is in a position to make this conclusion on the information available in this case. I myself feel unable to make this conclusion. The causes of death as given remain a possibility.'

In his judgment, Justice John Coldrey was particularly scathing of the opinions given by two expert witnesses who helped Victoria Police and had also appeared as witnesses in Kathy's trial. One of them was Dr Allan Cala. The other was Dr Susan Beal. Dr Beal suggested in her report that: 'All the evidence points to all the children having been killed by non-accidental suffocation.'

'In relation to Joshua Matthey,' Justice Coldrey commented, 'it appears that Dr Cala accepts the view that the respiratory arrest and bradycardia which occurred in the [Royal Children's Hospital] was due to the respiratory depressant effects of intravenous morphine. However, he, like Dr Beal, implies, despite a total lack of evidence, that Mrs Matthey may have had a part to play in this event.'

Justice Coldrey said: 'Dr Beal's reasoning appeared to be as follows. Whilst Shania's death had to be called undetermined, having ruled out to her satisfaction accident, infection or unrecognised congenital malformation, she was prepared to find non-accidental suffocation. Having done so, Dr Beal reasoned backwards to a probability that the other three children died by non-accidental suffocation.'

In an echo of the evidence presented at Kathy's trial, and the significance attributed to the way she reacted to her children's deaths, Justice Coldrey ruled some of the 'demeanour' evidence in Carol Matthey's case to be inadmissible.

This included evidence that 'Mrs Matthey, on the day after Shania's death, was observed to be smiling while talking on her mobile phone. There are a myriad of reasons why a person, even a grieving one, may smile. Without the benefit of any context this evidence has little probative value but a high prejudicial potential.'

In addition, there was 'the evidence of the witness Cassidy of observing Mrs Matthey on the day after Shania's funeral chatting with an unknown group of people at her house and laughing with them. Again, there are manifold reasons for a person to laugh – nervousness, relief, the desire to secure approval, are three that immediately spring to mind. Devoid of context this evidence also has little probative value and is capable of having a highly prejudicial effect.'

Justice Coldrey remarked that a rare case like Carol Matthey's 'may be seen to present real challenges for the legal process in dealing with expert medical opinion'. And he quoted from a recent academic paper, 'The Case of Kathleen Folbigg: How did justice and medicine fare?', which addressed 'the challenge of achieving a legally and medically fair result in a trial that is based largely on circumstantial evidence'.

In Kathy's case, medical experts had argued that, in the absence of clear, substantiated natural causes of death, it was open to conclude that all four children had been smothered.

The paper's two authors, Sharmila Betts and Jane Goodman-Delahunty, from the School of Psychology at the University of New South Wales, examined the medical evidence given at Kathy's trial, and were critical of the fact that in her case, all four deaths were tried together.

In their view: 'If autopsy investigations have not yielded physical evidence of external trauma or suffocation, there is no physiological or pathological basis for a medical expert to concede or to raise the possibility of inflicted suffocation.' But this is exactly what Dr Cala, Professor Berry, Professor Herdson and Dr Ophoven had done in her case.

'Further,' the authors wrote, 'as inflicted death or murder is less common than any known medical cause of death in infants, and this statistical difference was not rigorously pursued by the defence, there is a real risk that undue weight was given by the medical experts and jurors to the explanation of inflicted death.'

Sharmila Betts and Jane Goodman-Delahunty argued that: 'Alone, none of the infant deaths was suspicious', and pointed out that the hypothesis that all four children were suffocated 'does not entertain the real possibility that separate, non-inflicted mechanisms were involved (such as subtle breathing/airway/apnoea issues ...). It is not logically necessary to conclude that because a medical or natural account is unavailable, the cause must be inflicted death.'

Justice Coldrey warned the lawyers prosecuting Carol Matthey that, given the substantial amount of evidence he was going to exclude from the trial and the doubtful probative value of much of the evidence that remained, 'it will be necessary for the Crown to reassess the viability of this prosecution'.

Following this, the prosecution withdrew the case altogether, and Carol Matthey walked free.

Justice Coldrey's ruling raised a significant question: what if he had been the judge in Kathy's case? Would her trial have had a different outcome? And would it even have gone ahead?

20

'A SCHOLAR OF BIAS'

Four years after Carol Matthey's prosecution was dropped, an academic author called Emma Cunliffe published *Murder, Medicine and Motherhood*. Her book was researched initially as a PhD thesis before its publication in 2011. By this point, Kathy had been incarcerated for eight years, and had failed in two appeals against her convictions. The book's findings would play a pivotal role in reopening Kathy's case.

As part of my own research from 2017 onwards, I contacted Dr Cunliffe and warmed to her immediately. She is a forthright Australian feminist and a highly regarded forensic scholar of the criminal justice system. By nature, modest and quietly spoken, she is also fiercely determined when circumstances demand it.

By the time I spoke to her, she was an Associate Professor at the University of British Columbia in Vancouver, in the Faculty of Law. 'My research focuses on expert evidence and bias and stereotypes in criminal cases,' she told me. 'I'm interested in how judges and juries find the facts in trials.'

Emma told me that in 2003, when Kathy was on trial, she was doing her master's degree at UBC and was actually studying Lindy Chamberlain's case.

'I was thinking very much about the murder trials of mothers, and the coincidence of the fact that Folbigg's case was being reported in the Australian media as I was looking at the transcripts of the Chamberlain case drew the case to my attention,' she told me.

Dr Cunliffe looked at the other cases of mothers who had been wrongly convicted of killing their children, noting that 'as I was studying them, one by one, each of those mothers were either acquitted, had the evidence against them excluded by courts or were exonerated by courts of appeal. And so, by 2006, the only mother whose conviction still stood was Kathleen Folbigg.'

Dr Cunliffe, however, was not someone who for ideological or any other reason had dismissed the strength of the prosecution's case at Kathy's trial. Far from it. She had studied the medical evidence, and appreciated how persuasive it would have been to the jury.

'I think that the most striking evidence that the jury heard was from Dr Cala and four other medical witnesses, each of whom were asked by the prosecution whether the medical literature documented three or more sudden unexplained deaths in a family being natural deaths,' she explained. 'Every witness answered no to that question, so each witness told the jury that the medical literature did not document three or more natural unexplained deaths in a single family. I think that the jury would have been very struck by that evidence and would have found that that really compelled a conclusion that the children were killed.'

'Were the experts right to say so?' I asked her.

'No, they weren't,' she said. 'And one of the most concerning things that emerged from the research that I conducted after the trial is that, at the time of the trial, the medical literature documented at least eight and as many as eleven confirmed cases of natural recurrent death – three or more SIDS deaths. And since the time of the trial, more cases have been documented.'

The jury in Kathy's trial should have been told this.

In Dr Cunliffe's opinion, Dr Cala's evidence at trial was particularly damaging. When he carried out Laura's autopsy, he found that she was suffering from myocarditis when she died and noted that it might be an incidental finding. But the jury never saw his autopsy report.

'Instead, they heard testimony from Dr Cala that it was not reasonably possible that Laura had died from myocarditis. Dr Cala also testified that none of the children could have died from identifiable natural causes, and none of the children's deaths should have been ascribed to SIDS, because of the existence of concerns about those deaths.'

Dr Cunliffe said she believed that Dr Cala had overreached his expertise in concluding that each of the children had probably been smothered.

'Straight question,' I asked her. 'Was he biased?'

'You know I'm a scholar of bias, right?' she replied. 'And I really want to give you a scholarly answer.'

'I want you to give me a clear and unvarnished answer,' I told her.

'Indeed, I know you do,' she retorted. 'Okay, I'm going to give you the definition of bias that I'm going to use, and then I'm going to give you a clear and unvarnished answer.

'Cognitive science,' she explained, 'shows that when someone believes that there is a likely explanation for a phenomenon that they are observing, they are more likely to notice evidence that supports their conclusion, and less likely to notice evidence that can test their conclusion.

'This is what leads to the definition of confirmation bias, and I believe that Dr Cala may well have fallen prey to confirmation bias in the way in which he testified in the Folbigg case.'

In the double episode of *Australian Story* that the ABC broadcast on Kathy's case in 2004, Detective Ryan spoke about Dr Cala's reaction to being told that Laura's death was the fourth in the family: 'Most of the time you cannot find anything at autopsy to show ... to prove suffocation. But then he looked at the three previous deaths. Based on all that, he said, "Bernie, I've got some real problems with this. You've gotta do the best police investigation you can [to] find out, you know, what's happened in this family."'

Emma Cunliffe suggested that the investigation would have been extremely difficult for all involved in it. 'Dr Cala was presented with an autopsy of a nineteen-month-old girl, in a context in which he knew there had been other deaths in the family. He was aware of the diaries and their contents. He was working closely with the police, speaking regularly to them while the investigation was taking place. I believe that the information he had about the police suspicions, his concerns, perhaps, about the contents of the diaries may have influenced his medical judgment on the things he could observe on autopsy.'

It was an unflattering assessment, but Dr Cala himself had admitted on *Australian Story* that: 'I suspected one thing, but medically I couldn't prove it', and his comment lent weight to the theory that perhaps his suspicion that all four children had been smothered carried more weight in his final judgment than it should have.

Dr Cala's stated view that Laura's myocarditis was 'patchy' and 'mild' wasn't shared by other forensic pathologists, most notably, Professor Johan (Jo) Duflou, whom I consulted in my own research for the *Australian Story* episode we eventually broadcast on Kathy's case, fourteen years after the original double episode.

In 1999, at the time of Laura's autopsy, Professor Duflou was the Chief Forensic Pathologist and Clinical Director at Glebe Coroner's Court where Laura's autopsy took place. Surprisingly, he wasn't called to give evidence by the defence at Kathy's trial.

Professor Duflou retains a very clear memory of Dr Cala showing him and a number of other pathologists the histology slides of Laura's heart, soon after Dr Cala conducted the autopsy. Gathered together in the registrar's room at Glebe, the pathologists took it in turns to examine the slides on the department's multi-header microscope.

Professor Duflou later revealed that the 'abnormalities' found in Laura's heart tissue were 'entirely unexpected'. Not only that, 'there was no doubt to any of us looking at the slides that there was very significant myocarditis, and that the severity and extent of it was sufficient to be capable of causing death.' His opinion hasn't changed in the intervening years. 'I remain of the firm view that the initial slides showed myocarditis of a severity entirely capable of causing sudden death in a young child,' he declared more recently.

As part of the research Emma Cunliffe carried out for her book, she studied Kathy's diaries, and the way they were used at her trial. But she surprised me with the revelation of how she reacted when she first had the chance to study them in the New South Wales Supreme Court registry.

'I think what I can speak to most viscerally, is when I first sat down and read the diaries,' she told me. 'Like many, I was shocked by what I read in the diaries. And I did feel that there was good reason to be concerned about whether Kathleen Folbigg had killed her children. So, I started from the position that the evidence had been strong.'

Echoing the reaction that the jury members at Kathy's trial must have had, Dr Cunliffe said that she found the diaries 'distressing and difficult to interpret when I first read them. Kathleen Folbigg used her diaries to record her anxieties about herself and her mothering. She articulates her own sense that she carries some responsibility for her children's deaths, and when you read some of the entries that she wrote, it sounds very much like she is hinting at having harmed the children. I think that any reasonable person who read the diaries would have concerns and questions about her role in her children's deaths.'

What did she believe now, I asked her.

'I now believe that those diaries record a woman who was struggling with the grief of losing children, and who was clinging on to the things that she could control in a situation that was largely uncontrollable. The research that I've done into maternal reactions, to losing a child, suggests that self-blame and guilt are very common reactions to sudden unexplained death and that those reactions are highly tuned in circumstances where medical science can't explain why or how the children died.

'I read the diaries now as Kathleen Folbigg blaming herself for getting frustrated, for losing her temper with her children, and feeling as if, if she had only been a better mother, perhaps the children would not have died. But that's very different from admitting that she killed the children.'

That, however, was exactly the interpretation that Mark Tedeschi put to the jury, when he explained to them – in his own words – what he believed certain entries in Kathy's journals meant.

In his closing address, Mr Tedeschi said:

'Now, you should also compare that with the diary entry for 9 November 1997 where she wrote this – she is talking about Craig: "There is a problem with his security level with me, and he has a morbid fear about Laura. He, well, I know there is nothing wrong with her, nothing out of the ordinary anyway, because it was me. Not them." What does that mean? What could that possibly mean other than this: Craig has terrible fear about losing Laura like he's lost the others. I know there is nothing wrong with her, nothing out of the ordinary anyway, because I killed them. They didn't just die". That is what it means.'

If the jury wasn't confused by that account of who was saying what, Emma Cunliffe suggested, they should have been, because the official court transcriber certainly was. When Mr Tedeschi addressed the jury, the court transcriber found it difficult to decide where to place the inverted commas in the formal record that would identify at what point he was quoting Kathy's diary entry, and at what point he was inserting his own interpretation of what Kathy meant by the words she had actually written.

'I found the court reporter's difficulty instructive in respect of how the jury might have interpreted what Mr Tedeschi had said,' Dr Cunliffe told me. 'To me, it seems that he stitched his interpretation of what the diary entries meant together with the words in the diary themselves. I suspect that the jury may have had difficulty disentangling Mr Tedeschi's interpretation with the actual text itself.'

We will never know how exactly the jury did interpret the diary entries.

'I know there's nothing wrong with her, nothing out of the ordinary, anyway,' were Kathy's words, but the ensuing words: 'because I killed them. They didn't just die,' were from Mr Tedeschi. Kathy never wrote those words. Nowhere in the tens of thousands of words in her journals was there a single sentence in which she admitted to having actively harmed any of her children – let alone to having killed them.

'The prosecutor's duty is not to seek a conviction at all costs,' Dr Cunliffe declared. 'It is to press the case to its fullest and fairest extent; to ensure the jury understands the evidence and its good and bad, and that they're entrusted with the responsibility to decide criminal responsibility accordingly.

'In this case, I am concerned that Mark Tedeschi overstepped that responsibility; that the manner in which he presented the diaries to the jury, in his closing submission, would have made it difficult for them to disentangle what was the *actual* evidence in the case, and what was his argument about what the evidence meant.

'The jury's responsibility was to consider, very carefully, not just what's the most likely explanation for those diary entries, but also other alternative, reasonable, possible explanations.'

In Dr Cunliffe's view, they should have been told to have regard to the explanations that Kathy had given to police when some of the diary entries were put to her, but they weren't given that instruction.

Never once, anywhere in her journals, or at any time in private when her conversations were being intercepted, did Kathy admit to having physically harmed her children in any way.

21

THE FIGHTBACK BEGINS

In one of my regular chats with Peter Gill – the champion bridge player – he arranged to introduce me to a close friend of Kathy's in Newcastle called Helen Cummings. Helen, quietly spoken though she is, possessed a steely determination to lobby for Kathy, stemming in part from the fact that she came from a Labor family and knew how the political system worked.

Her mother Joy had been the first female Lord Mayor in Australia, and her daughter Sarah Wynter was an accomplished actress. Helen's favourite line was: 'I'm the daughter of a famous mother, and the mother of a famous daughter.' But that belied her own significant achievements. She was made a life member of the Labor Party as a reward for her own political service – but continued to call the Party to account when the need arose.

In this regard, she had an ally – Emma Cunliffe.

When *Murder, Medicine and Motherhood* was published, Emma wrote to Kathy, whom she had never met, to tell her that the book was coming out, and that she had concluded that Kathy had been wrongly convicted.

In reply, Dr Cunliffe says: 'She asked me to do what I could to bring attention to my conclusions. That was a request I took very seriously. And my first step in that direction was to write to the then New South Wales Attorney General, who was Greg Smith.' She sent him a copy of her book, together with a synopsis of her findings.

Unfortunately for Kathy, Mr Smith had been Deputy Director of Public Prosecutions when Kathy had gone to trial, and he responded only with the advice that Kathy could, if she chose, apply for her convictions to be overturned under the State's *Crimes (Appeal and Review) Act*. The next Attorney General, Brad Hazzard, was equally unhelpful. And a third Attorney General, Gabrielle Upton, would also do nothing to help.

In December 2011, Dr Cunliffe went public, calling for New South Wales to introduce a legal means to allow Kathy's case to be reconsidered, following two failed appeals. There was a precedent here: in Lindy Chamberlain's case, the Northern Territory Parliament had passed the *Commission of Inquiry (Chamberlain Convictions) Act*, in order to allow her murder conviction to be reviewed.

At the same time, Helen Cummings, who had read Dr Cunliffe's book and was dismayed by what she viewed as an obvious miscarriage of justice, contacted her local paper, the *Newcastle Herald*, and in February 2013 the paper's leading investigative journalist, Joanne McCarthy, wrote a front-page feature about Helen and her crusade to free Kathy. Like Emma Cunliffe, Helen had herself been lobbying Greg Smith, telling him that Kathy's case had 'all the hallmarks of another Lindy Chamberlain', and that there was a danger of history repeating itself. 'I have no doubt at all about her innocence,' she told the *Herald*.

Greg Smith's department told the *Herald* that Kathy had 'several' avenues of review available to her, although they were 'only possible in exceptional circumstances'. The New South Wales Supreme Court could order an inquiry or refer the matter to the Court of Criminal Appeal, and the Governor of New South Wales could also be petitioned.

Helen Cummings regularly visited Kathy in prison.

'I remember the first time that we met,' she told me. 'It was like we'd known each other for a long time. I'd already written to her and asked her if it was okay if I could visit. But that very first visit, I liked her, and I have a very good bullshit antenna. I can tell if someone's trying to pull wool over my eyes, or is a bit phoney, or is a little bit pretentious, or is a bit gushy.

Kathleen just came across as someone basically really honest. So I guess meeting her cemented in me that she is innocent of these crimes.'

To Helen, Kathy 'has this incredible ability to overcome her own adversity and make you feel that it's gonna be okay, so I have found her friendship to be one of the loveliest I've ever had with anybody. I simply love her.'

Helen arranged to take me to visit Kathy in Silverwater jail on a Sunday in June 2017. It was early on in the piece. There was no guarantee that I would produce an *Australian Story* episode about her. But I was fascinated by her, and a bit apprehensive at the prospect of meeting her.

I needn't have worried. From the moment we said hello, Kathy was warm and welcoming, confident and humorous – we hit it off. She gently mocked me for wearing a cardigan when I visited her. Helen, as she always did, had bought handfuls of goodies – including a packet of snakes and some chips and a soft drink – from the vending machine inside the jail, which she spread out on the round metal table bolted to the floor, for Kathy to enjoy while we chatted. I liked her on sight, and I came away from my first visit impressed by how self-contained she seemed.

And of course, a single visit proves nothing. But it was one small indication that this could be an innocent woman. Had I felt at any point then, or subsequently, that she was hiding the truth, or acting, lying or dissembling, I would not have gone ahead with the program I was hoping to make.

I visited Kathy several times after that, with Helen to begin with, and later, when Kathy was moved to Cessnock jail, with Megan Donegan and Tracy Chapman. Sometimes we could talk freely; at other times prison guards would be seated nearby and I would feel particularly cautious. In order to be able to enter the prison to visit Kathy, I was listed as being a 'friend' of hers, but my real reason for being there was to talk to her as a journalist, to gather information, to assess her state of mind, and to tell her how *Australian Story* was hoping to bring her case to a wider audience.

On one of those visits, when we were outside Cessnock Correctional Centre, filming the prison walls topped with barbed wire, I spoke to a prison guard who was detailed to escort us around the perimeter of the jail. He told me that the general view among the guards was that Kathy was innocent. And that too seemed significant, because prison guards are often the best judges of an inmate's guilt or innocence.

In discussions with Helen Cummings, she told me how her interest in Kathy's case had developed. 'When I read about Kathleen's conviction, I immediately, like perhaps, a lot of people, thought about Lindy Chamberlain. There were other cases I started to look at; Sally Clark in England, Angela Cannings, they were all mothers who were dealing with exactly the same thing Kathleen had been convicted for.

'And Carol Matthey was probably a more important one because that was a Victorian case where she was accused of killing her four babies. She had the same expert witnesses as Kathleen did. The judge in Victoria threw the case out. Carol Matthey walked.'

Helen's belief was that if Kathy had been charged in Victoria, and taken before the same judge, she wouldn't, when we spoke, have been serving her sixteenth year in prison.

In her opinion: 'The similarity with Lindy Chamberlain was that she was a mother and her basic mothering was on trial, not who she was, not the evidence.'

Helen – like Emma Cunliffe – had studied the Chamberlain case when she was doing an associate law degree and said: 'What struck me was that we haven't learned a thing.'

In particular, there was the mistake made in both cases of judging women by their outward appearance. This had happened to Kathy after Laura's death, when she put on a brave face for her friends. Helen had talked to her about it.

'Nobody saw that inside she was weeping, but she's not going to come out and just do that for everyone else's benefit. I understand that totally, and I know what Lindy went through. I'm not going to do that just because you're talking to me, you know? My grief is my grief. It's personal, it's deep, it's heartbreaking. So, I will cry when I need to cry.

'She cries ... I'm sure she sheds many tears in prison. But they're for her. They're not for anybody else.'

Helen's and Emma's approaches to successive Attorneys General fell on deaf ears. Not everyone in the New South Wales legal profession was implacably ranged against Kathy, however.

Isabel Reed, a local Newcastle barrister who was helping to set up an Innocence Project at the University of Newcastle, read the article about Helen Cummings in the *Herald* and told me that after doing so, 'I literally went across the road and into our chambers, and I said: "Holy shit, look at this – we've got to do something about this!"'

Ms Reed is that rarity in the rarefied legal profession – a lawyer with an open heart, and an equally open mind.

After linking up with Helen, who rushed over with Emma Cunliffe's book, Ms Reed and a close colleague, the barrister Nic Moir, contacted Emma directly and remained in close touch with her, exploring the voluminous material connected with the case.

That same year, Emma Cunliffe went to meet Kathy for the first time and spoke out on Australia's most viewed commercial current affairs program, *60 Minutes*, telling its viewers: 'An error has been made, and a woman has been wrongly convicted. She should walk.'

By contrast, Kathy's foster sister Lea Bown told *60 Minutes* that Kathy deserved to die, with the words: 'She took four lives; an eye for an eye.' Later, Lea would say the same thing to me, that if capital punishment by hanging had still been the law of the land, she would have been the first to 'pull the lever'.

Nic Moir suggested looping in the University of Newcastle's Legal Centre. There, an army of students under the guidance of the Centre's Director, Associate Professor Shaun McCarthy, reviewed the trial transcripts, examined the other cases in the UK which had been tainted by Meadow's Law, and helped with some of the most complex background research.

Also in 2013, the Legal Centre announced that it would seek a judicial review of the case, and from 2013 until 2017, Shaun McCarthy acted as Kathy's instructing solicitor.

Nic Moir and Isabel Reed, meanwhile, were in regular contact with Professor John Hilton, who was present when Dr Cala carried out his autopsy on Laura.

One day, Professor Hilton revealed a remark Dr Cala had made to him that would knock them for six. He said that after Dr Cala had carried out his autopsy on Laura, he had come in to see the professor and exclaimed, 'Fuck it – it's myocarditis!', or words to that effect.

Isabel Reed told me that she and Nic Moir were so shocked to hear this that they drove straight up to the Blue Mountains outside Sydney, where Professor Hilton lived, to ask him to repeat this on tape – but he wouldn't agree to do so. I myself would later ask him about this, and he wouldn't confirm it – but neither did he deny the story. 'I couldn't possibly comment,' he told me, cryptically.

Before long, Nic Moir recruited a barrister he had worked with many times before, Dr Robert Cavanagh, to join the team.

Dr Cavanagh is tall, imposing and undeniably unique. He is almost never visibly cheerful, exhibiting the demeanour more of Banquo's ghost, or – as one journalist described him – of a country undertaker. But I liked him.

In 2018, we met for the first time in his decidedly cramped barrister's chambers in Newcastle, where the ceiling was barely high enough to accommodate his lanky frame. Working with him on a part-time placement was a young, enthusiastic, indefatigable law student at the University of Newcastle, Rhanee Rego, who would later play a major role in the battle to overturn Kathy's convictions. Ms Rego had the benefit of bringing an entirely fresh mind to the case – she was only eleven years old when Kathy was convicted.

Dr Cavanagh is a veteran campaigner in the field of human rights, and is nothing if not direct. I soon experienced his gift for being brief and brutally frank. He could be irascible, and on occasion, explosive in his anger at what he considered to be the idiocy of the judicial system that had condemned Kathy to spend the best years of her life in prison.

He made it clear, however, that he wasn't acting as an advocate for Kathy. 'I am simply an advocate for trying to see that justice is appropriately applied, especially where fresh evidence comes in. I'm doing this as a person who's interested in human rights; interested in assisting wherever I can to ensure that miscarriages of justice don't go unresolved.'

An early meeting I had with Dr Cavanagh was attended by an adjunct law professor at La Trobe University, Ray Watterson. We had met briefly nine years previously, when I had interviewed him for a Four Corners investigation into the use of lethal force by police against people suffering mental illnesses or psychological distress. Ray had plenty to say about Kathy's case – none of it complimentary about the judges and courts that had put her behind bars.

He had one very helpful and notable notch in his belt; he had played a significant role in the ultimate push to exonerate Lindy Chamberlain. 'I came into the Chamberlain case in the final chapter. That's the fourth and final inquest in 2012,' he told me. 'I was asked by Michael Chamberlain and Stuart Tipple, Lindy and Michael's long-term lawyer, to help them put together a submission to the coroner, to have an inquest.'

With Ray's help, Lindy Chamberlain was able to secure the coronial finding that a dingo was responsible for Azaria's death. But it had taken a tortuous thirty-two years for this to happen.

I asked Ray what the lessons of the Chamberlain case were.

'One of the lessons is about prosecutors, you know, fighting for a conviction and using high drama to convince a jury of a proposition that they're putting about a person's guilt,' he said.

'So, in the Chamberlain case, the prosecutor was Ian Barker, QC, and Ian Barker was able to persuade the jury that Lindy killed her baby Azaria. Of course, the defence was saying it was a dingo.'

Ray read me the words used by Mr Barker during the Chamberlain trial, where he told the court: 'The dingo story is preposterous. It's not capable of belief and what we do know as Australians, and you don't need experts to tell you, is that dingoes are not notorious man eaters. If your general knowledge tells you that dingoes are not known as a species for killing and eating human beings, then you can take all that into account in deciding the likelihood of the truth of the dingo theory.'

Ray was struck by the close similarity between what Mr Barker had said at Lindy Chamberlain's trial, and what Mr Tedeschi had said in his closing address to the jury at Kathy's trial, where he used the same word 'preposterous' to ridicule the idea that each of Kathy's children might have died from natural causes. That was akin, he suggested, to Farmer Joe looking out of his window one morning and seeing piglets sprouting wings and flying away.

'In my view that language is not only inflammatory, but it's almost contemptuous of the jury,' Ray told me. 'It's almost treating them like they're mugs who can't understand possibilities and probabilities and it has to be put to them in terms of pigs flying.'

The other glaring similarity between the two cases, he believed, was the way in which both women were demonised as bad mothers. The fact that Lindy was nearby when the dingo took Azaria, and that Kathy was the first to discover her children moribund or deceased, was twisted to suggest that they must have been responsible for their children's deaths.

There was also the way the media had treated Lindy's and Kathy's physical appearance – and even the clothes they wore on their way to court. 'The depictions of them in the media usually show them not crying, often sullen faced; well, I think you would be sullen if you were on trial for murdering your babies, and that's how they're depicted in the media as, as bad mothers.

'People are in the middle of trials for killing their babies, they're gonna look terrible and there'd be plenty of chances to take shots of them looking terrible.'

I asked Ray, if Kathy was innocent, how great an injustice had been done to her. 'Well, if she's innocent, I could imagine no greater injustice,' he replied.

The common perception for many years was that the greatest injustice suffered in Australian criminal history had been Lindy Chamberlain's. And at the time it was. But Lindy served three years in jail, thanks to a royal commission that freed her.

'Ms Folbigg's already served almost fifteen years in jail. Fifteen years is a lot longer than three years and a much greater injustice,' Ray suggested.

It was clear from these discussions that the small legal team had the bit between their teeth. They were highly motivated, and nothing would stop them in their efforts to see justice served in this case.

22

THE PETITION

On 26 May 2015, twelve years after Kathy began her jail sentence, her barristers Nic Moir, Dr Cavanagh and Isabel Reed signed a petition calling for her convictions to be reviewed under section 76 of the Crimes (Appeal and Review Act) 2001. The petition was delivered to the Governor of New South Wales, General David Hurley. He, in turn, handed it on to the Attorney General's office at the New South Wales Parliament.

Notably in New South Wales, although the Governor is nominally responsible for considering petitions and reaching decisions on them, in practice the decisions are made by whoever is Attorney General at the time, and every Attorney General is a politician who belongs to whichever party is in power. These decisions, therefore, carry a strong political overtone.

In 2015, the Liberal Party was in power, and a legally trained former banking and finance lawyer called Gabrielle Upton was the Member of Parliament charged with assessing the petition's merits.

I came to the story in 2017 and in the intervening two years, the petition had dropped out of sight. Kathy herself was still regarded by most as a baby-killer, and arguably, for any Attorney General to have taken up her cause and championed it would have been political suicide. The petition asked for a review of Kathy's convictions, but it remains unknown whether Ms Upton, who served as Attorney General until January 2017, took any steps to actually consider it. The silence was deafening. And there was no sign that her successor, Mark Speakman, himself a senior counsel, had any greater appetite to grant the petition's request.

In September 2017 – more than two years after the petition had been lodged – Mr Speakman told a parliamentary committee that he had 'personally read, considered and discussed within my office the Department of Justice brief in this matter'. He added: 'I have personally gone through the petition and the accompanying material and I am personally considering the matter as to what recommendation I will make to His Excellency.'

Mr Speakman acknowledged that it was open to him to refer Kathy's case to the Court of Criminal Appeal, but wouldn't be drawn on any timeframe for reaching a decision. 'I cannot give you a timeframe,' he said. 'I am very conscious that this has been hanging around now for a considerable period of time. I will try to deal with it as quickly as I can.'

But Kathy's team of lawyers associated with the University of Newcastle, as well as her supporters, were growing increasingly frustrated. To them, it looked as if the petition had in effect, been flushed down the toilet. The delay was seemingly endless.

That only made me more intrigued. Why had it taken so long for two Attorneys General to decide what action, if any, to take? If the petition had no merit, why hadn't they said so already?

The petition claimed that following Kathy's unsuccessful appeals, 'further evidence has come to light'. That evidence fell into two main categories: the children's causes of death, and the use made of the diary evidence at Kathy's trial and appeals. Four new expert reports were also submitted, backing the arguments being made by Kathy's lawyers.

The petition to the Governor argued that: 'When the new evidence is looked at, along with the evidence adduced at trial, you and subsequently a judicial officer would feel a sense of unease or a sense of disquiet in allowing the convictions to stand.'

Crucially, it pointed out that: 'The proposition that there had never been more than three SIDS deaths in a family was allowed into evidence. This was damaging evidence ... and was wrong.'

The most substantial report attached to the petition came from one of Australia's foremost forensic pathologists, Professor Stephen Cordner, who had taken a year to compile an exhaustive re-evaluation of the medical evidence put forward at Kathy's trial.

As Professor Cordner was based at Monash University in Melbourne and at the Victorian Institute of Forensic Medicine, he came to the case as an entirely independent expert, unshackled by any duty of loyalty to the New South Wales department of health, which oversaw the autopsy carried out on Laura, and which was Dr Cala's employer at the time.

Given that Kathy had been convicted in 2003, had then lost two appeals, and had lost a bid to have her case heard before the High Court, it was startling to read Professor Cordner's conclusion: 'There is no forensic pathology evidence to suggest that the Folbigg children were deliberately smothered or killed.'

The professor added, pointedly: 'It seems not to have been explicitly stated in the trial, but there is no forensic pathology evidence, no signs in or on the bodies, to positively suggest that the Folbigg children were smothered, or killed by any means.'

And that wasn't all. He argued, further, that the lack of facial injuries on all four children was evidence *against* the conclusion of smothering.

This was particularly so with Laura, who was nearly nineteen months old and had teeth when she died. There were no signs of tooth marks on the inside of her mouth, which any pathologist would have expected to find if her mother had tried to smother her, and she had struggled to stay alive.

In Laura's case, Dr Cala had discovered myocarditis, but judged it to be patchy and mild, giving evidence at the trial that it hadn't actually killed her. Professor Cordner didn't just give his own opinion on this; he sought the opinions of ten other forensic pathologists, asking them to examine slides of Laura's heart tissue – but without telling them where the tissue originated from – and all ten pathologists concluded that the cause of death was myocarditis.

Taking that into account, Professor Cordner wrote: 'I believe the middle of the road conclusion in relation to Laura's death is that considered alone, most forensic pathologists would be comfortable ascribing the death in similar circumstances to Laura's as being due to myocarditis. This is indeed my view.'

In the final chapter of his extensive report, Professor Cordner wrote: 'In my view, it is wrong on the forensic pathology evidence available in this case to conclude that one or more of the Folbigg children are the victims of a homicide. There is no merit in forcing certainty where uncertainty exists.'

He added: 'If the convictions in this case are to stand, I want to clearly state there is no pathological or medical basis for concluding homicide. The findings are perfectly compatible with natural causes.'

Professor Cordner conceded that the findings couldn't rule out smothering in one or more of the cases, but added that, especially in Laura's case, not only was there an 'acceptable' natural cause of death easily visible, but in addition, 'absolutely no signs of asphyxia or compression of the face are present'.

Both Caleb's and Sarah's deaths were best regarded as SIDS, Patrick's ALTE – or near-miss incident – was unexplained; but Patrick's death was 'an unsurprising consequence of the state he was left in following the ALTE'; and Laura's death had been caused 'unexceptionally' by myocarditis.

Professor Cordner was particularly critical of Mr Tedeschi's use of the term 'acute catastrophic asphyxiating event' when he questioned the medical witnesses.

'Asphyxia is not a helpful word in forensic pathology, is not understood in a uniform way, is not a diagnosis, and is not diagnosable,' the professor wrote.

'Yet the word is at the core of the main question asked repeatedly by the prosecution: Did this child/these children suffer "an acute catastrophic asphyxiating event"? If this question was intended to be a technical question in forensic pathology, it has no content and is not capable of an answer.

'Ultimately, and simply, there is no forensic pathology support for the contention that any or all of these children have been killed, let alone smothered.'

Professor Cordner ended by saying it was surprising that in five alleged smothering events, there were no signs of smothering.

Here was a full-frontal assault by one of Australia's leading forensic experts on the medical evidence which had been given at Kathy's trial, and which had helped to condemn her to spend most of the rest of her adult life behind bars.

And this wasn't just a rogue view by a fringe forensic pathologist. Professor Cordner's study was peer reviewed by the Chief Forensic Pathologist for Ontario, Professor Michael S. Pollanen, who said that the report's conclusions were supported by the data and were correct. He went on to explain that: 'The concept that a series of unexplained deaths in infancy (such as SIDS) are homicides has its roots in modern American pathology.

'This was based [on] a small number of high-profile cases in the USA, most notably the Hoyt case. The mythology/dogma around these cases became known as "DiMaio's rule". The rule states that if the autopsies are "negative", then the first infant ought to be certified as natural, the second as undetermined and the third homicide ...

'Most forensic pathologists now believe that this approach is oversimplified and thus too flawed to be sustained. However, even if you accept DiMaio's rule, it is clear that the Folbigg case does not follow the rules, since there is a satisfactory natural cause of death in two cases in the series.' The professor was referring here, to Patrick's and Laura's deaths.

Kathy's lawyers argued that the reasoning that Kathy was guilty because there were multiple deaths was unsupportable, and yet the jury at her trial had been specifically asked to engage in such reasoning.

The petition also addressed the effect that Kathy's diaries would have had on the jury at her trial. In her lawyers' opinion, they were the catalyst that led to her being charged.

The petition quoted the remarks made by Justice Brian Sully at Kathy's first appeal against her convictions in 2005.

'These entries make chilling reading in the light of the known history of Caleb, Patrick, Sarah and Laura,' Justice Sully wrote. 'The entries were clearly admissible in the Crown case. Assuming that they were authentic, which was not disputed; and that they were serious diary reflections, which was not disputed; then the probative value of the material was, in my opinion, damning. The picture painted by the diaries was one which gave terrible credibility and persuasion to the inference, suggested by the overwhelming weight of the medical evidence, that the five incidents had been anything but extraordinary coincidences unrelated to acts done by the appellant.'

Here was one of the strongest, most unequivocal statements by a senior judge during the entire course of Kathy's case, and her lawyers acknowledged that Justice Sully's conclusion that the diary entries were damning 'is one that is rationally available'.

However, they argued, 'there is other equally compelling reasoning that allows for an innocent interpretation'.

In their petition, the lawyers pointed out that the defence at Kathy's trial had failed to call any experts to help the jury interpret the diary entries, and, that this in turn allowed Mr Tedeschi to suggest that the entries amounted to virtual admissions of guilt, allowing the jury to use the diary entries in a way that was highly and unfairly prejudicial.

An alternative explanation for the entries, they suggested, was that they were made by a 'weary and emotional person who sought to express her feelings in the written word as a cathartic process, expressing emotions that have often been reported as not uncommon amongst women experiencing childbirth and motherhood. She speaks of the feelings of alienation from her husband, of feeling fat and unattractive, of feeling alone …

'There are no admissions in the entries of guilt, and unease arises where the private and emotional writings of a mother traumatised by the death of a child are taken by third parties to indicate a guilty mind.'

A report attached to the petition, supporting this argument, was provided by the clinical psychologist, Dr Sharmila Betts, whose earlier paper on the medical evidence in the case had been quoted by Justice Coldrey in his ruling on the case against Carol Matthey.

Dr Betts, at Shaun McCarthy's request, had made her own separate study of Kathy's diaries.

Her view was that they documented Kathy's moods, her marital relationship concerns, and her guilt about being unsuccessful as a mother. 'She appears to interpret her feelings of stress, irritability and exhaustion in caring for her infants as evidence of poor mothering and possibly equates her psychological reactions to motherhood as the reason for their deaths,' she wrote.

She emphasised, however, that the diaries contained no direct confession of harming her children, or any negative beliefs about them. 'Rather her concerns centre on her lack of family, stress, and social isolation.'

'Self-blame,' she stressed, 'an oft-documented phenomenon in both bereaved and non-bereaved mothers, and a sentiment that pervades Ms Folbigg's diaries, is not tantamount to a confession.'

Dr Betts concluded that: 'Ms Folbigg is no different to many mothers. Ms Folbigg's entries suggest periods of depression but largely her beliefs consist of unremitting self-blame. She also exhibits confusion about how to reach her own exacting standards of motherhood. It is evident that Ms Folbigg has unrealistic notions of the function of motherhood and no doubt placed considerable pressure upon herself.

'Despite this, Mr Tedeschi's assertion that the Crown was able to read the "truth" behind the diary entries, which, according to the Crown, were tantamount to confessions, is misleading and unsupported by my reading of the diaries or the psychological literature on maternal adjustment, in both bereaved and non-bereaved mothers.'

The fourth report submitted with the petition came from a British Professor of Mathematics, Ray Hill, who first appeared as an expert witness in criminal cases following Sally Clark's conviction for the murder of her two babies.

'I was so shocked by the misuse of statistics at her trial, that I felt I should get involved,' Professor Hill told me when I spoke to him. 'I studied the statistics for myself, and this led to my submitting a report to Sally Clark's second appeal.'

Professor Hill explained that in Sally Clark's case, there was no doubt that the 73 million to 1 figure presented in evidence by Professor Roy Meadow 'was widely misinterpreted as being the chances of Sally Clark being innocent. This is a common statistical error known as the prosecutor's fallacy.'

Most significantly, Professor Hill turned the statistical claims made by Professor Meadow and Dr Ophoven on their heads.

In what, to me personally, was a kind of 'eureka' moment, the professor pointed out what should have been obvious to everyone: 'It's important to note that while multiple cot deaths may be a rare event, so also will be multiple homicide. What is important is to calculate the relative chances of cot death or murder in cases where two or more sudden unexpected deaths have occurred.'

Professor Hill's own rough estimates, which he had published in a paper, was that single cot deaths outweigh single infant murders by 17 to 1. Double cot deaths outweigh double infant murders by about nine to one, and triple cot deaths outweigh triple murders by about two to one.

'This shows that Meadow's Law is in fact complete nonsense; while each successive death does bring a small amount of extra suspicion, this is to nothing like the extent that Meadow's Law would suggest. In particular, when two, or three, or more cot deaths or sudden infant deaths have occurred, the statistics show that there is no more reason to suppose that these are murder than cot deaths.'

In Professor Hill's opinion, it was likely that some of the jurors would have been aware of the 'one in a trillion' figure put forward by Dr Ophoven at Kathy's committal hearing, even though it was ruled inadmissible at her trial.

'By the time of Kathleen Folbigg's trial, Sally Clark had recently been cleared and Meadow's statistical arguments totally discredited. So, the figure of a trillion to one, which was wildly inaccurate and misleading, was not used at trial, but it had already been widely circulated by the Australian media. I think there is every chance that this figure must have entered the privacy of the jury room.'

Professor Meadow had suggested that to lose two children to SIDS was like winning a bet on an 80 to 1 outsider in the Grand National four years in a row. By contrast, Professor Hill drew his own comparison between the tragedy of losing several children to SIDS, with the joy of winning a lottery.

'The odds of winning the lottery are very long, but there are so many entrants each week that it's inevitable that there will be big winners now and then. Similarly, there are so many women giving birth that it's inevitable that there will be cases of two, three, and occasionally even four cot deaths in the same family,' he asserted.

And Professor Hill wasn't alone in saying this.

His assertion that, tragically, cot deaths do run in families has been borne out by an exhaustive, long-running study in the UK known as the 'Care of Next Infant', or CONI, program. The program, which extends across almost every health district in the country, is designed to support families who have lost an infant, and to provide them with help and information to ensure that no more children in the family suffer the same fate.

The CONI program has for years studied the rate of sudden unexpected death in infancy (SUDI) for infants born after a previous sudden death in the same family and has worked to establish the causes of death and the frequency of child protection concerns in families with recurrent SUDI.

In a 2020 paper, the program revealed that between January 2000 and December 2015, the CONI study had 6608 live-born infants registered, with twenty-nine subsequent deaths of siblings occurring. Twenty-six families had two deaths, and three families had three deaths in all.

The number of infants born after one sudden unexpected death, who also died, was 3.93 per 1000 live births. The causes of death for nineteen first and fifteen subsequent deaths were unexplained. Accidental asphyxia accounted for two first and six subsequent CONI deaths; medical causes accounted for three first and four subsequent CONI deaths; and homicide was judged to be the cause of two first and four subsequent CONI deaths. Ten families had child protection concerns.

In families like the Folbiggs, where Craig smoked, the study reported that: 'Many parents continued to smoke and exposed infants to hazardous co-sleeping situations, with these directly leading to or contributing to the death of six siblings.'

Most notably, the study concluded that: 'Homicide presenting as recurrent SUDI is very rare.'

Professor Hill's conclusion was unequivocal: 'The jury in the Folbigg trial were almost certainly misled by statements made by experts regarding the rarity of multiple SIDS. It is highly likely that the jury reasoned that three or more SIDS in the same family was so unlikely that this explanation could be discounted, leaving multiple homicide as the only plausible explanation. After all, this was the line effectively pursued by the prosecution, with three experts saying that they knew of no previous occurrence anywhere of three or more SIDS in the same family.'

This raised the question, why hadn't Kathy's defence called Professor Hill to give evidence at her trial, given that it took place so soon after Sally Clark's acquittal? It looked very much to me as if the jury's decision at Kathy's trial might have been very different, if only Professor Hill had been called to give evidence. But he wasn't.

The petition concluded by suggesting that because the overwhelming weight of forensic pathology evidence pointed clearly to natural causes of death for Patrick and Laura Folbigg, those cases should never have been prosecuted. And, in the case of Caleb and Sarah, the only evidence that could possibly be seen to support their convictions were the 'ambiguous' diary entries.

The legal team submitted their petition and waited. And waited. And waited.

23

'AN EMINENTLY FATAL CASE OF MYOCARDITIS'

In early 2018, the decision was taken to re-examine Kathy's case on *Australian Story*, and in March I flew to Canada to film with Emma Cunliffe and an independent forensic pathologist called Matthew Orde.

It was an exciting prospect. Dr Cunliffe was Australian born and educated, but had made her home in Vancouver where, quite coincidentally, Dr Orde had landed as well. It would not only be an opportunity to film with them both, but also, to help bring them together to swap notes and to discuss the pathology of the Folbigg case, and the broader evidence that had helped to convict Kathy.

Matthew Orde was critical to our story, because while at her trial, the prosecution's medical experts had agreed that Kathy had probably smothered her children, by 2018, when we were putting our story together, there was a serious divergence of views among medical professionals.

On the one hand, Dr Allan Cala, the main medical expert who had given evidence at the trial, remained adamant that smothering was the most likely cause of death for all four children. But on the other hand, Professor Stephen Cordner was unequivocal in his view that there was no forensic evidence to support the allegation that Kathy had smothered any of her children. And in fact, there was positive forensic evidence to the contrary.

There was a clear scientific impasse here, and I wanted *Australian Story* to stand between the two opinions and feature an interview with a pathologist who could justifiably be said to be entirely independent of Kathy's case.

It was Professor Jo Duflou who suggested Dr Orde to me as being a highly regarded, eminently qualified pathologist, who might be prepared to read through Professor Cordner's report and tell me whether he agreed with it, and also, more significantly, who could examine the slides of Laura's heart muscle for himself and give his own, unvarnished opinion as to what the chances were that Laura had died from myocarditis.

This was critical, because the positive evidence of a natural cause of death appeared to be strongest in the case of Laura, who had died with – or from – myocarditis. But the question was: which was it?

If the preponderance of independent expert opinion turned out to support the view that she had indeed died from myocarditis, then, in Dr Cavanagh's view, the case against her would collapse like a pack of cards, because the prosecution's case depended on the assertion that Kathy had smothered all four of her children – and not just one, two or three.

The coincidence evidence depended on the idea that there were marked similarities between all four deaths. Once you took one of those deaths out of the equation, it no longer carried the same weight. And if you could demonstrate, beyond reasonable doubt, that two or three of the deaths were from natural causes, it would be game over.

Ten independent pathologists canvassed by Professor Cordner had already backed his view that Laura's death was caused by myocarditis. My view was that, if Dr Orde were to share this view, it would add considerable weight to the argument that Dr Cala – to put it bluntly – had got it wrong. And if Dr Orde decided that Dr Cala was right, and that the slides showed that Laura's myocarditis was only patchy and mild, and incidental to her death, well then, so be it.

Professor Duflou had already given me an eye-opening

insight into what had happened inside NSW Health Pathology when Kathy's petition had been submitted nearly three years earlier. He had been asked to write a brief, bullet-point assessment of Professor Cordner's report and in doing so, he not only broadly agreed with his conclusions; he also strongly urged the department to undertake a detailed review of all four cases, while cautioning that this would cost a lot of money to carry out.

There was one unarguable reason to take the matter further. In his bullet-point note, Professor Duflou wrote: 'The report by Professor Cordner implies strongly that Dr Cala has not been impartial in his assessment of Laura's death. In my opinion, there is definite myocarditis present, and this could reasonably have been the cause of death.' Sensationally, he added: 'I therefore agree with the implicit views of Professor Cordner that there may have been bias on the part of Dr Cala.'

Dr Cala was and remains a departmental employee, and only recently was I given an insight into the level of consternation this caused behind the scenes, after obtaining internal emails and briefs following an application under the state's freedom of information laws.

On 16 June, the same day Professor Duflou gave his own damning assessment of Dr Cala's forensic judgment, Catherine Foster-Curry, Director of Forensic Medicine at the NSW Forensic and Analytical Science Service, wrote a brief for senior colleagues, acknowledging that Professor Cordner's report 'implies strongly that Dr Cala has not been impartial in his assessment of the death of the fourth child'.

She repeated Professor Duflou's comment that Professor Cordner 'has without a doubt a solid and very highly regarded reputation in the field of forensic pathology. This is a well-deserved reputation, and consequently it can be expected that much weight will be given to his report.'

Underneath, one of the executives had written: 'Anticipate that an appeal will be lodged to overturn the conviction.'

On 10 July, Ms Foster-Curry wrote an email to Isabel Brouwer, Statewide Clinical Director of Forensic Medicine, telling her that Professor Cordner's report had been 'quite scathing of Allan'. If action was to be taken, why not now?

Instead, one month later, a further brief to the Minister's office noted that 'It would be possible for the Department of Forensic Medicine to conduct an internal review of the children's deaths should this be requested or directed by the judicial system. However, the Department advises such an investigation would be highly complex and resource intensive.'

Dr Orde had undertaken most of his training in the UK but had also worked in Sydney for nine years, and so he was familiar with Australia's forensic landscape. He had started working at Vancouver General Hospital five years before we met.

His favourite saying was one of Voltaire's: 'To the living we owe respect; to the dead we owe only the truth.'

In my opinion, when so much doubt attached to Kathy's convictions, she was owed far more respect than she had received so far from the courts and the judiciary, and her children, although long gone, were still owed, above all else, the truth. That was why I wanted to tell her story.

When I met Dr Orde, he told me, off camera, that broadly speaking he agreed with Professor Cordner's report and with his conclusions, but it was also very clear that he took the task we had set him very seriously. A pathologist's reputation can hang on one wrong diagnosis and, in a case like this, where all four children's deaths had been considered together at Kathy's trial, the postmortem evidence wasn't just incidental — it was central to a judgment of Kathy's guilt or innocence.

When it came to filming the interview with Dr Orde, he suggested we do so in the hospital's basement, on the floor housing the morgue, and at one point, he opened the door to the morgue itself, and I peered inside with some trepidation, taking a short, squeamish look at the hundreds of body bags stacked inside. If ever a lay person needed a reminder of how strong a stomach a forensic pathologist needs to do their job, here it was: visible evidence of death, piled row on row from floor to ceiling in the cavernous, refrigerated storeroom.

Outside, in an area populated not, thank God, by corpses, but by slabs and sinks and metal instruments, we set up the lights and cameras and started filming. The room had a dark, blueish, slightly ghoulish look, but Dr Orde himself was anything but ghoulish. He was calm and open and frank, but also, appropriately enough, forensic in his commentary about the evidence.

Dr Orde declared that fundamentally he was in agreement with Professor Cordner, 'in that all four of these child deaths could be explained by natural causes'.

I asked him about the fact that none of the medical experts at Kathy's trial said that they had ever come across a case where three or more infants in the same family had died from natural causes.

He replied that, in 'the olden days, the odds were given as a very low probability, that these deaths could be explained by natural causes. Whereas now, I think, there is more of an understanding that, in fact, multiple child deaths in the same family, may well be explained by natural causes.'

The understanding at the time was that these deaths could be considered independently, and that sudden infant deaths in the same family bore no relationship to one another.

Nowadays, he told me: 'That doesn't necessarily hold true. And the reason for that is that multiple deaths in the same family would be subject to the same genetic underpinnings and the same environmental influences. So, in fact, where there's been one cot death, maybe in fact, the second, and perhaps third, cot deaths are more likely.'

This argument mirrored the observation made by Professor Ray Hill, that if a family suffers the tragedy of an infant dying from SIDS, the chances of a second death from SIDS are increased. It ran against the grain of the evidence given by the medical experts at Kathy's trial but was much more in line with the evidence uncovered by the Care of Next Infants (CONI) studies in the UK.

'There was a paper in 2005, looking at exactly that,' Dr Orde told me, referencing this, 'looking at multiple recurrence of infant fatalities in the same family. And their conclusion, after looking at a huge deal of data, was that multiple infant deaths in the same family, would be most likely explained by natural causes rather than foul play.'

In Laura's case, Dr Orde noted that she suffered from a cold-like illness during the week prior to her death. 'And I think that may be of relevance to this investigation. Because she ultimately was found to have myocarditis at autopsy and that's typically caused by a viral infection and that same viral infection may have been the cause of her respiratory symptoms prior to death.'

Dr Orde's view was very clear: 'Upon examination of the sections of Laura's heart and in the absence of any other identifiable potential competing cause of death, I think it's entirely reasonable and proper to conclude that her death would have been due to myocarditis. We know that myocarditis is a potentially lethal condition. In the sections of heart that I have examined, the disease was present in each and every one. And the degree of severity was such that I think it would have posed a real risk of sudden death at any time.'

So, was Dr Cala justified in giving the opinion he had?

'I think Dr Cala's position is justifiable,' he conceded, 'and I think the reason for this, is that the judgment as to the cause of death is an opinion, it's a very subjective experience rather than a scientific black or white.

'At autopsy, he would agree that Laura had myocarditis, but the question really is how bad was that myocarditis and could that have been the cause of death? Dr Cala, I think, felt the severity was not to such a degree as to have posed a cause of death. I would disagree with that, I think the myocarditis would have been so severe, as to have posed a real risk of sudden death.'

On Good Friday, four days after I had arrived in Vancouver, Dr Orde and Emma Cunliffe viewed the images of Laura's heart muscle at Vancouver General Hospital. We filmed as Dr Cunliffe listened intently to Dr Orde explaining what he had found.

As they peered into the microscopes, he told her: 'We have here the sections of Laura's heart. This is a times 200 magnification image, and this is the inflammation of the heart muscle that makes this disease myocarditis. And if you look now at the lower part, you can see that this disease is actually present quite extensively across this heart muscle. It's not the most florid example I've ever seen, but it's certainly, most definitely there, and as I say, it's present on each and every section I've looked at.'

Emma Cunliffe asked him: 'What's the significance of seeing inflammation on every slide?'

'Well, I think it comes down to judgment,' Dr Orde replied, 'as to whether or not this disease could be ascribed as the cause of death. And I think the more extensive the disease is, the more likely it is that this will explain death ... I think this is an eminently fatal case of myocarditis. Of course, we can't say for sure that this would have been the cause of death in Laura's case. All I can say is I think this provides a very good explanation for her untimely death.'

Even so, Dr Orde was cautious. 'I think we have to concede it's a possibility that these children were smothered, that their deaths were unnatural,' he told Dr Cunliffe. 'But there's no positive evidence to indicate that would have been the case. If one were to attempt to smother a healthy, robust, normal eighteen-month-old child, you would expect I think, reasonably, that this infant would put up a struggle. This struggling would be expected to give rise to some injuries; in Laura's case, there weren't any such signs whatsoever.'

Describing the disease he had found as an 'eminently fatal case of myocarditis' sealed the deal as far as I was concerned – at least in terms of establishing reasonable doubt.

It confirmed what Professor Cordner and the ten other forensic pathologists consulted had found: Laura, most probably, had died, suddenly and tragically, from a lethal case of myocarditis.

I wanted to ask the former Director of Public Prosecutions, Nicholas Cowdery, about this. After some persuasion, he had agreed to be interviewed on *Australian Story*.

To my surprise, when I did this, he put a very different slant on the evidence in Laura's case.

Referring to Dr Cala's evidence at trial, he said: 'One child had evidence of mild myocarditis, inflammation of the heart muscle. But again, the evidence was that that would not have caused death. There was some evidence that it was possible that it could, but then that conclusion has to be put against all of the circumstantial evidence, surrounding the death of the child.'

I pressed him on this, asking him what might happen if the petition in Kathy's case resulted in an inquiry where it was accepted that Laura died from myocarditis, or alternatively, if her case was referred to the Court of Criminal Appeal, and the judges there accepted that this was so.

He told me: 'If in the review process, the judicial officer or the Court of Criminal Appeal took the view that Laura's death was in fact caused by myocarditis, it leaves open the question of whether or not, a degree of smothering might have been involved as well. And I don't want to speculate about that. It may, if smothering is not involved, take Laura's death out of the sequence of deaths, but the other three deaths could still be examined with the coincidence evidence as well.

'So, it wouldn't necessarily mean that all of the convictions should be set aside. It may mean that the conviction in relation to Laura should be set aside. But it doesn't necessarily follow that the other three should be.'

I was frankly, staggered by this assertion; there was no physical evidence whatsoever that 'a degree of smothering' had taken place before Laura died, and to me, Mr Cowdery's argument reeked of a desperation to salvage the jury verdict in the face of very clear evidence to the contrary. I asked Dr Cavanagh for his reaction.

His response was typically forthright: 'You can't just simply say, well, we got one wrong, but the others can still stand. It doesn't work that way.'

24

'THAT'S, AS MOTHERS, WHAT YOU DO'

In 2018, it was still frowned on to be offering airtime to 'Australia's worst female serial killer'. Almost no one was paying any attention to her story, and most people who had heard of her wanted her to die in prison.

Nevertheless, we decided to do what no one else in the media had done – to invite Kathy to have her voice heard on *Australian Story*.

It meant that – for the first time – the Australian public would hear her speak openly and freely about her former life, her former husband Craig, her children, her trial, her diaries, and her hopes for the future. I had met her several times in prison, but those were private meetings. This was Kathy speaking publicly, from the heart, for the first time.

The conversations came about after my Executive Producer at *Australian Story*, Caitlin Shea, told me that she felt as if the story I was producing lacked its most important element: Kathy's voice.

She was right, but up until then I had been reluctant to ask Kathy – via her best friend Tracy Chapman – to be included in our program, because there could be repercussions for her if she agreed to talk on the phone, knowing that the conversations would be recorded.

But courageously, considering the punishment she might suffer inside the prison, and the level of hatred for her in the wider community, she agreed. Phone calls from prison are monitored and cut off after just six minutes, and so our task entailed recording multiple phone calls over two days which – with Kathy's and Tracy's permission – we did.

In July 2018, we filmed Tracy receiving the calls in a small apartment we had rented for her in George Street, Sydney. Tracy had arranged for Kathy to call her soon after 9.30 am on day one, and to continue on through day two for as long as it took, or until we all ran out of energy.

Kathy showed remarkable initiative and stamina. Somehow, she managed to arrange to hog the prison phone, and over the course of the two days, we recorded fifteen six-minute calls – a total of ninety minutes. Many of the questions were arranged beforehand, and the conversations covered some of the most controversial areas of evidence that had led to her being convicted.

When the first phone call came through, a robotic voice at the other end intoned the words: 'You are about to receive a phone call from an inmate at Cessnock Correctional Centre. Your conversation will be recorded and may be monitored. If you do not wish to receive this call, please hang up now.'

'Good morning bub, how are you?' Tracy asked.

'Good, how are you?' Kathy replied.

'I'm good. What have you been up to?'

'Not too much. Just did my cleaning and all the laundry and all the stuff you do when you're in here,' Kathy told her. 'Bit same-o, same-o.'

Over the next few hours, and again the next day, with numerous pauses between phone calls, Kathy told us about her life in prison, about her police interview, about the trial and the crushing experience of hearing the verdicts, and about the most contentious diary entries, how they had been interpreted, and what they actually meant. 'My life just seems like it's been never-ending battles and things that I've been having to get over and conquer,' she told Tracy.

It was revealing to hear her be so open, and it allowed viewers, when they watched and listened to our report, to appreciate her as the warm, witty, strong and stoical person I had met, rather than as the monster she was portrayed as by the media, following her convictions.

Tracy asked Kathy about her children, and how she remembered them. 'What's the best memory you have? Do you have any particular ones?' she asked.

In reply, Kathy told Tracy she remembered Caleb as being dark-haired, and dark-skinned. She was proud of the fact that he looked like her, and thought he was going to be 'a little me'.

Patrick, she told Tracy, was stubborn, and 'Sarah was the cheekiest one ever. Run around sticking her tongue out at you if she just thought that was going to get a laugh.'

With Laura, there was much to remember. 'She was around the longest and when she got to 12 months we actually thought we were home and hosed.'

Kathy told Tracy that when the accusations started flying, she had put walls up, and, that if she had chosen to give evidence at her trial, it would have resulted in a 'full-on attack' from Mr Tedeschi, 'and why would anybody want to put themselves through that?'

Tracy, at my request, asked Kathy about some of the most contentious entries she had written in her journals, including the entry where she wrote:

> I feel like the worst mother on this earth. Scared that she'll leave me now. Like Sarah did. I knew I was short tempered & cruel sometimes to her & she left with a bit of help.

When Tracy asked her about this, Kathy's frustration broke through. It meant the same as it had fifteen 'fricking' years before.

'That quote, that was a reference to God or to some higher being or a higher power or a something, going on,' she told Tracy. 'I was thinking about, why was I not allowed to have the other three, but now I've fallen pregnant again, am I going to be allowed to keep this one?'

Kathy described it as 'a very dark time back then', which was why she had started writing in her journals. It was where she dumped anything negative, and everything that was troubling her.

She told Tracy she had to understand that 'those diaries are written from of a point of me always blaming myself. I blame myself for everything.' She would blame herself if it was raining. 'I took so much of the responsibility, because that's, as mothers, what you do.'

Tracy shared with me a letter that Kathy had written to her from jail, in which she gave written explanations for some of the diary entries which had been interpreted at her trial as virtual admissions of guilt. 'I know my diaries hung me,' she wrote.

As she had in the conversation with Tracy that we recorded, Kathy told Tracy in her letter that the phrase: 'She left with a bit of help' was a reference to God, who had already taken Caleb and Patrick from her. It definitely didn't mean that she was 'the help'.

Kathy spilled out the emotions she had felt when pregnant with Laura. Night and day, she felt tortured – fear ruled. All of this she dumped in her diaries. But what she didn't often write about in her journals was all her 'wonderful times of absolute joy', when she felt that everything would be fine, and her need for a family would finally be fulfilled.

Perhaps most tellingly of all, she told Tracy in the letter that, given her constant propensity for self-blame, if indeed she had killed her children, she wouldn't have been able to stop herself admitting she had done so, and she would have used the journals to try to figure out why she had committed such terrible deeds. She told Tracy she would have killed herself or confessed to her, and turned herself in.

Not only that, but there was also a logical fallacy in the accusation that she had killed her children, because, as she described it to Tracy, she had a 'total obsession' with having children. It didn't make sense for her to deny herself the one thing above all others that she desired: a family.

We heard, in one of the recorded conversations, that Kathy kept photos of her children, and said good morning and goodnight to them every day. She would cry her eyes out looking at them whenever she felt unsettled, and it would calm her down.

She now realised, she told Tracy, that she had been grief-stricken from 1989 onwards – the year that Caleb died.

At one point, referring to the petition lodged in 2015, she admitted: 'I do feel incredibly frustrated. And I think it's because we're just simply waiting for a decision. For three years now, we've been clinging to that little bit of hope. If I can get myself heard in any way, then I guess my last fifteen years in prison will have been worth it.'

25

EUREKA!

On Monday, 13 August 2018, viewers were able to sit down to watch Kathy speak publicly for the first time, on *Australian Story*. The episode was entitled: 'From Behind Bars'. As described above, one of the people I had interviewed for the program was Nicholas Cowdery, who in 2003 was the New South Wales Director of Public Prosecutions when Kathy went to jail.

On *Australian Story* he defended the jury's decision but said that the three years that had elapsed since Kathy's petition was lodged in 2015 amounted to an 'inordinate' delay.

It was a stinging rebuke, and nine days later the New South Wales Attorney General Mark Speakman called a press conference to announce, finally, that an inquiry would be held into Kathy's convictions, to be headed by a former Chief Judge of the New South Wales District Court, Reginald Blanch. It was big news, announced in a newsflash on the ABC. It was also a cause for major celebrations among Kathy's friends and supporters, and her new legal team were, coincidentally, talking to Kathy on the phone for the very first time when the announcement was made.

Helen Cummings, who had been pleading with Mr Speakman to announce a review, said she was 'speechless, I'm just so happy. It's been a long, hard road.'

Mr Speakman, in his remarks to the media, announced that after carefully considering the petition, and taking extensive advice, 'I have formed the view that an inquiry into Ms Folbigg's convictions is necessary to ensure public confidence in the administration of justice.'

He stressed, however, that 'Today's decision is not based on any assessment of Ms Folbigg's guilt.'

He explained that the petition 'appears to raise a doubt or question concerning evidence as to the incidence of reported deaths of three or more infants in the same family attributed to unidentified natural causes in the proceedings leading to Ms Folbigg's convictions'.

This sounded like a roundabout way of conceding that the jury at Kathy's trial had been misled by the medical experts about the incidence of multiple infant deaths in a single family from natural causes – and that the prosecution got it wrong. It wasn't, as Mr Tedeschi had alleged, a fantasy to imagine a family like Kathy's where three or more children had died from natural causes – other cases had already been recorded.

At the press conference, I asked Mr Speakman whether in addition to this, the forensic evidence would be a focus of the inquiry, and he wouldn't confirm this. That to me was disconcerting, when Professor Cordner had produced such an extensive, detailed report, pointing out that no forensic evidence existed to support the allegation that Kathy had smothered her children.

His report had been a cornerstone of the petition.

It seemed clear to me where Mr Speakman's personal sympathies lay. 'I have spoken with Mr Craig Folbigg to explain this immensely difficult decision,' he announced. 'I am sorry for the renewed distress and pain he and his family will endure because of the inquiry.' Mr Speakman said he had asked the Commissioner of Victims' Rights to offer support to Craig and other family members throughout the forthcoming inquiry.

No words of sympathy or support were offered to Kathy. But at least an inquiry would now take place.

When *Australian Story* interviewed Mr Speakman many years later, he explained: 'I was particularly interested in distilling what was new or what hadn't been dealt with before. And the doubt or question that was raised in my mind was the fact that it had been put to the jury that, to paraphrase it, lightning doesn't strike three times.

'There was something called Meadow's Law that if one death was tragic, two deaths were suspicious, three deaths, there's a presumption of guilt. And I think the jury had been told that there hadn't been a case anywhere in the world where through natural causes, three or more children in one family had died after the guilty verdicts.

'It came to light that that was wrong. It was difficult to deconstruct the extent to which the jury had relied on that and may have relied on other matters. I thought there was a doubt or question that warranted an inquiry. So, after getting a lot of legal advice, I then asked the Governor in 2018 to direct an Inquiry.'

In the course of writing this book, I asked Mr Speakman to explain why it had taken him so long to do this.

He replied that there was a 'huge volume' of material to consider, and that 'extensive and very detailed' legal advice, and then supplementary legal advice, had been obtained from the Crown Solicitor's office and from external senior and junior counsel. This advice was discussed 'over a lengthy period' before the *Australian Story* episode went to air.

Behind the scenes, and away from the powers-that-be in government, something truly remarkable happened. The day after *Australian Story* went to air, Dave Wallace, a young lawyer with a science honours degree in immunogenomics, wrote an email to Isabel Reed and Dr Cavanagh, the two barristers who headed up Kathy's legal team and whom I had interviewed for *Australian Story*.

He told them that he had been interested in Kathy's case since law school and had always had issues with the prosecution's case and its presentation of probability, 'so I greatly admire your commitment to having the case re-examined'.

He suggested that genetic sequencing of Kathy, Craig and their children could yield evidence of a genetic cause for the children's deaths.

It's no exaggeration to say that this one email altered the course of Kathy's life.

In 2013, just two years after Emma Cunliffe's book was published, and two years before the petition was lodged on Kathy's behalf, Dave Wallace was completing a science honours degree in genetics. Quite independently, he started to wonder whether whole genome sequencing of the Folbigg family would yield evidence suggesting a genetic cause for the children's deaths. His idea was that a genetic variant – or mutation – might have triggered the deaths of one or more of the children.

A paper published in 2018 dealing with cases of sudden unexplained death (SUD) had examined thirty-four unexplained deaths and found links to genes associated with cardiac channelopathies – defects in the microscopic channels that carry calcium, potassium and sodium in and out of the cells of the heart, and which disrupt the heart's electrical activity and cause fatal arrhythmias. Here was clear, recent evidence that genetic variants could cause cardiac disease and lethal arrhythmias, leading to sudden, unexpected deaths. Was this the case for any of Kathy's children, Dave Wallace wondered.

'I'm sure you have both looked into genetic explanations for the children's deaths, and I note that genetic causes were discussed by the experts at trial,' he told the two lawyers, 'but the rapid advances in genetics that have come with the plummeting costs of whole genome and whole exome sequencing over the last few years means that any genetic tests conducted even just five years ago would have discovered only a small fraction of what they are capable of discovering now.'

The cost of doing the tests provided an extra incentive. In the past, the cost of whole genome sequencing had been prohibitive. Now, a whole genome sequence could be performed for under $2000.

'Whole genome sequencing would be your best bet and most comprehensive,' Mr Wallace told Isabel Reed. 'Whole exome sequencing only looks at the coding regions of DNA which may not reveal the potential genetic mutations that could have caused or increased the likelihood of the children's deaths.'

Mr Wallace explained that, ideally, Craig's DNA would need to be collected, in addition to Kathy's, because 'if there is a hereditary genetic cause for the children's deaths, then finding it via whole genome sequencing becomes a lot easier if you have both of the parents' DNA'.

Dave Wallace's view was that genomic investigations are especially useful for trying to find the cause of a sudden death where no cause of death was found after a complete autopsy. 'In a criminal context, genomic investigations can result in the exoneration of people who may have been wrongfully convicted of having killed someone who actually died of natural causes, especially in the context of SIDS cases.'

When Isabel Reed read Dave Wallace's next remark, she could hardly contain herself: 'Given the nature of familial genetic conditions, there is a real chance that whole genome sequencing the Folbigg family could result in evidence capable of exonerating Kathleen,' he wrote.

Thirty minutes later, Isabel Reed replied: 'This is very exciting … I'm just wondering what sort of genetic sample would be required?'

Ms Reed's efforts to interest the rest of Kathy's legal team in a genetic investigation met with strong and surprising resistance. They were sticking with the old lawyer's adage that you don't ask a question you don't know the answer to, and were focused on other things. But to her credit, and despite the resistance from within her own team, she persisted.

Dave Wallace told Isabel Reed: 'I'm very passionate about the intersection of the law and genetics, so if there's any way I can help I'm happy to do what I can in my spare time.'

Shortly afterwards, he got in touch with a genetic immunologist who would help change the entire course of the Folbigg case – Professor Carola Garcia de Vinuesa. He had studied in the same lab department where Professor Vinuesa was a group leader and held her in high esteem.

Isabel Reed recalls, 'Carola was instantly interested in assisting in any way she could – I think spurred on by David's tireless enthusiasm.'

Dave Wallace suggested to Professor Vinuesa that she watch our *Australian Story* episode. When she did so, the professor told me later: 'I saw firsthand some of those images of the pathology of Laura's myocarditis. I was intrigued. I thought there could be a genetic basis for that disease. The coincidence was that just a few weeks before I had been referred a family in which there had been four neonatal deaths in children aged from twenty days to four months, and we had found a genetic cause for their deaths.'

In an extraordinary twist of fate, and in the most unlikely of circumstances, Professor Vinuesa emerged out of nowhere to spearhead a new scientific endeavour on Kathy's behalf.

Carola Vinuesa was born in the Spanish city of Cádiz and raised in Madrid, the daughter of a lawyer who held the government post of Financial Secretary to the Treasury after the country's transition to democracy, following the death of General Franco. Her father helped steer her on a path to a life of service in the world of science and medicine.

Fiercely intelligent, highly qualified, charismatic and extraordinarily hard-working, she branched out from her medical studies in Madrid to work in a leprosy clinic in Calcutta, and later, took on the task of training health workers in Ghana.

After obtaining her medical degree, she undertook specialist clinical training and PhD studies in the UK, and in 2001 she moved to Australia, after receiving a Wellcome Trust Fellowship to do postdoctoral work at the John Curtin School for Medical Research at the Australian National University.

Significant awards followed, including, in 2008, the Science Minister's Prize for Life Scientist of the Year. In 2015, she was elected a Fellow of the Australian Academy of Science.

When Dave Wallace contacted her, she was Professor of Immunology at the Australian National University and co-director of the Centre for Personalised Immunology, specialising in undertaking genomic investigations of people with immune disorders, and perfectly placed to carry out the genetic research which both she and Dave Wallace believed might yield results.

An exciting new avenue had opened up for further investigation, and Isabel Reed's priority now, at Dave Wallace's urging, was to obtain a medical history and samples of DNA directly from Kathy in prison.

'Because Carola was based in Canberra at the time, it was going to be difficult for her to come to visit Kathleen herself,' Ms Reed told me, 'so she asked for the assistance of Dr Todor Arsov, initially just to do genetic counselling with Kathleen. I went with Todor to visit Kathleen on 8 October 2018 and he did an extensive family history interview with her.'

Dr Arsov was a Senior Research Fellow at the John Curtin School of Medical Research and the Centre for Personalised Immunology. It was he who had alerted Professor Vinuesa to a family from Macedonia in which, tragically, there had been four neonatal deaths in children aged from twenty days to four months.

When he visited Kathy in prison, Dr Arsov now admits, he did so with mixed feelings, wondering on the one hand if he was about to meet 'the worst psychopath on the planet', and on the other hand, 'am I going to meet someone who's been facing this injustice for the last twenty years or so?'

When he took down her personal history, she told him that she had experienced several fainting fits – or syncopes – during her life, including one event where she had lost consciousness at the end of a swimming race. He took a buccal swab from Kathy, from inside her cheek, and a saliva sample. At that stage, no blood sample could be collected, as a formal procedure had to be gone through in order to do so.

But even so, Professor Vinuesa was excited at the prospect of what they might find. She told Isabel Reed there was 'a real possibility that those children all died from some kind of genetic anomaly.' The buccal swab was couriered to the professor on Monday, 15 October.

Whole exome sequencing was carried out on the samples, and, with a ream of sequencing data to interpret, Professor Vinuesa sat down with Dr Arsov in her kitchen one Sunday afternoon in early December to try to work out what, if anything, Kathy's DNA file revealed that might be significant.

To the scientists' astonishment, as they pored over the lines and lines of data on their computer screens, they came to a sudden, simultaneous realisation of what the data showed: Kathy carried a unique and potentially deadly mutation in a gene known as Calmodulin 2 – or *CALM2* – a protein which is vital in regulating heart function. Calmodulin mutations can cause sudden cardiac death.

Dr Arsov recalls it as being a genuine 'Eureka' moment, as they both simultaneously looked at each other and exclaimed: '*CALM2!*' For Professor Vinuesa, it felt like a highly significant breakthrough. 'I was quite excited,' she told me later. 'It had never been identified in any other individual in the world.'

That same day, the professor sat down and summarised the findings and their analysis of the data for Kathy's lawyers. Her report was short, but dramatic.

'We have performed whole exome sequencing on Kathleen Folbigg's genomic DNA extracted from both buccal swab and saliva,' she wrote. 'Excellent coverage was obtained from both samples ... Analysis of the exome for variants in genes previously shown to cause sudden unexpected death has identified two candidates.' The two mutations were known as *CALM2* G114R, and a second mutation in a gene known as *MYH6*.

'The variant in *CALM2* is novel,' Professor Vinuesa wrote, 'and has not been reported to date (either in healthy populations or in patients with Long QT syndrome). In silico analysis predicts that the amino acid substitution is damaging. Other heterozygous mutations in *CALM2* have been associated [with] LQTS and sudden death in infancy and childhood.'

Long QT syndrome, or LQTS, is a heart rhythm disorder that generates fast, irregular heartbeats. It can cause fainting and particularly in the very young, can be fatal.

But that was only the first step. The next step was to find out if any of Kathy's children carried the same mutation, and it wasn't until the inquiry process got underway that Professor Vinuesa was able to gain access to DNA from each of the children. 'We managed to get DNA from some preserved tissue samples that were taken from two of the children on autopsy,' Dave Wallace told me. 'For the other two children we were able to get DNA samples from their neonatal heel-prick cards, the blood spots on cardboard stored in a hospital.'

It was an epic scientific effort, as Professor Vinuesa later explained: 'From a technical perspective it was an incredible achievement. The Victorian Clinical Genomics Service sequenced entire genomes from neonatal heel-prick blood cards that were over twenty years old.

'We performed bioinformatic analysis of the approximately three billion base pairs of DNA for each subject,' Professor Vinuesa reported. But their analysis was hindered by Craig's refusal to provide his DNA for analysis. The scientists had assumed that the inquiry would compel him to provide a saliva sample, but it declined to make such an order.'

Despite this major hurdle, Professor Vinuesa's team found the exact same calmodulin mutation that they had found in Kathy, in her daughters Sarah and Laura – proof that she had passed it on to them.

The genetic mutation present in Kathy and her two girls was 'novel', meaning that it had never before been reported in any scientific literature anywhere in the world.

An extraordinary genetic journey had begun.

PART 3

26

AN INQUIRY AT LAST

Inside the expansive surroundings of Lidcombe Coroner's Court, in western Sydney, seven months after our *Australian Story* episode went to air, a large complex opened up for the first full day of the inquiry's hearings into Kathy's convictions. It included the court where the hearing itself would take place, and a separate media room for the bevy of reporters who attended every day. Press officers were present to offer guidance and hand out official documents.

It felt like a defining moment for Kathy and her supporters. Kathy had been in prison for nearly sixteen years, and it was nearly four years since the petition calling for a review of her convictions had been lodged with the Governor of New South Wales, General David Hurley, on her behalf. Now at last, following what felt like an interminable delay, an inquiry was about to take place.

Importantly, this wasn't an appeal or a retrial; it was, in theory at least, an objective, unbiased inquiry into her convictions, prompted by the revelation that the jury at her trial had been misled, and Kathy's supporters were hoping, optimistically, for an open, impartial and transparent process that would result in her exoneration.

Among the questions I asked myself were: Would the inquiry endorse *Australian Story*'s conclusion that Laura had died from myocarditis? Would it acknowledge that the jury at Kathy's trial had been misled about the number of families in which three or four children had died, suddenly and unexpectedly, from natural causes, as Emma Cunliffe had pointed out?

Would that lead the inquiry to recognise that there was reasonable doubt surrounding her convictions, and would Kathy's case be referred to the Court of Criminal Appeal, where her convictions could be overturned?

The atmosphere in court was solemn. The inquiry's commissioner, Reginald Blanch, was a former chief judge of the New South Wales District Court. Seventy-six years old, he was undeniably old-school, and disappointingly, lacked the gift of leavening the often dense and detailed evidence with the slightest touch of humour. He was also – more importantly – a judge with a long prosecutorial history, having been appointed the state's first Director of Public Prosecutions in 1987.

Mark Tedeschi, who led the prosecution at Kathy's trial, was appointed Deputy Senior Crown Prosecutor by Reginald Blanch in 1990, and when Mr Blanch ended his term as the state's DPP in 1994, he was succeeded by Nicholas Cowdery – the DPP who oversaw Kathy's prosecution, and who I had interviewed for *Australian Story*. Mr Cowdery still believed that Kathy was guilty beyond reasonable doubt.

It was a small world inside the New South Wales judicial fraternity and, following several frosty exchanges I witnessed during the inquiry's earlier directions hearings, it certainly seemed to me (and many others) that the judicial establishment was unsympathetic to Kathy.

Counsel Assisting Mr Blanch was Gail Furness SC, an imposing figure who had been, on occasion, a brutal inquisitor. Tall, serious and severe in her manner, she had attracted national coverage not long before as Senior Counsel Assisting the Royal Commission into Institutional Responses to Child Sexual Abuse. There, against a backdrop of multiple scandals in churches and other institutions, she interrogated the abusers and those who had failed to rein them in – including most notably, the late Roman Catholic Cardinal George Pell who, in *The*

Guardian's words following his death in 2023, 'chose career over the safety of children'.

Now, here she was again, standing as chief interrogator of those who, with the backing of substantial fresh evidence, believed that a real injustice had been done to Kathy – herself a probable victim of child sexual abuse.

In her opening remarks at the inquiry's first directions hearing, six months before, Ms Furness had acknowledged that the Crown's case against Kathy at her trial in 2003 was circumstantial, listing four areas of evidence put forward by Mark Tedeschi: 'Firstly, the circumstances of each child's death. Secondly, coincidence evidence. Thirdly, medical evidence, and finally the diaries. The Crown case was that the totality of the evidence pointed to the applicant's involvement in all five events.'

The diaries of course, were central to the prosecution's case, and one of the planks on which Kathy's petition was built was the opinion of the clinical psychologist, Dr Sharmila Betts, that – contrary to Mr Tedeschi's assertions at her trial – her diaries contained no admissions to having harmed or killed any of her children. It was a fundamental matter of interpretation that went right to the heart of Kathy's guilt or innocence.

But Ms Furness argued that while 'opinions may well differ as to the meaning of the diaries ... the inferences to be drawn from them when considered with other evidence in the trial were necessarily a matter for the jury.' Dr Betts would not be called as an expert witness to give evidence.

From the announcement of the inquiry, Kathy's legal team had been steered by an instructing solicitor from Newcastle called Stuart Gray, who had been recruited by Isabel Reed, one of the petition's original signatories. Mr Gray had put together a team that included Ms Reed herself, Dr Cavanagh, and the tireless Rhanee Rego.

Over the course of the inquiry, Mr Gray struck me as the legal equivalent of an ankle-biting terrier, a whip-smart solicitor who hated losing and who certainly wasn't intimidated by the considerable presence of Gail Furness and her team.

The senior counsel appearing for Kathy was Jeremy Morris SC, assisted by Dr Cavanagh and Ms Reed. I was invited to meet Mr Morris at his chambers, with Dr Cavanagh, and over the course of the inquiry he came across as innately kind, humorous, and benevolent, with a distinct twinkle in his eye when circumstances permitted, but also, as someone who at times felt burdened by the weight of an enormous challenge, made worse by the fact that he and his team had far fewer resources at their disposal than the State's team headed by Gail Furness.

When I arrived at his chambers to meet him, Mr Morris was deep in conversation with one of the medical experts who would later appear before the inquiry. Even for a counsel with extensive experience in medical negligence claims and appeals, his focus and forensic attention to detail was impressive.

But from the start, Kathy's legal team were met with significant challenges.

In early December 2018, after receiving Professor Vinuesa's report of the results of Kathy's DNA test, Mr Gray rang Craig Folbigg while driving from Newcastle to Sydney and finally got through to him. He pulled into the car park of a 7-Eleven at the top of the expressway and the two men had an hour-long conversation, during which Mr Gray invited Craig to provide a DNA sample, to help the scientists map out the family's genetic history.

'I told him about the Vinuesa report, and I asked him whether anyone from the inquiry had spoken to him,' Mr Gray told me later. 'He said no.

'During the conversation Craig seemed open to the idea of giving a sample and I pitched it to him in terms of the children he had with his new wife and that he would be given all the results from a top-class facility for nothing. He said he'd think about it. We spoke about who I acted for and the testing that we'd recently got that had just been received from Kath.'

Imagine Mr Gray's surprise when one week later, at an early directions hearing for the inquiry, Mr Blanch announced that

'So far as Craig Folbigg is concerned, we've received a complaint from the Commissioner for Victims Services that the solicitor … who's appearing for Mrs Folbigg had approached him and he took an extreme exception to the way that was done.'

Mr Blanch told the court, in front of the media who reported it, that Craig had lodged a complaint with the Legal Services Commissioner about Stuart Gray's approach, and that as a result he was 'absolutely refusing to provide a DNA sample.'

As it turned out, no complaint had been lodged with the Legal Services Commissioner about Stuart Gray's conversation with Craig. What it did reveal, however, was Craig's abiding animosity for his former wife, and his refusal to countenance helping her, or the scientists, in any way.

At the same directions hearing, Mr Morris argued that it would be wrong for the inquiry to focus solely on the medical evidence, and to exclude the diaries from the scope of the inquiry, pointing to the fact that at Kathy's trial and appeals, the courts had ruled that 'the combination of the scientific material and the diaries gave rise to a damning inference against my client. In other words, they were not matters which were to be considered in isolation.'

Mr Blanch, in response, announced that if Kathy wanted to come to the inquiry to discuss the diaries, he would be happy to call her, 'but it is a matter entirely for her'. It seemed at the time to be a helpful invitation. Mr Blanch assured her legal counsel repeatedly that the inquiry would be 'non-adversarial', and as a consequence Kathy may have assumed that if she were to appear to give evidence about the diaries, she would be treated with courtesy and respect.

The road to this point, for Kathy's friends and supporters, had already been long and hard, and despite the fact that Mr Blanch was overseeing the inquiry, hopes were high that at last, justice would be served, and her wrongful convictions would be swiftly overturned.

On the first full day of hearings, Gail Furness acknowledged that before 2003 there had indeed been reported cases involving the deaths of three or more infants in the same family attributed to unidentified natural causes, 'or at least not established as attributable to unnatural causes'.

In other circumstances and other courtrooms, that might have signalled the end of the inquiry, there and then. Here was clear confirmation that the jury at Kathy's trial was misled by the expert evidence, and not in an insignificant way. It was simply wrong, as was Mr Tedeschi's assertion that the idea of Kathy's four children dying from natural causes was 'preposterous' and 'fanciful'.

But this weighty concession by Gail Furness didn't mean that she and Mr Blanch were recognising that there was room for doubt surrounding Kathy's convictions – far from it.

Later that morning, just before 11 am, an article I had written for the ABC was published online. It contained a summary of startling fresh evidence contained in expert reports which I had obtained, exclusively, and the announcement that Kathy had accepted Mr Blanch's invitation to appear at the inquiry in person to give evidence about the entries in her diaries.

This new evidence, sensationally, provided strong support for the argument that Kathy had suffered a terrible miscarriage of justice.

27

'IT IS AN APPALLING SITUATION'

In the article I wrote for the ABC, I reported that:

- Three senior forensic pathologists who were to give evidence that week were expected to agree that the most likely cause of death for Kathy's fourth child, Laura, was myocarditis.
- A new expert witness, Professor Caroline Blackwell, had submitted a statement revealing that Detective Inspector Bernie Ryan had turned down the opportunity for tests to be carried out to establish whether infections had played a part in the children's deaths, because, he said, it was 'too expensive'.
- Another neurological expert's opinion cast doubt on the allegation that Kathy tried to smother her second child, Patrick, when he was four months old.

In the case of Patrick, a report had been written by an acknowledged neurological expert, challenging the prosecution's view that Kathy had attempted to smother him when he was four months old. Kathy said she had found him gasping, blue around the lips, lifeless and floppy.

He was revived and lived for a further four months.

Professor Monique Ryan, director of the Neurology Department at the Royal Children's Hospital, in Melbourne, reviewed Patrick's medical records, reporting that: 'Patrick was admitted to hospital on multiple occasions. On no occasion was he reported to have shown any obvious evidence of inflicted injury. His CT scans and ophthalmological examination did not show the changes often seen in children subjected to non-accidental injuries.'

This was a clear challenge to the Crown's case at Kathy's trial, namely, that she had tried to smother Patrick, depriving him of oxygen to the brain.

Specifically in relation to the acute life-threatening event when Kathy found him apparently lifeless, Professor Ryan said: 'I am not convinced that Patrick's clinical history is consistent with him having neurologic deficits resulting from a single hypoxic-ischaemic episode occurring on October 18, 1990.

'He was ... very unwell at the time of presentation. On the same day, however, a head ultrasound and EEG were normal, and within a few hours of admission he was described in the nursing notes as feeding well.

'Had Patrick sustained a severe hypoxic-ischaemic insult on the morning of October 18, 1990 — one sufficiently severe to cause the changes seen on his subsequent imaging and his post-mortem examination — it is difficult to imagine that he would have been able to feed well that day, and that his EEG could have been entirely normal.'

That wasn't the only challenge to the Crown's case contained in the new experts' reports.

Professor Caroline Blackwell is an infectious diseases specialist, who had been a key witness at Sally Clark's successful appeal in the UK, just before Kathy's trial in 2003. In 2000, she was asked to review the material relevant to the deaths of Christopher and Harry Clark after their mother Sally had been convicted of their murder.

In her submission to the Folbigg inquiry, she outlined her own role in that case, saying: 'It was my observation that the microbiology report was missing from Harry Clark's file that led to its recovery and to the evidence that he had suffered from a disseminated infection with *Staphylococcus aureus*. This and other reassessments of the medical evidence in relation to the infection led to the acquittal of Mrs. Clark at the High Court in London in January 2003.'

Professor Blackwell's view, shared by the English Court of Appeal, was that: 'Ignoring the microbiological findings was a major oversight in the prosecution of Sally Clark in which the pathologist relied on the hypothesis promoted by Roy Meadow rather than the hard evidence of *S. aureus* isolated from multiple normally sterile sites in the second child ... These were facts, not vague hypotheses.'

As Professor Blackwell had played a central part in helping to free Sally Clark, her expert opinion on how Kathy's children died could be regarded as carrying some weight.

Part of her evidence to the inquiry addressed a suggestion which had been made before Kathy's trial, that a gene known as Interleukin-10, or IL-10 – known colloquially as the 'cot death gene' was associated with SIDS and might have played a part in Sarah's death. The suggestion had been made originally by Dr David Drucker, a microbiologist and cot death expert attached to Manchester University in the UK. Dr Drucker, too, had played a part in the Sally Clark case, as an advisor to her legal team.

At the last minute in 2003, Kathy's solicitor Peter Krisenthal had commissioned Dr Drucker to write a report on the children's deaths for the defence team.

In his report, Dr Drucker suggested that in Laura's case, on microbiological evidence alone, there was 'some evidence of SIDS associated bacteria', and in Sarah's case, there was a 'species associated with SIDS present', following an upper respiratory tract infection, and that: 'It is entirely possible that Sarah died as a SIDS case.' Professor Hilton, of course, had already ascribed her death to SIDS.

In a separate email, Dr Drucker wrote: 'The test on Sarah Folbigg found she had two copies of the "cot death gene" which would obviously increase her risk of SIDS.'

He called for further, genetic testing to be carried out – which didn't immediately happen – and he noted that IL-10 'is not a sentence of death. It is merely a naturally occurring variant of a gene we all have. However, the "wrong" variant is associated with increased risk of SIDS.'

To Kathy's defence team in 2003, this must have seemed like potentially groundbreaking evidence that might give rise to reasonable doubt that Kathy had killed her two daughters. But Dr Drucker never made it to court to give his expert opinion at her trial.

In September 2002, six months before the trial got underway, Justice Graham Barr had declared the trial a 'complex' one and ordered the defence to hand over all of its medical evidence, in order to allow the prosecution to research it and assess it, prior to the trial.

Dr Drucker's report was duly handed over to the prosecution, who promptly commissioned an opposing opinion from Dr Cala – himself neither a geneticist nor a microbiologist.

Even so, Dr Cala delivered a letter to the prosecution team in which he made every effort to discredit the theory that the IL-10 gene might play a part in SIDS. 'If this is true, one would expect that SIDS would run in families, given its genetic aetiology, whereas this is not the case,' he wrote.

'SIDS is sporadic and is not a genetically inherited condition.' He described Dr Drucker's paper as 'confusing and contradictory' and the theory that the IL-10 gene might 'somehow explain the deaths of these infants' as 'in my view unscientific and implausible'.

But in one important respect, Dr Cala was wrong. SIDS can, and tragically, often does run in families. A first SIDS death makes a second death from SIDS more likely. And Dr Drucker hadn't suggested that the gene provided an explanation for the children's deaths, simply that 'the "wrong" variant is associated with increased risk of SIDS'.

The real aim of the prosecution team was to discredit the theory – and also, to discredit Dr Drucker. The final question asked of Dr Cala was: 'Is there anything known professionally about Dr Drucker which may undermine or discredit his authority in reaching the results and conclusions which he purports to reach?' The DPP was fishing for dirt on the UK expert.

'Not that I am aware of,' Dr Cala replied. 'There is no broad acceptance that SIDS is infectious in origin. At this stage, I reject this particular theory as having any role in the aetiology of SIDS.'

Not content with Dr Cala's takedown, the prosecution commissioned a further report from Dr Janice Ophoven, also not a genetics expert. That, though, didn't stop her declaring that 'All opinions are stated to a reasonable degree of medical certainty.'

She described Dr Drucker's conclusions as 'pure speculation'.

A more nuanced opinion was provided by Professor Peter Berry, who commented that Dr Drucker's theory 'and other theories implicating novel mechanisms and infection have rightly attracted considerable interest among SIDS researchers'.

A paper that Dr Drucker had written about the IL-10 gene, which was published in the journal *Human Immunology* in 2000, had received a great deal of attention from the media, which described it as the 'cot death gene'. Professor Berry said this label was misleading, 'not least because many cot death victims do not have this gene variant, and the vast majority of people with it lead healthy lives'.

Armed with these opposing views, a solicitor in Nicholas Cowdery's office attacked Dr Drucker's report with barely concealed contempt, telling Mr Krisenthal, 'Dr Cala advised us today that the theory associating the IL-10 gene with SIDS is nothing more than a theory ... He does not give the theory any credence.'

The DPP solicitor was particularly contemptuous of the idea that IL-10 could be regarded as the 'cot-death gene'.

'Dr Cala stated that anyone can go fishing for a gene and suggest a genetic link with SIDS,' he wrote. 'At this stage, it is no more than "junk science".'

After receiving this letter, Kathy's legal team decided not to call Dr Drucker to give evidence on Kathy's behalf at her trial.

A retrospective study of Justice Barr's orders, published by the New South Wales Parliament the following year, observed that this resulted in large numbers of scientific expert reports being exchanged, and 'a vast reduction in the court time necessary to resolve complex issues of medical science.'

The politicians suggested that if all of the complex medical issues on the defence side had been presented at Kathy's trial, the trial itself might have been aborted, adding, 'From the Crown's perspective the making of the pre-trial disclosure orders had a very beneficial impact on the case.'

As far as the prosecution was concerned, the application of the pre-trial disclosure orders had the positive effect of narrowing the issues before the trial began, and in doing so, significantly narrowed the scope of reasonable doubt which might otherwise have been put to the jury.

It meant that the defence instead had to rely on incidental findings from the children's postmortem examinations, to explain how and why they had died.

Professor Blackwell said her conclusions, 'particularly for Sarah and Laura', were in line with the opinion given by Professor Roger Byard, who appeared for the defence at Kathy's trial, that 'potentially significant organic illness was present in these children'.

When Dr Cala was questioned about this on the second full day of the inquiry in March 2019, he denied using the term 'junk science' in relation to the theory. 'I wasn't suggesting that Dr Drucker and anybody else attached to this was junk science but I was flagging caution in interpreting this in relation to SIDS deaths,' he told Gail Furness. Professor Cordner commented that: 'The sort of things that Professor Blackwell is talking about isn't in the zone of junk science.'

Another expert, mucosal immunologist Professor Robert Clancy, also believed that infection may have played a role in Sarah's death, arguing in his statement to the inquiry that: 'The bacteria of the type found in Sarah's lung tissue are commonly present in children that die unexpectedly and without any readily identifiable alternate cause of death.'

But there was another revelation from Professor Blackwell that was genuinely shocking.

In her statement, which I obtained before it had been admitted in evidence to the inquiry, she recalled that in 2000, while she was working in Newcastle on sabbatical leave from the University of Edinburgh, Craig Folbigg telephoned her.

'He called me to inquire about the study on genetic assessment of families in which there had been a sudden infant death. This was in response to an article in a local newspaper about the study I and others were conducting on genetic assessment of families,' she recalled.

'Mr Folbigg said that his wife was accused of murdering their four children; and he asked that, if they participated in the study, could the results provide an explanation to the deaths? I advised Mr Folbigg that I could not provide them with the results as the ethics committee required all participant information be anonymous. Neither Mr Folbigg nor Mrs Folbigg provided samples for the study.'

However, this wasn't the end of the matter.

'After this telephone conversation with Mr Folbigg, I received a visit from Detective Bernie Ryan who asked for information about sudden infant deaths. He said that there was a family that had four infant deaths and he was investigating the circumstances of the deaths.'

Either Bernie Ryan had read the same article in the local paper, or he and Craig had been talking.

At the time, Professor Blackwell was based in the Newcastle Royal Hospital as a visiting Professor of Immunology and Microbiology, and it was there that she and the Deputy Director of Immunology Services, Professor Maree Gleeson, had a meeting with Detective Ryan. He came to the meeting alone.

'He informed me he was investigating the circumstances of four infant deaths. I recall being surprised that Mr Ryan wanted information about four infant deaths in one family, because

Mr Folbigg had approached me a few days prior about the four infant deaths in his family,' she told the inquiry.

Professor Blackwell told Detective Ryan that Mr Folbigg had inquired about the study she was conducting but had decided not to take part. 'I asked Mr Ryan about the results of the autopsies but did not see the reports at this time. The only suggestion I could make was based on work recently published by our research group. I advised him that my research team had screened tissues and body fluids from infants who died of unexplained causes and identified toxins of *Staphylococcus aureus* in over half of the SIDS/SUDI infants tested. More recent findings have indicated that *S. aureus* is one of the major isolates from infants who die suddenly and unexpectedly.'

Professor Blackwell told Detective Ryan that tests could be carried out for the toxins at the University of Edinburgh, where the tests had been developed. 'I suggested that the costs would be modest ... He said it was too expensive as there would need to be someone accompanying the samples and to watch each step of the process. I indicated that there would be no objection to an observer.'

Professor Blackwell said that Detective Ryan didn't ask how much the laboratory tests would cost. By her calculations, it would have been around US$5000.

As a result, the tests did not go ahead.

With the publication of my article, all of this fresh evidence was in the public domain by late morning on 18 March. So, I was surprised at lunchtime to be approached by a press officer attached to the inquiry, who asked me if she could have a word with me. I agreed, and we sat together in the Coroner's Court café.

There, she told me that Gail Furness and her team had read the article and wanted to know if I could tell them where I had obtained the experts' reports. She explained that this was because the reports had not yet been formally tendered to the inquiry. I told her that I couldn't reveal my source, and she said that was fine.

Back in the inquiry hearing after lunch, Gail Furness rose to her feet and announced: 'Your Honour, it's just been brought to my attention that the ABC has – on its website has written a lengthy article and it's clear from the article that they have had access to Professor Clancy's reports, which I indicated this morning were received by the inquiry over the last few days, Professor Blackwell's and Professor Ryan's reports. They are reports that were prepared for the purpose of the inquiry and have been provided to that inquiry …

'None of them have been tendered, and certainly I wasn't proposing to tender at least one of them in their fullness, and I don't know whether anyone else had any objections to any part of those reports, but they have clearly been made available to the media before your Honour has had an opportunity to consider what the inquiry may make of them.'

Mr Blanch reacted furiously to this news, asking Kathy's counsel, Jeremy Morris: 'Mr Morris, are you appearing in this court or are you running your case in the media?'

'Your Honour, I'm sorry,' Mr Morris replied. 'I'll make enquiries.'

Mr Blanch continued to scold Mr Morris, telling him: 'It appears that there are parts of material that were to be tendered which will not be admitted into evidence,' and adding: 'It is an appalling situation. In the ordinary course of events, if this were a court, it would be a contempt of the court to be putting forward material such as that through the media before it even has had an opportunity of being considered here.'

But it wasn't a court; it was an inquiry. Also, those reports were already in the hands of many of those connected with the inquiry; not just Kathy's new legal team. As Mr Blanch continued to vent at Mr Morris, other journalists in the media room, disappointed perhaps not to have received the same reports, turned to stare me down, disapprovingly.

I was bemused though, why the Crown was not intending to tender these reports in their entirety. What did they contain that could not be reported on or considered by Mr Blanch in reaching his findings?

Now three of the four pathologists that had prepared reports were saying that the children may well have died from natural causes, two of the medical experts were saying that infections may have hastened their deaths, and a neurological expert had questioned the notion that Patrick died from suffocation.

In my view, the only conclusion to be drawn was that the evidence produced in these new reports challenged the judiciary's view that Kathy had smothered her children and made for uncomfortable reading on the other side.

None of the fresh evidence, in my opinion, was welcome news for a judicial establishment that had consigned Kathy to a thirty-year prison sentence, and reaffirmed her guilt time and time again.

28

'SHE COULD BE PART OF THAT SMALL NUMBER'

On day two, I was back at the inquiry to hear Gail Furness question four senior forensic pathologists about the case. Two of them – Professor Stephen Cordner, whose report had been attached to the 2015 petition; and Dr Allan Cala, who conducted Laura's autopsy in March 1999 – had been at loggerheads over Laura's cause of death. While Dr Cala believed she had been smothered by Kathy, Professor Cordner saw the most obvious cause of death as myocarditis – or inflammation of the heart tissue.

A third pathologist, Professor Jo Duflou, was clinical director of the Department of Forensic Medicine in Glebe when Laura died, and the fourth expert was Professor John Hilton, who carried out Sarah's autopsy.

Under questioning from Gail Furness, Dr Cala stressed that the evidence he had given at Kathy's trial was driven by the forensic pathology of Laura's postmortem, and not by his knowledge that three other children had died.

'I wasn't biased to express any particular view or prejudiced in any way. It was a finding that I determined myself just by looking at the material provided,' he insisted.

However, when Gail Furness asked him: 'Was there any evidence of deliberate smothering on autopsy?' he replied, 'No.'

The questioning by Gail Furness highlighted inconsistencies in the opinions Dr Cala had offered over a period of time. She asked him about the statement he had given to Detective Ryan in March 2003 – one month before Kathy's trial – in which, after watching the video of Laura by the family pool the day before she died, he stated: 'That Laura Folbigg appeared in such good health less than 24 hours prior to her death makes me believe more firmly that the myocarditis which was found at autopsy played no role whatsoever in her death and was an incidental finding.'

'You had described myocarditis before as it might have been the cause of death,' Ms Furness pointed out.

'Yes.'

'Here you say "played no role whatsoever" which is more emphatic. What was it that caused you to be more emphatic in your view?'

'I found the video to be important,' he replied. 'As depicted, it showed a child who appeared to be in very good health but who, 24 hours or less than 24 hours later, was deceased. She exhibited no outward sign of symptoms as I've said in that and so I was of the view then based on the video that it made it even less likely for me to be of the view that she's died of myocarditis.'

Ms Furness continued to press him: 'Do you understand that people including children can die of myocarditis without showing any symptoms beforehand?'

> A small number can, yes.
>> Why couldn't she be part of that small number?
>> She could. She could be part of that small number.
>> It's a very emphatic description, Dr Cala, 'played no role whatsoever'.
>> Yes. I accept that.
>> And that's still the view you hold today?
>> No, I temper that. I would say, when I've said 'played no role whatsoever' that categorically excludes it as being a
> cause of death and I think that's — I think that's incorrect.
>> So what would you say today?

> I'd say I cannot positively exclude myocarditis as being the cause of death. I did say that at trial and although I believe it's — in my view she did not die of myocarditis I do not believe I could categorically exclude it as being the cause of death.
>
> You consider it to be an incidental finding.
>
> That's my view.

To Kathy's legal team and her friends and supporters, this was a highly significant climb-down by Dr Cala. He was admitting that he had been wrong in his letter to Bernie Ryan, to express the unambiguous view that myocarditis 'played no role whatsoever' in Laura's death: 'I think that's incorrect'. It wasn't a complete about-face – he wasn't saying that myocarditis was indeed the cause of death, but he was admitting that he could no longer categorically exclude it.

All three of the other experts were in agreement that myocarditis can cause sudden death in a child, and that Laura had myocarditis when she died.

Professor Cordner went one step further, telling Gail Furness that in his opinion, it was 'unexceptional for a child to die suddenly and unexpectedly from myocarditis with no preceding indicators or indications or symptoms.'

'As I understand it,' he added, 'Laura did have a bit of a sniffly viral sort of cold, but not that anybody thought was of any significance, so you can have that as either a preceding symptom or actually that it was completely and totally sudden and unexpected.'

Professor Cordner also wouldn't accept the suggestion by Ms Furness that it was 'rare' for a child to die suddenly and unexpectedly from myocarditis. 'I don't think it's rare, I think it's uncommon,' he said. And Professor Duflou was even more emphatic. 'Look, in my view it's one of the more common causes of sudden cardiac death in young people,' he declared.

Professor Hilton's view was that 'in the overall picture myocarditis is perhaps an uncommon cause of death, however there's another side to that coin; are people with myocarditis subject to sudden unexpected death and the answer to that is yes'. In a report he had written for the inquiry, Professor Hilton suggested that Laura 'died with and highly probably because of florid myocarditis'. It was a stronger view than the more cautious opinion he gave at trial, and now, under questioning from Gail Furness, he tempered this slightly, saying that Laura 'may well have died' from myocarditis.

Pressed even further, Professor Hilton exhibited a flash of irritation at her line of questioning, telling Ms Furness: 'There is no physical evidence, no pathological evidence of any other cause of death, dead she certainly is, myocarditis she certainly has, can myocarditis kill, yes it can, may it well have killed her, is it the favoured diagnosis in this particular case, yes, it is.'

In relation to Caleb, Professor Hilton said that laryngomalacia, if it were present, 'and there was certainly clinical indications that it was present, is likely to persist and laryngomalacia has been recorded as being a potential cause of death in small children'. His further observation was that Caleb had died at a very young age, 'which means if in fact laryngomalacia were present, he really didn't have the time to grow out of it'.

Professor Duflou's opinion was that, while he hadn't encountered any confirmed cases of laryngomalacia himself, he was aware of research which indicated that some cases can prove fatal.

Dr Cala, again, was the opposing voice. 'I'm not convinced by anything I've seen that his laryngomalacia was in any way serious,' he suggested.

But Professor Hilton countered that: 'The fact that the child had laryngomalacia is a very interesting factor. Did it play a part? It may have. Can I prove it? No, and neither can anyone else. Nor can I disprove it.' Both he and Professor Cordner said that, in their opinion, SIDS was the diagnosis they felt most comfortable with, in relation to Caleb's death.

In Patrick's case, Professor Cordner explained that the cause of death written on the death certificate, namely 'Asphyxia due to airway obstruction', was not a reference to a deliberate act of smothering, but in fact referred to how Patrick's airway may have been obstructed by the epileptic fits he was suffering. He explained that in his opinion, the underlying cause of the epileptic fits was an encephalopathic disorder, or disorder of the brain, and stressed that: 'I do want to make it very clear that the death is very understandable in the circumstances of a baby having severe epileptic seizures.'

Professor Cordner pushed back at Ms Furness, when she asked him to say whether he would exclude smothering as a possible cause of Patrick's death. 'There is no real need to go searching for another cause,' he suggested. 'In the circumstances of a child having intractable seizures, death from that is well recognised and something that we see not infrequently.' He added, later: 'There's nothing to suggest that epilepsy wasn't the cause of death.'

Professor Hilton's view was that: 'The indications are that this little lad died as part of an epileptic-type illness.'

In Sarah's case, Professor Hilton, who carried out the autopsy, said that he discovered that her uvula – the droplet shaped piece of flesh hanging down at the back of the mouth – looked congested, and overlapped the epiglottis – the flap at the top of the windpipe that helps to prevent food and liquid entering the lungs.

Sarah was a significant snorer, and the professor suggested that: 'It is possible – and I put it no more than that – it is possible that the snoring was because this uvula was bouncing off the epiglottis or bouncing off the larynx in the region of the same epiglottis.' Professor Cordner wondered aloud if this could have made Sarah more vulnerable to SIDS.

Throughout her questioning of the forensic pathologists, Gail Furness appeared to me to resist the clear evidence being given, that there were entirely reasonable potential natural causes of death for each of Kathy's four children. And, occasionally, the experts' frustration with the line of questioning broke through.

At one point, in relation to Caleb, Patrick and Sarah, Gail Furness asked Professor Duflou: 'You couldn't exclude smothering in relation to any of the three deaths, could you?'

'I couldn't exclude it,' the professor replied, 'but I can't include it either. There's no evidence for it.'

29

THE CALM BEFORE THE STORM

When in April, the inquiry began to hear the genetic evidence, no one present in the courtroom knew how pivotal to the question of Kathy's guilt or innocence it would prove to be. Genetics hadn't been the first focus of Kathy's legal team, it was extremely complex, and to any untrained observer, it was frequently impenetrable.

It was, nevertheless, vital for the inquiry to establish whether there was a genetic cause for any of the children's deaths. Genetics was in its infancy in 2003 when Kathy was on trial, but since then, the potential to test for genetic disorders had exploded.

Some genetic investigations relating to Kathy's children were undertaken before her trial, but the results were inconclusive and, largely, unhelpful. However, counsel assisting Gail Furness acknowledged that advances in genetics since the trial 'permit a much broader scope of investigation than was possible in 2003'.

Since then, two major genomic sequencing technologies had become mainstream. One of them, whole exome sequencing, Ms Furness explained, 'sequences the whole exome, which is that small part of the genome, approximately 1% to 2% of the whole, that is involved in coding for proteins. Proteins are the key components of cells and damage to them can cause serious, if not catastrophic problems.'

As we saw in Chapter 25, using whole exome sequencing, Professor Vinuesa and Dr Arsov had identified a unique cardiac genetic mutation, *CALM2* G114R, which Kathy carried and had passed on to her daughters. As the scientist who had overseen this process, Professor Vinuesa expected to be given an early opportunity to explain what the implications of this discovery were.

In her opinion, the *CALM2* variant was 'likely pathogenic'.

However, she was not invited to give evidence on the first day of the genetics hearings. Instead, Ms Furness took evidence from four other expert witnesses: paediatric cardiologist Professor Jonathan Skinner, clinical geneticist Professor Edwin Kirk, genetic pathologist Dr Michael Buckley, and clinical geneticist Dr Alison Colley.

These expert witnesses came to be known as the 'Sydney team'; all four were employed by or closely connected with NSW Health – the state's health department.

In 2015, Professor Jo Duflou had urged NSW Health Pathology to carry out a thorough review of the forensic pathology in the Folbigg case following his favourable assessment of Professor Stephen Cordner's report, which concluded that there was no evidence that any of Kathy's children had been smothered. That review didn't happen, and nearly four years had elapsed until the inquiry's hearings got underway.

And this raised a fundamental question: did the health department have an interest in maintaining the status quo? Is that why a review of the four deaths had never occurred, and would it colour the approach being taken at this inquiry?

Professor Vinuesa and her two colleagues Dr Arsov and Professor Matthew Cook had no ties to the New South Wales health department; all three were affiliated with the Australian National University in Canberra, and they were referred to as the 'Canberra team'. Professor Cook was medical director of the Canberra Clinical Genomics Laboratory, which was accredited to undertake the kinds of analysis that had led to the discovery of the Folbigg mutation.

At the outset, the Sydney team's Professor Skinner explained what sort of cardiac genetic conditions can cause a child's sudden death: 'Most sudden cardiac deaths in children occur in children with structurally normal hearts, which after death looks normal both to the naked eye and under the microscope.'

Part of the process that allows a person's heart to work efficiently is 'depolarisation', which leads to the heart's cells contracting, and blood being pumped around the body, while 'repolarisation' allows the cells to relax.

Professor Skinner explained that the rapid movement across the cardiac cell wall of sodium, potassium and calcium ions – atoms carrying a positive or negative electrical charge – are required for depolarisation and repolarisation of cardiac cells with every heartbeat.

'If the channels through which the ions travel are defective, then repolarisation or depolarisation is abnormal and there is a risk of serious ventricular arrhythmia, a rhythm so fast and uncoordinated that there is no output from the heart and sudden syncope, cardiac arrest or sudden death can occur.'

Kathy's medical history showed that she had suffered multiple syncopes – the medical term for fainting or falling unconscious – during her life. One question to be answered by the experts was: were Kathy's bouts of fainting a damaging effect of the *CALM2* mutation which she carried?

Professor Skinner explained that three genetic heart diseases most commonly resulted from cardiac ion channelopathies – the defects which can cause fatal cardiac arrhythmias. The three diseases were: the heart rhythm disorder Long QT syndrome, Catecholaminergic Polymorphic Ventricular Tachycardia, or CPVT, and Brugada syndrome, 'and there's a long list of genes which can cause these conditions.'

CPVT is a severe genetic disorder which occurs in childhood, and results in fainting or sudden death. Brugada syndrome causes the heart's normal rhythm to be disrupted, resulting in fainting, seizures, breathing difficulties, or sudden death.

These conditions, the professor explained, could cause ventricular tachycardia, 'which means the bottom part of the heart is beating extremely quickly', or alternatively, ventricular fibrillation 'which is basically a seizure of the bottom part of the heart.' Typically, it wasn't a slowing of the heart that was fatal, 'it's the very rapid rhythm that causes the death.'

Put simply, a cardiac genetic disorder can cause fatal cardiac arrhythmias in children, as well as in adults.

Professor Vinuesa was excluded from this initial discussion, and told me later how shocked she was by her first, preliminary meeting with Gail Furness. She had come to the inquiry reluctantly – not wanting to give evidence in person when she found out Professor Cook could not attend to back her up and Dr Arsov had not been invited, but had agreed to after being pressed to do so by Kathy's legal team. The previous meetings and written exchanges between the Canberra and Sydney teams had been tense and unpleasant, and highly critical of the Canberra team's interpretation of the genetic findings. She insisted that Dr Arsov be permitted to attend.

In one crucial area, Professor Vinuesa was highly qualified to give evidence; she brought specific, relevant experience to the table that none of the other experts did. Since 2009, she had pioneered the use of next generation sequencing for the diagnosis of novel rare diseases and for the discovery of novel genes and novel mutations that cause disease. Together with her colleagues, they had sequenced more than 2000 individuals.

The knowledge and experience held by her and by Dr Arsov about next-generation sequencing was greater probably, than anyone else in the hearings, because they had done it themselves from scratch. 'We had to learn it as the technologies came,' she told me later.

She was, in other words, an extremely accomplished and innovative genetic research scientist. 'Our primary goal was to identify novel causes of disease, so, to uncover novel variants that could be pathogenic,' she explained.

This didn't deter Ms Furness from taking Professor Vinuesa and Dr Arsov into a private room at the Coroner's Court to lay down the ground rules for how they should give their evidence to the inquiry. 'She told us that there were experts with much more expertise than we had in all of these domains, in cardiology, in metabolic medicine, even in genetics,' the professor later revealed.

Ms Furness emphasised that Professor Vinuesa and Dr Arsov didn't have formal qualifications as clinical geneticists – a field that is relatively new. She told the professor and Dr Arsov that they would need to restrict themselves in what they said, that the level of expertise in the courtroom would be 'massive, including cardiac and metabolism experts, which you are not,' that the level of expertise in genetics was also very high, and that: 'I am going to ask you questions. Only answer my questions.'

Dr Arsov was told he could only contribute his opinion when asked to do so, and says he felt demeaned by the experience.

'So I think that sent a very strong, bleak message to Todor and myself that our opinions were not really welcome,' Professor Vinuesa told me. 'Through that I understood that we couldn't really speak freely, that we could only answer her questions.'

As the genetic discussion got underway, a long debate ensued between the Canberra and Sydney teams about the potential for the *CALM2* mutation to be pathogenic. Professor Vinuesa forecast – accurately – that eventually, it would be laboratory testing of the variant that would settle the matter. Experts in the calmodulin protein could be asked to carry out 'assays', or experiments, that 'could tell us if this mutation is pathogenic or not'.

The Sydney team wouldn't accept Professor Vinuesa's opinion that the variant was 'likely pathogenic'. They preferred to classify it as a 'variant of unknown significance', basing their classification on a table of terminology laid down by the American College of Medical Genetics and Genomics. Under ACMG guidelines, a variant could be classified as being pathogenic, likely pathogenic, a variant of unknown significance, likely benign, or benign. The ACMG guidelines are used to assess the clinical significance of different genetic variants.

Professor Vinuesa made it clear that, until the variant was tested in a laboratory, she would not feel comfortable with 'excluding its potential for pathogenicity'.

'So it's a potential rather than something that's been published to date, is that correct?' Ms Furness asked.

'All of this ... is analysing the potential for pathogenicity,' the professor replied. 'This is a novel variant. Precisely because they are novel, the potential for pathogenicity is greater than those that might be already known.'

Professor Vinuesa emphasised that, even if a person is a carrier of a novel variant and exhibits no symptoms, 'you still will have the pathogenic variants that might kill or cause catastrophic events in other members of the family'. This, she was saying, could apply to Kathy who carried the *CALM2* variant but was still alive and on the surface, apparently well. That didn't rule out the possibility that her daughters might have died as a result of carrying the same genetic mutation.

The fact that Kathy had suffered no major adverse cardiac event, such as a heart attack, allowed the Sydney team to characterise her as being 'healthy'. But when it was revealed that Kathy had suffered syncopes in the past – including, on one occasion, fainting at the end of a swimming race, Professor Skinner acknowledged that this could be highly significant.

'I think this is a really important event that we need more detail about,' he said. 'Two conditions are quite specific, Long QT syndrome type 1 and CPVT can cause sudden loss of consciousness, particularly while swimming, so the detail of that event actually is pivotal here.' But he cautioned that the simple act of fainting wasn't necessarily a symptom of a potentially fatal condition.

'If she sank to the bottom of the pool, was pulled out by somebody and given resuscitation, that's one story, if she'd just won a race, felt a bit dizzy and was pulled out and recovered, that's a completely different story.'

The first would suggest that she did indeed suffer from Long QT syndrome or from CPVT; the second, however, would not.

But with a growing body of evidence linking fainting with calmodulinopathy – a life-threatening cardiac arrhythmia caused by mutations in any of the three calmodulin genes, *CALM1*, *CALM2* and *CALM3* – the fact that Kathy had fainted many times indicated that her genetic mutation could be life-threatening, regardless of what exactly happened at the swimming pool.

For Professor Vinuesa, it was her first experience of appearing as an expert witness in court or at an official inquiry. Like all of the expert witnesses appearing for Kathy, she was unpaid. Later, she told me that she felt that the inquiry had not afforded her evidence and opinions the weight and respect they deserved.

For reasons that she maintains were never explained to her, Professor Vinuesa and Dr Arsov were 'excused' from giving any further oral evidence before the Sydney team had finished giving theirs. 'I feel that my evidence has not been given proper consideration by the Commissioner in his report,' she said later.

'While the legal system has an unparalleled ability to draw and distil information from varying sources, my experience left me thinking it has several blind spots when it comes to evaluating scientific evidence. My hope is that we can build a more scientifically sensitive and informed legal system. One that is not only skilled in applying the scientific method but also welcoming of scientists.'

After the hearings had ended but before Reginald Blanch handed down his findings Professor Vinuesa reached out to the top world experts in calmodulin mutations to canvass their opinions on the pathogenicity of the *CALM2* variant. She also asked them who would be the best scientist to undertake a functional assay, or in layman's terms, tests in the laboratory, to investigate if it was indeed pathogenic.

She received several replies. One of them was from Professor Peter Schwartz, a world-leading authority in genetic causes of cardiac arrhythmias and sudden unexpected death. Professor Schwartz reviewed the Folbigg family's clinical and genetic information. He told Professor Vinuesa about their recently accepted peer-reviewed article, reporting data from an international registry of seventy-four people with variants in calmodulin genes. Of those, twenty had died suddenly, five of them while asleep. Three of those five were less than two years old, as Sarah and Laura were when they died.

This was significant, because Professor Skinner had told the inquiry that this had never happened with a calmodulin mutation. 'All of the deaths produced in the literature have been over the age of two and the majority of those are in teenagers or above during exercise, while awake, not while asleep,' he asserted.

The results from the registry showed otherwise. Inadvertently, the inquiry had been misinformed about the reported incidence of infant deaths from rare calmodulin mutations.

But the most important piece of information Professor Schwartz revealed to Professor Vinuesa, was that they had identified 'one boy who died at age four, and his brother, who suffered a cardiac arrest at age five, and both had a calmodulin mutation at the exact same amino acid location as Sarah and Laura. The boys had also inherited the mutation from their seemingly healthy mother.'

In his email, Professor Schwartz indicated that in his view, the *CALM2* variant was the likely cause of Sarah's and Laura's deaths.

Writing to Professor Vinuesa from the Italian Auxological Institute in Milan, where he was Director of the Centre for the Study and Treatment of Cardiac Arrhythmias of Genetic Origin, Professor Schwartz suggested Kathy undergo a full cardiological assessment, to determine whether she was a 'mosaic'; meaning, that the variant she carried could be pathogenic, without herself exhibiting any life-threatening symptoms.

'She could very well be a case of mosaicism. This could account for a milder phenotype in the mother and a more serious one in the children. It is essential to obtain different sources of DNA from the mother to test for possible mosaicism,' he declared.

He told Professor Vinuesa: 'The identification of the *CALM2* variant justifies fully re-opening the case because it raises significant doubts to a significant extent,' adding, for good measure, 'My conclusion is that the accusation of infanticide might have been premature and not correct.'

Professor Schwartz's letter landed like a bombshell, and given that he was a pre-eminent authority in the exact scientific domain which had been under scrutiny at the inquiry, it might have been expected that there would be an interest in reopening the hearings and inviting him to come to Sydney to give evidence.

That didn't happen. To the dismay of the Canberra team, Mr Blanch did not feel it necessary to reopen the inquiry to explore the evidence provided by Professor Schwartz and the registry data.

Another calmodulin expert contacted by Professor Vinuesa recommended approaching Danish professor Michael Toft Overgaard for the functional tests. He was immediately interested in the mutation, and in its potential for pathogenicity, and agreed to undertake the laboratory experiments to test if *CALM2* G114R was arrythmogenic.

There followed an exchange of further reports between the Sydney and Canberra teams. For their part, the Sydney team argued that, while the *CALM2* variant might be pathogenic, the clinical evidence in relation to Kathy suggested otherwise.

'If the clinical information … is *not* taken into account … the variant would be classified as Likely Pathogenic,' they conceded.

However, they wrote, 'It is possible that the variant contributed to, but was not the sole cause of, the deaths of Sarah and Laura,' and furthermore, 'It is possible that the variant is pathogenic but is unrelated to the cause of death of Sarah and Laura.'

Surprisingly, they added, 'We … do not see a straightforward way of resolving the issue by further genetic or other testing.'

The subtext in this rebuff appeared to be that, even if Sarah and Laura carried a pathogenic mutation, Kathy might have killed them. The girls might have died *with* the genetic mutation, but not because of it.

This, though, was pure speculation. And by now, Professor Vinuesa had recruited another world-leading expert on calmodulin genes, based in Denmark, to give his opinion on the G114R mutation. Professor Michael Toft Overgaard had not been invited to give evidence by the inquiry, and had only become involved at Professor Vinuesa's invitation.

The Canberra team's response to the Sydney team's submission was acerbic. 'The Sydney team has revised their classification of the *CALM2* G114R variant as likely pathogenic,' they wrote. 'Based on opinion and speculation, however, they have classified the variant as non-pathogenic.' Professors Schwartz and Toft Overgaard had agreed to be joint authors of this report and provided their qualified opinions.

'We recommend that any conclusions should be based on available facts together with an acknowledgement of the current limits of our knowledge. Furthermore, we suggest that reaching a conclusion based on speculation rather than acknowledgement of these available facts and knowledge gaps is *fundamentally flawed*. Very recent information on the precise *CALM2* genetic variant in question exemplifies why we should be careful not to discount possibilities until the facts are in.'

Professor Vinuesa and her colleagues declared that 'the Sydney team's assertion that a *CALM2* gene variant cannot be disease-causing if present in a phenotypically healthy carrier is incorrect.' And they insisted: 'A "healthy" related person can be the carrier of a mutation that can be lethal in another related person.

'In conclusion,' they argued, 'based on the available facts, we cannot reasonably exclude, and we think it is likely, that the two female Folbigg children died as a result of the *CALM2*

G114R variant, while the two male children died from different causes that could also be genetic.'

Armed with the registry data and the views expressed by Professors Schwartz, Toft Overgaard and Vinuesa, the Canberra team were cautiously hopeful. The Sydney team had tried to downplay the significance of the genetic mutation the Canberra team had discovered. But perhaps at last, the powers-that-be would acknowledge the reasonable possibility that all four children had died from natural causes.

30

UNDER SIEGE

On Monday, 29 April 2019, at 10 am came the moment the public and the media had been waiting for – Kathy entered the witness box, to answer questions in a court for the very first time about the diary entries she had written all those years ago, that had led the jury at her trial to condemn her as a baby-killer.

TV crews were not allowed to film inside the Coroner's Court and were reduced to catching fleeting images of her through the glass from outside, as she passed, like a phantom, along a corridor, escorted by prison guards.

Kathy hadn't given evidence at her trial, and the conversations she had with Tracy Chapman which we had recorded the previous year for *Australian Story* marked the first time she had opened up at length, and in public, about her diaries.

That, though, had been a friendly discussion with her best friend. This was very different.

As she arrived at Lidcombe Coroner's Court and entered the witness box, she presented an utterly different image to the distraught thirty-five-year-old who had been half-carried down to the cells sixteen years earlier after hearing the jury's verdicts.

Here, now, was a middle-aged woman with sunken eyes and a permanently sad expression, dressed in a light-blue patterned dress with a black cardigan, the unkempt curls of her hair flecked with grey, cascading over her shoulders. She looked much older, serious, calm and self-possessed, but underneath, her emotions were in turmoil. She smiled briefly at her friends in the public gallery as she entered the courtroom. She knew she was going to be asked to explain the most troubling and contentious entries in her diaries, and she knew she would be challenged about those explanations.

Even so, she could not have had any idea how ferocious the questioning would be.

Present in court was Christopher Maxwell SC, the new Senior Crown Prosecutor for New South Wales, who had replaced Mark Tedeschi in 2017. As the DPP's legal representative at the inquiry, he would be one of the counsel asking her questions.

Margaret Cunneen SC was there to represent Craig's interests and protect his reputation. She wasn't expected to question Kathy at any length.

Mr Blanch had repeatedly emphasised that the inquiry was not an adversarial process. However, it was to become very much adversarial, as Kathy's impending cross-examination would demonstrate.

Which counsel would go first? Mr Blanch asked Jeremy Morris, 'What's your view about it?'

Mr Morris replied, 'I'm happy to lead evidence from her, if that's the most convenient course.' He emphasised that, 'We do need some context as to how the diaries were generated and what the issues were in this woman's life at the time.'

This seemed like the most reasonable way to proceed. It would clearly be wrong to deny Kathy the opportunity to put her diaries in their proper context, and to explain what was happening in her life when she wrote those entries.

But her opportunity to do so was denied.

'I must say that I take the view, Mr Morris, that the context is irrelevant,' Mr Blanch declared.

This seemed bizarre to me. How could the context be irrelevant, and why wouldn't the Commissioner want to understand what the context of the diaries was? Didn't he want to know what was going on in Kathy's life when she wrote those entries?

'Well, your Honour, if that be the case, then I should wish to go last, given that Ms Folbigg's my witness,' Jeremy Morris replied.

It wasn't only the context of Kathy's life that would be missing. A few weeks before, Mr Blanch had knocked back the idea of any expert psychiatric or psychological evidence regarding the diaries, telling Kathy's counsel: 'Can I say, Mr Morris, that I would not be assisted at all in this inquiry by a psychiatrist who wanted to come along and tell me (a) what the words of the diary mean or (b) about the fact that a mother who had lost her babies would be upset and emotional and so on. Those are things that are readily apparent, I think, unless there is some other aspect of it.'

In a later directions hearing, Mr Blanch restated his opinion that, 'I am certainly not going to be helped by a psychiatrist's view of the meaning of entries in the diaries, etcetera.'

Rhanee Rego, along with the rest of Kathy's legal team, was angered by this, later remarking to the *Sydney Morning Herald* that Mr Blanch 'isn't a psychiatrist, he's not a mother, and he hadn't lost four children. But he still felt able to interpret Kathleen's words and why she wrote them.'

There was another disturbing revelation on the first day of Kathy's evidence. For months, Isabel Reed had been attempting to obtain the original diaries – without success. What she wasn't told was that Craig Folbigg had had the diaries all along and handed them over to the inquiry only after being summonsed to do so. As a consequence, Kathy was denied the opportunity to read the diaries in their original form and to ensure that they were complete and that the inquiry's record of what she had written was accurate.

In one respect, Kathy found herself in an unfortunate predicament. She had come from jail to give evidence as a convicted child-killer in the eyes of the law, and her convictions rested in large part on the diaries she had written. But she had also volunteered to help the inquiry understand why she wrote those entries, and what they meant. Whether she knew it or not, she had entered the lion's den, and the lions were circling.

Just before 10.15 am, Kathy was sworn in, and Mr Maxwell launched into an aggressive interrogation which lasted through to mid-afternoon. He was followed by Ms Cunneen, who – quite unexpectedly – grilled Kathy for the rest of the afternoon, and the whole of the following day.

Mr Maxwell started by asking Kathy about diaries which no longer existed.

'How many diaries did you get rid of?' he asked.

'I only have a clear recollection of getting rid of one,' she replied.

While acknowledging that six diaries covering 1989, 1990, 1992, 1996/97, 1997/98, and 1999 were before the inquiry, Mr Maxwell noted – with apparent disapproval – that there were no diaries covering the years 1991, 1993, 1994, 1995 and 1998/99.

The suggestion seemed to be that this was sinister, that Kathy had got rid of the diaries because she had made admissions in them to killing her children. But her explanation, quite unremarkably, was that she had written in diaries ever since she was a teenager and hadn't kept them all.

'I never hid my diaries, they were never hidden, people always knew I was writing in them, they were always in places where people could see them,' she told Mr Maxwell.

Kathy resisted the Crown's narrative that she had deliberately thrown away, or hidden her diaries, because they contained incriminating entries.

Mr Maxwell turned to the diary entries themselves, and it quickly became clear that his overriding aim was to extract an admission from Kathy that she had smothered her children. He was, in effect, conducting the cross-examination that Mr Tedeschi had been unable to carry out during the trial.

Much of the interrogation focused on Sarah, and Mr Maxwell began by asking Kathy about her entry of 25 October 1997. Laura by then was two and a half months old, and Sarah had died almost four years earlier.

I cherish Laura more. I miss her, Sarah, yes, but am not sad that Laura is here and she isn't. Is that a bad way to think? Don't know. I think I am more patient with Laura. I take the time to figure what is wrong now instead of just snapping my cog. Wouldn't have handled another like Sarah. She saved her life by being different.

Mr Maxwell homed in on one particular phrase.

You say, 'I take the time to figure out what is wrong now, instead of just snapping my cog'?
Yes.
What did you mean by 'snapping' your 'cog'?
'Snapping my cog', to me, could have been simply as even showing a slight frustration.
Well, could it have been more than 'a slight frustration'?
No.

Mr Maxwell would return again and again to the phrase: 'snapping my cog'. This, he suggested, was an admission of her agency in Sarah's death.

'Snapping your cog' suggests some kind of action, doesn't it?
Not to me.
Doesn't it suggest losing control?
It's a loss of control, yes. 'Frustration', 'loss of control', 'anger', 'snapping cog', all these references I don't differentiate between.
But they're not one and the same concept, are they?
I believed at the time they were.
You see, what we're talking about is the meaning of your use of words in these diaries, isn't it?
If you like, yes.
And what I'm suggesting to you is that there's a distinction between feeling frustrated and snapping your cog. What do you say about that? They're different

concepts, is the point I'm trying to put to you. What do you say about that?

At the time, I didn't believe – I didn't differentiate between them. If I was slightly frustrated, that equalled me being out of control in some fashion, which equalled me snapping my cog. There was no differentiation for me.

I suggest to you that you used the term 'snapping your cog' as a mitigating term for something that you had done to Sarah in order to stop her living. What do you say about that?

No, I won't agree with that at all.

Mr Maxwell challenged Kathy directly and repeatedly to admit that she had murdered Sarah.

Do you say that you didn't smother Sarah, you didn't kill her? That's your position, isn't it?

Absolutely.

Do you say that at the time you wrote these diaries you missed her desperately?

I miss all my children all the time.

But I'm asking about Sarah. Do you say that at the time on 29 October 97 you missed Sarah desperately?

Yes.

This is a child you say that died in an unexplained way but had nothing to do with you, correct?

Yes.

You didn't kill her is what you say?

No.

As the cross-examination continued, Kathy was repeatedly hammered with the accusation that she 'snapped her cog' and killed the children.

'The bottom line of this is, these are diaries and these are thoughts. They're not actions,' she told Mr Maxwell.

Mr Maxwell asked Kathy to comment on one of the most contentious entries in her diaries, from New Year's Day 1997.

> Another year gone & what a year to come. I have a baby on
> the way, which means major personal sacrifice for both of us.
> But I feel confident about it all going well this time. I am
> going to call for help this time & not attempt to do everything
> myself anymore. I know that that was the main reason for all
> my stress before & stress made me do terrible things.

Kathy explained: 'If I left my child to cry for a second it was a terrible thing. If I hadn't met my child's needs in some way, that was a terrible thing. It all meant exactly the same to me.'

Mr Maxwell continued:

> What I'm suggesting to you is the word 'terrible things' is
> far more consistent with killing your children than it is with
> having some kind of angry thought. What's your answer to
> that?
>> As I stated before, no.

Mr Maxwell asked her about the entry she had written, saying, 'What scares me most will be when I'm alone with the baby. How do I overcome that? Defeat that?'

> 'What you are saying is that the time of greatest danger to
> the baby is when you were with them. That's what you're
> saying isn't it?'
>> 'No.'
>
> 'That's what scared you the most. Is that right?'
>> 'No.'
>
> 'Because you'd snap a cog?'
>> 'No.'

This was all too much for Kathy. As Mr Maxwell asked her a further question, she wiped away her tears.

> 'You were expressing a fear of being alone with the baby.
> That's what you're frightened of?'

'I'm expressing the fear that I was scared to death of finding my child not alive.'

Mr Maxwell focused on another diary entry about Laura, where Kathy wrote about the deep depression she experienced, and her dark moods:

> Hopefully preparing myself will mean the end of my dark moods, or at least the ability to see it coming & say to him or someone hey, help I'm getting overwhelmed, help me out. That will be the key to this babies survival.

'So in dark moods did you lose control?' he asked her.

'No,' Kathy replied. 'What I'm referring to there is I had a belief that even a mood from me could affect my child.'

> What, cause its death?
>   Cause it to be not happy, I had a desperate weird thought that my moods contributed to my children making a choice that they didn't want to stay, that's how desperate I was.
>   ...
>   So you're considering her survival, whether she'll survive or not?
>   Whether she'd stay with me yes.
>   And I suggest you're considering her survival because you know that you've killed the other three when you've been in a dark mood, what do you say about that?
>   No.

Mr Maxwell asked Kathy about an entry she had written which contained the phrase: 'With Sarah all I wanted was her to shut up. And one day she did.'

> You say, 'With Sarah, all I wanted was her to shut up'. Do you see that?
>   Yes.

Were you sad that Sarah had died?

Yes, of course.

But, you see, that seems somewhat – I've used this word before – a heartless way to describe this baby of yours who died, 'All I wanted her to do was shut up'?

It's not heartless at all.

Okay.

There wouldn't be a mother in this room who hasn't – with their baby incessantly crying, hasn't wished that they'd stop.

And then you say, 'All I want her to do is shut up, and one day she did'?

Well, she did, she died.

So, one day you got what you wanted?

No, that's not what I wanted.

Am I misreading, am I misunderstanding that, am I?

Absolutely.

You're saying you wanted – 'all' you wanted, was her to 'shut up, and one day she did'. You're the mother, you've described her death like that. What I'm putting to you is, do you not even concede that may be a heartless way of describing it?

Not from where I stood, no.

One thing I had learned about Kathy, from her history and from her closest friends, was that she could be very blunt in the way she faced up to the tragedies in her life.

'With Sarah all I wanted was her to shut up. And one day she did' may have sounded shocking and heartless, but her friends would say that this was typical of her: she told it as it was – the plain, unvarnished truth, and it didn't mean that she didn't love Sarah, or grieve for her; it was, quite simply, her own style of truth-telling, of addressing the reality of what had occurred.

Mr Maxwell eventually landed on the phrase most often quoted by Kathy's detractors as being a confession to killing Sarah: 'she left with a bit of help'.

So you're saying there that you were that bit of help?

No, I'm saying that God, higher power, or another decision, or even my children, Sarah deciding that she didn't want to [stay] was the bit of help, not me.

What I'm suggesting to you is that that's one of the closest places that you have come in the diaries to admitting your guilt of killing Sarah. What do you say about that?

I say it's me admitting how badly responsible I felt, and I will always feel that way.

Anyone sitting in the courtroom that day, witnessing the intense and, at times, hostile cross-examination, might have assumed that they were witnessing a trial and not an inquiry.

And there was more to come.

31

'THE ORDINARY, PLAIN MEANING'

As Mr Maxwell stepped away from the lectern where he had spent several hours challenging Kathy to admit that she had murdered her children, Craig Folbigg's counsel, Margaret Cunneen, stepped forward and launched into a second cross-examination, which covered a great deal of the same ground.

To Jeremy Morris, Kathy's counsel, this seemed patently unreasonable, and he objected that Margaret Cunneen 'does not have a general right of cross-examination on all issues outside her interest in protecting her client's reputation or character'. Her client was Kathy's former husband Craig, and nothing so far had brought his reputation or character into question.

Mr Blanch dismissed the objection, telling Mr Morris: 'Yes, well, I think she's allowed to ask those questions. I'll allow the questions.' He didn't elaborate on his reason for doing so.

There followed many more hours of cross-examination, none of it having a direct bearing on Craig's reputation or character. Ms Cunneen was permitted to go over nearly all of the same ground that Mr Maxwell had already covered. And Kathy, having acquitted herself robustly with the aggressive approach Mr Maxwell had taken, was back in the ring, fending off punches from a second opponent.

Even so, she applied herself to the task of offering helpful explanations about the entries she had written.

Ms Cunneen read out one extract that Kathy had written, in which, as she so often did in her journals, she blamed herself for her children's deaths:

I truly deserve anything life throws at me, so my philosophy
is, whatever happens, happens & it's the way it shall be. I'm
going to try my hardest this time. If anything does happen,
I will just leave & try to let Craig go in peace and start
again. No, I wouldn't. I'm not that brave.

Ms Cunneen said: 'I'm suggesting to you that you were showing an insight and some kind of remorse for what you had done, that you deserve anything life throws at you after what you'd done with your other children?'

'Incorrect,' Kathy replied. 'I felt that I deserved whatever bad things were happening in my life because of how much of a failure and – sorry ...'

Her composure broke, and she wept.

Returning to the same extract after a short break, the following exchange took place:

So 'I'm going to try my hardest this time' means that you
are going to try hard not to lose control and kill the baby?
  No, it is, I just had a belief that I had to try my best and
succeed, I was determined to succeed.
  You knew what you had done before was wrong?
  I didn't do anything before, I don't know why any of my
children died, but I didn't kill them.
  You did kill them all, didn't you?
  No, no I didn't.
  And your references throughout both of these books, don't
point in any other direction but that you killed them and you
knew you had, but you wanted to try again and do better?
  No I didn't kill my children and these diaries are a
record of just how depressed and how much trouble I was
having and all of the issues that go with that.

The following day, Kathy arrived at court with her hair swept back severely, to face the ordeal of Ms Cunneen repeating the same accusations again and again and again.

The cross-examination was blunt:

> You knew that you had asphyxiated your other three
> children when you lost control of your temper, when they
> wouldn't sleep as you wanted them to.
> No.
> Isn't that right?
> No, that's not right.

Ms Cunneen took exception to the way Kathy described her father in one of her diary entries.

> 'So many things point to the fact that I am not meant to be.
> Unwanted at birth, a father who was so selfish,
> unthoughtful, that he took my mother from me and ruined
> my life from that one action.'
> Yes.
> You considered him selfish and unthoughtful for
> murdering your mother?
> I had no other way to look at it, yes.
> You didn't say he was an evil dreadful murderer?
> I didn't know him. Why, why would I say such words
> about someone I don't even know?

At one point, Ms Cunneen made a comment that I found quite shocking. The to and fro between her and Kathy centred on the meaning of 'terrible things' and what Ms Cunneen described as Kathy's 'lexicon'. She addressed Kathy as 'Madam'.

It began with Kathy explaining when she had or hadn't 'lost it' with her children:

> I never lost it with Caleb. I don't recall ever losing it with
> Patrick. Did I lose it with Sarah due to frustration and all
> the issues I was having, yes. I've never denied that, and I've
> written and fully admit that, yes, I, I lost it that time with

Laura and that particular time was quite stressful even, and distressing even, for me.

You say that you similarly lost it with Sarah?

Yes.

In the same sort of way that you later lost it with Laura?

In a, in the way that, incessant crying and I've had to walk away to take a deep breath, then yes.

How did you lose it? Walking away and taking a deep breath seems like you're handling it.

I didn't look at it like that. I looked at it as I'm not handling this at all.

So what were the 'terrible things' that you did?

For me the 'terrible things' are anything. As I said, it's a broad spectrum of things that I'm using the word terrible for. It could be me placing my child down to let her cry for even thirty seconds. That's a terrible thing in my view.

You only thought that it was selfish and thoughtless of your father to kill your mother.

What has that got to do with what you're trying to refer to here?

I'm just trying to get into your lexicon, into the way you use words.

As I say before, the actions of my father and my father in general, he does not crop up much in my life and my thoughts at all, so I'm refusing to have it enforced on me which is what I'm feeling you're trying to do, that he has anything to do with my writings in these diaries at such a late stage.

My point, madam, is this: that you don't even describe your father's killing of your mother as terrible, only selfish and thoughtless, and here you have admitted that you did terrible things as a result of stress in relation to your other children, don't you?

My father killing my mother, it's just an assumed terrible thing. I, I don't think I would need to be stating that anywhere. Why would that not be a terrible, why would that, not be an awful thing?

Of course it's an awful thing, but you only referred to it as a selfish and thoughtless thing because you were only thinking of yourself, weren't you?

Of course I was. I was lamenting my father's actions as to how my own life had ended up. Of course I was talking about myself. They're my diaries. It's my thoughts and they are about myself.

Yes.

Yes.

Well, poor Kathy.

At times, yes.

It seemed to me, and others I spoke to afterwards, that the remark 'Well, poor Kathy' was delivered with undisguised sarcasm.

When Ms Cunneen allowed her to, Kathy explained what her diaries meant to her, and why she wrote them:

My diaries are a pouring out of every fear, every thought – negative, positive – every emotion, anything that was concerning me, anything at all, they were all poured into this diary. They were a way for me – as has been explained, I used those diaries as a friend and a confidant and, if you're having a discussion with your friend and confidant, are you expecting that friend and confidant to then go around telling everybody about it? You don't. So, I'm not expecting that people are going to be reading my diaries.

Yes, and so this was your 'friend and confidant', this journal?

Yes.

And because it was your confidant, you felt free to divulge the deepest secrets of your mind?

I felt alone, I felt lonely, I had limited people to talk to – or I felt that I had limited people to talk to. These diaries were something that I could empty my head, get rid of emotions, try to figure out what was going on, how to figure out where I was going with life and they are — that's all they are.

Ms Cunneen turned to the entry in Kathy's journal where she wrote: 'Wouldn't of handled another one like Sarah. She saved her life by being different.'

She asked Kathy what she meant by this.

> That's a mystical representation. That's me reflecting on my beliefs as in karma and the children talking to each other and God and all of those sorts of beliefs that I had.
>
> That's a fanciful answer which cannot be believed, I'd suggest to you.
>
> It's of no concern to me whether it can or cannot be believed. It was my belief at the time when I wrote this diary.

Mr Blanch interjected:

> Are you saying to me that you believe that there was some supernatural power that took the other three children away from you and you were concerned that that same supernatural power would take Laura away from you, and that she saved her life by being different?
>
> Yes.
>
> On that basis?
>
> Yes, along those lines, yes your Honour.

Ms Cunneen was at her most direct when she interrogated Kathy about Sarah's death:

> Then you say, 'With Sarah all I wanted was her to shut up and one day she did'?
>
> Because that's what happened, I'm merely making an observation that's —
>
> With Sarah you didn't walk away, did you?

Yes, I did.

With Sarah you wanted her to shut up, you wanted the battle of the wills to cease and you shut her up didn't you?

No, yes, I wanted maybe the battle of the wills to cease, yes, I wanted her to sleep better, I wanted to sleep better, I wanted our life to go as it should've.

And you made her sleep, didn't you?

No.

You put something over her face so that she couldn't breathe?

No.

And you killed her?

No.

Ms Cunneen returned to one of the most quoted entries in all of Kathy's diaries, from 28 January 1998, when Laura was five months old: '... she left with a bit of help'.

'And she left with a bit of help.' You mean she died, don't you?

She died, yes.

'Bit of help'?

From God, fate or something else. Not me.

There's a sardonic element to that isn't there, 'with a bit of help'? There's a black humour to that?

No, absolutely not. There's no humour in it at all.

I wasn't alone in feeling that the way in which Kathy was cross-examined was entirely inappropriate. Professor Cunliffe holds strong views about what she sees as the lack of respect shown to Kathy when she volunteered to come and explain her diaries.

At times, her treatment at the 2019 inquiry felt more like 'an exercise in ritual humiliation', Professor Cunliffe suggested.

Dr Betts also took issue with Kathy's cross-examination, and the inference that she should have expressed herself in a different way in her diaries, if indeed she was an innocent mother.

'Where's the rule book about what you're meant to write when your babies are suddenly dying,' Dr Betts asked when I spoke to her some time later. 'It's almost like, there's this template of motherhood that she violated.'

On the final day of Kathy's cross-examination, she was guided by her counsel Jeremy Morris through some of the more positive entries she had written in her diaries. One of them was an entry she wrote in August 1990, when Patrick was two and a half months old:

> Bumer of a day except that I have my son, husband & my home there isn't much going for us at the moment. Lifes being a real bitch! Seriously thinking that moving down to Melbourne is the only way that we are going to get ahead. Being scared of leaving here isn't a good enough excuse to stay. Opportunities are gone here. We need a fresh start somewhere else. A place where opportunities to have a great life are boundless because of the size & population of the city. I think that pats future would be better if we moved away. Melbourne has top schools & education system. Think about it?

Mr Morris made the point that here she was looking to the future, and anticipating a time when Patrick would go to school.

Mr Morris also referred to the allegation made by Mr Maxwell, that she was heartless.

> It was suggested to you in broad terms at each of those places that one of the entries in your diary in which you compared Sarah with Laura was heartless, and a heartless form of expression. It was also suggested to you that you were asked to comment on whether you had no bond with Sarah, or that otherwise you had been disparaging to Sarah. Did you love Sarah?
>
>> Absolutely, yes.

>   Did you feel grief at her death?
>   Of course, still feel it now, yes.
>   While we're at it, did you love Caleb and feel grief at his death?
>   Yes, of course.
>   And Patrick?
>   And Patrick, yes.
>   And Laura?
>   And Laura as well.

Mr Morris offered Kathy the opportunity to give her diaries some context.

>   You told his Honour over the last couple of days that you had a view that your mood would impact upon others, including your children?
>   Yes.
>   Where did that come from?
>   From a basis of my own upbringing.
>   Tell his Honour about it, what happened?
>   Your Honour my own upbringing was if I, even as a child, if my mood affected my mother there was a response to that, there was a consequence to that, so I therefore grew up believing that I had to always keep any negative or emotions or moods in check because I didn't wish them to inflict on other people and I never wanted to burden other people and I had learnt that if I did so there was always a consequence of some sort to that.

On the final day of her evidence, Gail Furness addressed the question of what exactly Kathy meant by different words in her journals, and whether she used them interchangeably:

>   You gave evidence that you meant 'similar things by different words'. Do you recall that?
>   Yes.

So, for example, words like 'frustrated', 'angry', 'terrible', 'cruel', all meant more or less the same things?

Yes.

Now, you understand again that his Honour's task is to look afresh at the evidence, which includes your diary entries. You understand that?

Yes.

And part of that task is to look at what the entries mean?

Yes.

You accept that the ordinary plain meaning of those words which you have put together can objectively be seen as different? Do you understand what I mean?

Yes.

You accept that?

Yes, but I – I'm also – was trying to explain that, at the time of writing my diaries, in the use of those words, that's not how my mind worked.

I understand that and I'm not revisiting the evidence you've given as to what you meant —

Yeah.

— by each of those entries. I'm asking whether you accept, and I think you do, that objectively looking at those various words they, by their ordinary meaning, have in fact different meanings. Do you accept that?

Yes.

Kathy's explanations of what she meant by what she wrote were being set against the 'ordinary, plain meaning' ascribed to them by the counsel who cross-examined her.

It seemed to me that a public standard of what the words meant was being preferred to her own, private way of expressing herself.

The cross-examination endured by Kathy had been brutal. Sixty-nine times, she was challenged to admit she had killed her children, and sixty-nine times she denied it.

For Kathy, it must have felt like a kind of prolonged inquisitorial torture. Once or twice, she cracked, shedding tears at the memory of her children who had died. But overall, she met the challenge head-on, with what her friends regarded as admirable resilience, maintaining a remarkable composure.

And at the end of the third day, she was driven back to prison, to await Mr Blanch's findings.

32

'HOPE CAN DESTROY ONE'S SOUL'

On Monday, 22 July 2019, just eleven days after Professor Vinuesa and her colleagues had sent their final report to the inquiry, arguing that the *CALM2* mutation was likely pathogenic, Reginald Blanch released his verdict on the evidence he had heard.

The announcement came suddenly and unexpectedly, with almost no notice given to Kathy's legal team, who had worked around the clock for weeks after the hearings finished on 1 May, to complete her final submissions. The submissions were due on 18 June, and one week before, on 11 June, Jeremy Morris's father Linton Morris QC passed away. It was a difficult time for him. Even so, he and Stuart Gray continued to work non-stop, and Mr Blanch sent a note conveying his condolences, with a short extension of time for Kathy's lawyers to get the 400 pages of submissions filed.

Any hope of Mr Blanch concluding that there was reasonable doubt surrounding Kathy's convictions was dashed. His most damning verdict was that 'The significant investigations conducted by the Inquiry into the four deaths and the ALTE have failed to identify a reasonable natural explanation for the five events, individually or together.

'The investigations of the Inquiry have instead produced evidence that reinforces Ms Folbigg's guilt.'

Shortly before the report was officially released, the New South Wales Attorney General, Mark Speakman, walked into a park in London, where he was on leave, and gave a press conference, declaring that there was now no doubt about Kathy's guilt.

Mr Speakman acknowledged that the jury at her trial had been misled by the Crown's assertion that there had never been a case of three deaths in a family that could be attributed to unidentified natural causes and reiterated that that had been the catalyst for his decision to order an inquiry.

Significantly, he conceded that: 'Mr Blanch found that taking the medical evidence alone for each of the four children, you couldn't decide one way or another whether Ms Folbigg was guilty. But,' he added, 'taking all the evidence into account, and in particular the damming evidence of her diary entries, that were tendered at the trial, it was beyond reasonable doubt that Ms Folbigg was guilty.'

Summarising the remarks made by Mr Blanch in his final report, he described the evidence given by Kathy over two and a half days of cross-examination as 'basically a pack of lies, and a pack of obfuscation, trying to disguise the real truth that she had killed her four children'.

He added that in his opinion, 'I think that this reinforces confidence in the justice system, it puts beyond doubt Ms Folbigg's conviction.'

Mr Speakman made a point of paying tribute to Craig Folbigg, telling the assembled media: 'I don't think any of us can imagine what it must be like to lose four children. And then to lose four children at the hands of your wife, their mother, and then go through twenty years of litigation, of criminal proceedings, the pain and distress is just unimaginable. My impression of Mr Folbigg is that he's incredibly stoical and I admire him greatly for that.'

Mr Speakman said that the suffering that Craig and his family had gone through 'weighed heavily on me in deciding whether or not to have this inquiry'.

Kathy learned about the verdict while watching a TV report in Silverwater jail. She wept, and it took all of her self-control not to break down completely.

I was on holiday in Venice at the time and was stunned to hear the result. The judgment that the evidence Kathy had given was 'basically a pack of lies' seemed beyond belief, and I gave an interview to the ABC, saying that the verdict handed down by Mr Blanch was highly contentious and would certainly be contested.

Kathy's legal team and supporters reacted with disbelief and dismay. They were aghast at what they saw as Mr Blanch's reluctance to acknowledge the strength of the evidence that Sarah and Laura might have died from a genetic mutation.

How, they reasoned, could that not amount to reasonable doubt?

'It was a heartbreaking result, because at that time it really felt like this had been our shot,' Emma Cunliffe told me. 'It felt like Kathleen's legal team had not had a fair opportunity to press the fullness of the evidence for her innocence. And knowing how rare post-conviction inquiries are in New South Wales, it truly felt like this was the end of it.'

Emma told me that 'What rang in my ears for weeks after that report was handed down, was that first letter that Kathleen wrote me when I wrote to her about my book, which contained that line, "I've learned in here that hope can destroy as much as enliven one's soul." It felt like it was the destruction of a hope.

'It was devastating because it felt that justice had not been done.'

Professor Vinuesa too, was completely shocked. 'I thought this is it. I mean, it's reasonable doubt,' she told me later. 'We've got the leader in the field, the two leaders, because both Michael Toft Overgaard and Peter Schwartz signed our last report, so I could not believe it. I was devastated, and I just felt it was such an injustice.'

Professor Vinuesa was so appalled that for a time she couldn't bring herself to read the report. She asked Dave Wallace to summarise it for her. In her opinion, it was biased against Kathy, and as a Spaniard living in Australia, she was asking herself: 'Is this the legal system of the twenty-first century?'

As far as she was concerned, the top two experts in the world had written that the *CALM2* mutation was the likely cause of death for Sarah and Laura, and that was the end of the matter. How could that not engender reasonable doubt?

Mr Blanch himself acknowledged that there *was* a reasonable identifiable natural cause of death for Laura. 'Having regard to the medical evidence in isolation, it is a reasonable possibility that the myocarditis found in Laura's heart at autopsy was either incidental to her death, or that it was fatal,' he wrote. This was the evidence we had focused on in our *Australian Story* episode.

However, he added, 'It is also reasonably possible on the medical evidence that Laura's death was caused by an asphyxial event.'

Mr Blanch also conceded that the medical evidence 'when considered in isolation and not in light of any other evidence, neither proves nor disproves that any of the children were smothered'. It was of course literally impossible to *disprove* smothering, because smothering can leave no physical traces whatsoever – and no traces of smothering were found in any of the children.

In a further comment Mr Blanch said, 'In respect of the *CALM2* variant found in Ms Folbigg, Sarah and Laura, I prefer the expertise and evidence of Professors Skinner and Kirk and Dr Buckley ... I find there is no reasonable possibility that this variant caused the death of Sarah or Laura.' Professor Vinuesa, for one, found this comment inexplicable.

Having listened to the evidence Kathy had given about her diaries, and the evidence in the listening device transcripts, Mr Blanch concluded that she had been 'in many respects untruthful, unbelievable and made deliberate attempts to obscure the fact that she committed the offences of which she was convicted.

'It remains that the only conclusion reasonably open is that somebody intentionally caused harm to the children, and smothering was the obvious method. The evidence pointed to no person other than Ms Folbigg.'

There was of course one listening device transcript, which had been redacted by the inquiry and kept from public view, in which Craig Folbigg laid out in detail exactly how *he* could have killed the children and what his motive for doing so might have been.

'The evidence at the Inquiry does not cause me to have any reasonable doubt as to the guilt of Kathleen Megan Folbigg for the offences of which she was convicted,' Mr Blanch concluded. 'Indeed, as indicated, the evidence which has emerged at the Inquiry, particularly her own explanations and behaviour in respect of her diaries, makes her guilt of these offences even more certain.'

Spurred on as much by anger as distress, Professor Vinuesa vowed not to let the case drop and, in an inspired move, she went straight to Anna-Maria Arabia, Chief Executive of the Australian Academy of Science, to ask for the Academy's help. She knew Anna-Maria slightly, and 'I thought that, look, she's a woman, and she's very intelligent, and she understands science.'

Anna-Maria Arabia remembers the meeting well. 'She came to see me because she was extremely concerned about the outcome of the first inquiry, on two fronts. She was concerned about the fact that science had not been heard and concerned about the way she was treated, and the way that expert evidence had been received and heard at the inquiry, and she didn't know what to do, as in, she was desperate to do something, but I guess, was looking at avenues for support.'

Professor Vinuesa asked Ms Arabia for her opinion: 'What can science do? Can the Academy do something? So she said, "Carola. You are very lucky, because today we've got a Council meeting here and the president John Shine is here. Why don't you come and talk to John?"'

Professor Shine, an Australian biochemist and molecular biologist, rose to fame in the scientific community after cloning the first human hormone genes, a breakthrough that led to the development of gene-cloning techniques that helped transform the world of biotechnology.

Accompanied by her colleague Professor Matthew Cook, Professor Vinuesa met with Professor Shine. 'He got it immediately,' she says. Professor Shine told the two scientists that he wanted to know more about the case before committing the Academy's support to Kathy's cause, but also, that the Academy was engaged in an ongoing conversation with the legal system, and wanted to make sure that science was heard and taken seriously. It certainly hadn't been, so far, in Kathy's case.

From the Academy's point of view, Anna-Maria Arabia was careful to assure Professor Shine that, 'We cannot and should not have a view on her innocence – that's for the justice system to figure out. We just need to talk about the science.'

Ms Arabia said, 'That enabled [Professor Shine] to have confidence in me, to pursue this with Carola.'

At the end of October, Kathy's lawyers filed a summons in the Supreme Court of New South Wales, seeking a judicial review of the Blanch inquiry's report and its findings.

The summons sought an order to quash the report, reasoning that Justice Blanch had demonstrated 'apprehended bias' in his conduct of the inquiry, by constraining its scope, by refusing Jeremy Morris leave to lead evidence about the context of Kathy's diaries, and by allowing Margaret Cunneen, who was representing Craig, to cross-examine Kathy beyond his 'limited interest ... to protect his reputation'.

The summons argued that Mr Blanch had failed to consider the fresh genetic evidence which was submitted to the inquiry towards the end of the proceedings, and he had failed to admit into evidence the redacted transcript of the conversation between Kathy and Craig, which was secretly recorded by the police.

The summons also stated that Justice Blanch had 'failed to apply the correct legal test of "reasonable doubt" to the evidence before the inquiry'.

On 29 February the following year, as the COVID pandemic began to take hold around the world, Professor Vinuesa was one of five speakers who were invited to talk to a gathering to mark the sixtieth birthday of Peter Yates, a former Macquarie banker who had previously run Kerry Packer's media empire, who also chaired the Australian Science Media Centre, and the Centre for Personalised Immunology at the Australian National University, whose directors were Professors Vinuesa and Cook.

The gathering took place in Old Parliament House in Canberra, and the theme of her talk was 'personalised medicine through genetics'. She told me later: 'I thought, "This is an opportunity to talk about this case, because, you know, it's terrible. Nobody's doing anything about it."'

Professor Vinuesa pointed out that Kathy's convictions for smothering her children occurred despite the fact that there was no history of abuse in the family and no signs of smothering.

'At the time of the trial, genomics was in its infancy,' she told her audience, 'and the geneticists involved in Kathleen's case couldn't find a cause for the deaths of any of the children. Instead, a British paediatrician's theory appears to have coloured the evidence.

'Meadow's Law was that one SIDS death is a tragedy, two is suspicious, and three is murder until proven otherwise. Roy Meadow has since been thoroughly discredited by statisticians and scientists. Kathleen has always denied smothering her children, but entries in her diaries in which she described how she felt, that fate was punishing her, and how she blamed herself for her children's deaths, were dissected and interpreted as confessions of guilt.'

The professor stressed that there was medical and pathological evidence of illness for all four children: for Caleb, difficulty in swallowing; for Patrick, epilepsy; for Sarah, bacterial lung infection; and for Laura, myocarditis, and that Kathy herself had suffered several witnessed episodes of fainting suddenly, including the episode after a school swimming race.

'Fainting in this manner is typical of cardiac arrhythmias that can cause sudden death in infancy and adulthood,' she explained.

The professor said she found it 'bewildering that the maudlin writings of a grief-stricken mother could be given more evidentiary weight than a novel mutation – a mutation that was classified by all the geneticists involved as more than 90% likely to be pathogenic.'

Professor Vinuesa's address to her highly engaged and qualified audience was brief, but passionate, and she concluded it with the avowed hope that, in the next few decades, 'we will see an increased understanding of genetics among the general public, lawyers and forensic pathologists.'

She ended by saying: 'I would also like to see more communication and collaboration between the legal and medical fields so that cases like Kathleen's can be peer reviewed, to give scientific evidence the necessary weight in court.'

Peter Yates told me that his response to the professor's address was that 'There's something really wrong here, because either Carola is overstating what's actually happened, or, otherwise, if she's not, what's actually happened is awful.'

Two of the guests at the birthday celebration listened closely to Professor Vinuesa's address, and approached her afterwards to tell her they wanted to do something about it.

'They were fascinated by this case, and they were shocked that science had not been able to persuade the legal system,' the professor told me later.

The two guests who responded so positively were Leon Kempler, a former Director of the Royal Children's Hospital Foundation, and Mark Rudder, a founding partner of the strategic and public affairs consulting firm GRACosway. Both, with Peter Yates, would prove to be central to the ongoing effort to shine a light on Kathy's case, and on the science that had been so rudely rebuffed at the first inquiry.

'They were very genuine,' Professor Vinuesa told me. 'Leon Kempler was super stressed about the whole thing. He spent the whole lunch asking me about Kathleen, and he took a lot of personal interest. He's now a good friend of hers. He visited her a few times. He talked to a lot of his old colleagues and legal people, and is connected to very influential people in the legal system and elsewhere.'

Mr Kempler, in turn, is a fervent admirer of the professor: 'I put Carola on a pedestal,' he told me frankly. 'A gifted scientist, a decent and fearless woman who in the Folbigg case wanted "right to be done".'

Mr Kempler said that when he listened to Professor Vinuesa's account of her experience, he felt that there was 'a moral obligation that the science and the scientists should be respected.'

The problem, he said, was that 'science and the law do not share a common language'.

'I told Carola that I would help her,' he told me, and help he did. Mr Kempler at the time chaired the advisory council for Questacon, which aims to further Australia's engagement with science, technology and innovation, and he raised Kathy's case at their meetings, 'and with everyone I met from the fields of science, academia, law, industry, and all levels of politics and the community'. As he did so, he encountered an ingrained prejudice about Kathy's story.

'People who were aware of the case said losing four children in one family was impossible, and that her diaries were the equivalent of a confession. What was even more surprising to me was that paediatricians that I respected were closed-minded and convinced of Kathleen's guilt without ever having looked at the data.'

Mark Rudder and his team would also prove to be invaluable, lobbying journalists to report on the fresh genetic evidence, and if needed, tapping some on the shoulder whenever an article was written that needed correcting.

Crucially, Professor Vinuesa had the backing of Anna-Maria Arabia, CEO of the Australian Academy of Science, who described her to me as 'tenacious, persuasive, relentless and thorough,' and as someone who was 'devoted to accuracy and in this case, unsurfacing the truth'.

At the beginning of March 2020, Professor Vinuesa wrote to Leon Kempler, telling him that Professor Michael Toft

Overgaard now had additional laboratory data showing that the *CALM2* variant found in Kathy's daughters 'impairs the function of the protein and would therefore be expected to cause cardiac arrhythmias'.

She added: 'This will soon be submitted to a top international, peer-reviewed journal.'

Professor Cook and Dr Arsov had contributed to the analysis and interpretation of the data and shared the same view.

At the same time, Professor Vinuesa and Professor Cook wrote to Professor John Shine at the Australian Academy of Science, expressing the view that the Blanch inquiry had been premature in reaching its findings, and that 'there is strong scientific evidence to suggest that Sarah and Laura had a calmodulinopathy and died from sudden cardiac death'.

With Dave Wallace's help, Professor Vinuesa had started the ball rolling, and the fightback had begun.

33

EUROPACE

Carola Vinuesa, the charismatic Spanish immunogeneticist who had headed the Canberra team at the Blanch inquiry, wouldn't take the inquiry's findings lying down. Defiant and determined, she set about taking the discovery that she and her colleagues had made much further.

Two years later, I interviewed her at length, asking her how she felt when Reginald Blanch handed down his judgment.

'To be honest, I felt outrage,' she said. 'I knew that those conclusions were wrong.'

Professor Vinuesa and her colleagues had taken issue with the Sydney team's assessment of the *CALM* variant as being a variant of 'unknown significance', and in particular they had taken issue with the evidence given by Professor Jonathan Skinner.

Professor Skinner told the inquiry that there had been no calmodulin deaths recorded in infants while asleep. But Professor Schwartz revealed that the registry had records of young children dying while asleep.

In his report, Mr Blanch had preferred the Sydney team's view, writing: 'It remains the case per Professor Skinner's evidence, that there is no reported case of a death of such nature – asymptomatic sudden cardiac death in infancy during a sleep period – being associated with a calmodulin variant. If so associated, Sarah and Laura's deaths would be the first and second reported cases of their kind.'

'So what did you decide to do?' I asked Professor Vinuesa.

'At that point, we felt that we had to get this knowledge in the public domain,' she replied. 'We had to get it published, and an important missing piece of evidence at the time was the functional validation of the variant.' The scientists needed to answer this question: was the variant actually pathogenic in practice, and not just in theory?

She explained that, 'When we find a variant that has never been reported before, one can perform tests in the laboratory to prove that it is damaging. I approached the expert, Michael Toft Overgaard, who has validated several calmodulin mutations in the past, and he agreed to do this.'

Professor Toft Overgaard, then Head of Chemistry and Bioscience at Aalborg University in Denmark, led the experiments which explored how the mutation affects the heart. But he wasn't alone.

In Canada, the team collaborated with Professor Wayne SR Chen, from the Department of Physiology and Pharmacology at the University of Calgary. In the US they collaborated with Associate Professor Ivy E Dick, from the Department of Physiology at the University of Maryland School of Medicine.

'Now, these experiments showed that the Folbigg calmodulin mutation was as damaging as other mutations that have been shown to cause sudden, unexpected death in children and in infants, both while asleep and while awake,' Professor Vinuesa told me.

What happened next revealed how anxious some in the medical community apparently were to prevent this new information from being published.

With the help of the accomplished young lawyer and scientist Dave Wallace, and her colleagues Professor Cook, Dr Arsov and Professor Toft Overgaard, Professor Vinuesa had assembled an international team of twenty-seven scientists from America, Canada, France, Australia, Denmark and Italy to conduct the tests and assess the results.

The team combined Professor Toft Overgaard's laboratory findings with their own genetic analysis and with the information from the Italian registry detailing the previous deaths of infants that were caused by calmodulin mutations. In June 2020, they submitted a paper detailing their findings to the respected medical journal *Europace,* which is based in the university city of Oxford in the UK. The paper was peer reviewed by experts in the field and accepted for publication, with a scheduled date of August 2020.

In the normal course of events, the paper would have been published without further delay. However, this was a paper that had the potential to stir considerable controversy in both the scientific and legal fields. At its heart, it was saying that at least two of a convicted child murderer's children most probably died from a rare genetic mutation, that the courts and the inquiry had got it wrong, and therefore by implication, that a terrible miscarriage of justice had been done to Kathy.

The authors wanted to make this clear in the paper by naming Kathy in the main body of their report, and I wanted to be the first to write an article breaking the news of this development. But in order to do so, I needed to ask Professor Skinner and his colleagues whether they agreed with the paper's conclusions. They had to be offered a right of reply to the allegation being made in the paper, that the information they had given to the inquiry was wrong.

As the paper contained specific criticisms of the information given to the inquiry by Professor Skinner, I contacted him directly. The only comment he would make on the record was that 'I would be interested to review the new evidence'.

My belief was that he might not have been aware of the registry's research when he declared that there were no records of young children who had carried a calmodulin mutation dying suddenly in their sleep. But he wouldn't confirm this to me on the record.

On Wednesday, 19 August 2020, Professor Vinuesa announced that the paper was due to be published the same day in a speech she gave to a joint symposium of the Australian Academies of Law and of Science.

But in fact, that hadn't happened. Without her knowledge, a 'letter from Sydney' was sent to the editors of *Europace,* in an apparent attempt to prevent the publication of the paper. The unknown sender of the letter, who has never come out into the open, took issue with the views expressed in the paper's discussion of the data revealed in the experiments, and it had the effect of delaying its final publication for another three months, until November 2020.

That, though, didn't prevent the ABC from publishing the paper's findings online in an article I had written, on the same day that Professor Vinuesa gave her address.

The delay in publishing their paper was profoundly disappointing for the authors. The amended version omitted Kathy's name and the names of the children from the main body of the manuscript, although numerous references to her case remained in links and footnotes provided in the paper. It was entitled: *'Infanticide vs Inherited Cardiac Arrhythmias'*, and the first line, even without naming Kathy directly, made it clear that the paper was referring to her case: 'In 2003, an Australian woman was convicted by a jury of smothering and killing her four children over a 10-year period.'

'We needed to de-identify Kathleen Folbigg and we also needed to remove any mention of the inquiry, as well as certain remarks in the discussion where Professor Schwartz was trying to explain what had gone wrong in reaching the conclusions that had been reached at the inquiry,' the professor explained to me later.

'The problem,' she added, was that 'anyone interested in the genetics of the Folbigg case could no longer find the article using search engines, unless they knew the title.'

The work carried out in Denmark and in laboratories in Canada and the United States established, to the authors' satisfaction, that the G114R mutation was pathogenic, significantly increasing the likelihood that in the case of Kathy's two girls, it had been fatal. The lethal mutation appeared to have been triggered by the infections they were suffering from at the time – in Laura's case, her myocarditis.

While not the main focus of their experiments, the international team also reported a different genetic mutation found in Kathy's two boys, Patrick and Caleb, that could conceivably explain their deaths as well – although this was never established.

Both boys carry two mutated copies of a gene known as *BSN*, which when defective, causes early onset lethal epilepsy in mice. Coincidentally, Patrick had suffered epilepsy for four months before he died.

I spoke to Professor Toft Overgaard, who told me that their findings showed that the Folbigg *CALM2* mutation 'significantly impairs the function of the calmodulin protein to the same degree as two other calmodulin mutations that are recognized as severely arrhythmogenic, predisposing to sudden cardiac death in infancy and childhood, including during periods of sleep'.

The professor suggested a metaphor for this.

'If the heart cell was a car, the Folbigg car has a partly dysfunctional brake,' he said. 'This works out fine for most situations, and you might adapt to this in your driving style. But if you end up in a critical situation, where you need the full potential of a normal brake, this will be catastrophic.'

The scientists, in their paper, said their new evidence challenged the Sydney team's assertion – as expressed in a late submission to the inquiry – that the G114R variant found in the girls was unlikely to be pathogenic because it would be 'very unusual to have a disease causing variant responsible for deaths at such young ages also present in a healthy person in her 50s'.

Professor Schwartz said Professor Skinner's statements 'incorrectly but effectively reduced the possibility that the [inquiry] would consider that the two Folbigg girls had died a natural death, related to their genetic defect'. And he argued that the understanding of inherited cardiac arrhythmias must impact on the way legal systems react to the occurrence of multiple infant and child sudden deaths in one family.

'Whenever someone dies suddenly, without obvious explanations, and a molecular autopsy identifies a mutation in a gene known to cause sudden death, then this is sufficient to diagnose that particular disease,' he wrote.

Professor Schwartz said that, if only one child in the Folbigg family had died, and with the evidence of such a mutation, 'this would be an "open-and-shut" case with the diagnosis of "sudden death due to a lethal arrythmia related to a Calmodulin mutation".

'This makes it absolutely necessary to perform a molecular autopsy searching for genes associated with sudden death, before almost automatically assuming that the children have been smothered.'

When I wrote my piece for the ABC, I asked Professor Arthur Wilde, Head of the Department of Cardiology at the University of Amsterdam, and a member of the European Reference Network, GUARD-Heart, to comment on the *Europace* paper, and its challenge to Professor Skinner's evidence.

He suggested that Professor Skinner might not have had access to all the necessary data from the registry, and to all the relevant data that had been published, before suggesting that the G114R variant was unlikely to be pathogenic.

He added: 'Caution should be taken to use expert witnesses in sensitive cases like this one without full disclosure of all information.'

One of Professor Skinner's concerns with identifying the *CALM2* variant as the cause of death had been that Kathy herself showed no clear cardiac abnormalities. However, the paper's authors noted that there were several reports of families with lethal *CALM* variants that had asymptomatic carriers.

Professor Wilde told me: 'I certainly do believe that the case should be referred back to another court for a further appeal.'

In his judgment at the end of the inquiry, Justice Blanch conceded that in light of the genetic evidence presented late in the day it was 'plausible that Sarah and Laura may have had a cardiac condition and that raises a possibility it caused their deaths'.

But he said that this was an 'exceptional clinical scenario', and that, when considered 'with all the other evidence in the inquiry', including the diary entries and what he judged to be Kathy's 'lies and obfuscation', the 'only conclusion reasonably open' was that she smothered Sarah and Laura.

He added: 'I do not consider the Inquiry should be re-opened for the purpose of holding further hearings about the *CALM2* variant identified in Sarah and Laura.'

The scientists who made up the *Europace* team strongly disagreed.

Professor Schwartz told me: 'I have no idea whether Kathleen Folbigg is innocent or guilty, but I think that she was sentenced on the basis of incomplete evidence and of incorrect opinions. A fair judicial system would acknowledge this and look again at the case on the basis of the novel evidence.

'Then, it is entirely possible that the Court will confirm the original sentence, but without ignoring the new facts.'

Despite the clear view expressed in the *Europace* paper that the *CALM2* mutation had likely killed Sarah and Laura, there was one more crucial test to carry out. In his letter to Professor Vinuesa in June 2019, Professor Schwartz had speculated that Kathy 'could very well be a case of mosaicism. This could account for a milder phenotype in the mother and a more serious one in the children. It is essential to obtain different sources of DNA from the mother to test for possible mosaicism.'

In September 2020, the professor went to extraordinary lengths to try and establish whether Kathy was indeed a genetic 'mosaic', which she would be if she could be shown to have a mixture of cells in her body with different genetic information. It would mean that she could have been healthy all her life, while carrying a genetic mutation which killed her children. If that could be proved, then almost certainly those scientists who up to now, had remained deeply sceptical, would accept that the mutation had probably proved fatal to Kathy's two daughters.

In order to establish whether this was the case, Professor Vinuesa's team had obtained multiple samples from Kathy, including from her hair, nails and saliva and a drop of blood, which she had produced by cutting herself in prison and sending it to the team on a plaster. They had also obtained a sample of her urine. 'And out of all the samples, the urine looked like a mosaic – a black and white mosaic,' the professor told me.

This was extremely exciting for the Canberra team, because if this was accurate, it could explain why Sarah and Laura had died with the genetic variant, but Kathy hadn't.

'But of course in science,' the professor cautioned, '$N=1$ is not good science.' One test just wasn't enough.

She had a test result which at first sight could break the case wide open, but it hadn't been repeated and confirmed, and she decided against publishing the findings. 'That's something I am proud of,' she told me.

Instead she set about obtaining a second urine sample, but found herself in difficulties, because Kathy was abruptly moved from Silverwater prison to Clarence Correctional Facility, near Grafton, in northern New South Wales. Urine cells don't last well, Grafton was at least a nine-hour drive away, and it would prove to be a real challenge to collect the sample and take it back to Canberra quickly. 'You have to get them back to the lab within hours to extract the DNA before it's degraded,' she explained.

The professor had a friend who was training to get his pilot's licence and had flown small aircraft short distances, and the flight to Grafton would be the longest he had ever attempted. But it seemed to be the only option on offer.

The flight up to Grafton was uneventful, and the professor and her colleagues were met by Tracy Chapman who drove them to the prison. Kathy's sample was handed over and they set off back to Canberra. But as the flight took off and made its way through the clouds, a storm broke, and rain started hammering the small aircraft they were flying in.

'It got very scary, very, very scary to be honest,' Professor Vinuesa told me.

When they finally made it safely back to the lab, the urine cells were not in good shape. Tests were performed, but the result appeared to be negative.

'The quality of the signal was dreadful, but it didn't look like a mosaic,' the professor conceded. The decision to carry out a second test was the right one, but the result was undeniably disappointing.

Even so, Leon Kempler told me that, in his opinion, the *Europace* article was a 'game-changer', and the global experts he had connected with were fascinated and impressed with the paper. 'When I mentioned that Kathleen was still in prison there was surprise, and comments like, how primitive Australia is, that poor woman, and so on.'

It was now more than a year since Reginald Blanch had handed down his judgment that the evidence he had heard had reinforced Kathy's guilt. Professor Vinuesa, too, believed that the fresh genetic evidence could be a game-changer.

It was time to take advantage of this and push even harder for a just outcome for the fifty-three-year-old woman who – the professor believed – should be freed from prison immediately.

34

A NOBEL CAUSE

On 2 March 2021, an extraordinary event unfolded – one unprecedented in the annals of science and the law.

Following on from the petition in 2015, which had led to an unsuccessful inquiry, a second petition was presented to the new Governor of New South Wales, Margaret Beazley, calling for Kathy's unconditional pardon and release.

The petition was signed by – among others – two Nobel laureates, two former Chief Scientists, and in all, ninety eminent scientists, medical practitioners and science advocates. It was drawn up by two of Kathy's legal team, solicitor Rhanee Rego and barrister Dr Robert Cavanagh, and it reflected the outcome of the fresh scientific inquiries which had been led by Professor Vinuesa and her team of scientists, and published in *Europace* the previous November.

It was the first time ever, anywhere in the world, that Nobel laureates had lent their support to a petition calling for a convicted murderer's pardon and release.

Emeritus Professor Elizabeth Blackburn had won her Nobel Prize in 2009; while Professor Peter Doherty became a Nobel laureate in 1996 and Australian of the Year in 1997. Both supported the call for Kathy to be pardoned and freed.

Other prominent supporters included the 2006 Australian of the Year and inventor of the cervical cancer vaccine, Professor Ian Frazer; the former Chief Scientist of Australia Emeritus Professor Ian Chubb; and the former Chief Scientist of Israel Dr Orna Berry.

Suddenly, Kathy's case was propelled into headlines around the world. It was reported by the BBC – in an article I wrote for them – and by CNN, the *New York Times* and other major global news outlets. The articles and TV reports were reaching readers and viewers across the United States and in the UK, where memories of the Sally Clark case were still painfully vivid.

My BBC article asked readers to place themselves in Kathy's position: 'Imagine for a moment what it must feel like if, as a mother, you give birth to four children, one after another, each of whom, as infants, dies from natural causes over a ten year period.

'Then imagine being wrongly accused of smothering them all and being sentenced to 30 years in gaol for four terrible crimes you did not commit.

'That narrative is emerging as potentially, the true story of Kathleen Folbigg, an Australian mother from the Hunter Valley region of New South Wales.

'Branded at her trial in 2003 as "Australia's worst female serial killer", Ms Folbigg has already spent nearly 18 years in prison after being found guilty of the manslaughter of her firstborn Caleb, and the murder of her three subsequent children, Patrick, Sarah and Laura.

'But now, fresh scientific evidence is turning this case on its head.'

Behind the scenes, an ad hoc team of lawyers, businesspeople and philanthropists had been building, with the aim of promoting the scientific breakthrough reported in *Europace*, and publicising the petition as widely as possible. The ultimate aim was Kathy's pardon and release. Headed by Peter Yates, it soon became known as 'Team Folbigg'.

Anna-Maria Arabia remembers the team's new members privately questioning each other's strategies and motivations early on, but says that, once the group started working together, 'We got to performing pretty quickly, and then, when we *were* performing, that team was unstoppable and a source of great inspiration and energy for everyone.'

Anna-Maria Arabia appreciated the unique approach taken by Peter Yates. 'He's a leader. He's a mover and shaker. He's very good at leveraging his network and calling in aid and assistance, whatever it is that we needed,' she told me.

'He's very strategic. He brought a business perspective that others on Team Folbigg didn't have. We all brought a unique perspective, and we all were respected for that unique perspective. So, where I saw science needing to be heard, Peter saw a deal to be closed, but we all wanted the woman to be freed.'

Peter Yates was driven in part by two concerns: first, that the petition wouldn't get listened to by the Attorney General's office, and that would be bad for Kathy.

And secondly, that if such an eminent group of scientists, with such a powerful petition, were ignored by the Attorney General, then 'that was a bad day for science. And so I thought quite hard about, how could I make sure that it was a good day for science; and a good day for science would mean it's going to be a very good day for Kathleen.'

The answer, he concluded, was to create a media storm, 'which is going to bang down the door of the Attorney General's office'.

If nothing else, Mr Yates was always direct, and was never short on ambition, and in a later interview he gave to the *Australian Financial Review*, he explained his strategy in very blunt terms.

'It's a bit like the old days at Macquarie Bank when I used to take over companies,' he told the newspaper. 'You're taking over an institution, the New South Wales judiciary and the Attorney General's office, that's what this was. We had to blow apart the Attorney General's office.'

The media storm was carefully planned by Mr Yates and his team in close collaboration with the Australian Academy of Science. He would later describe it as a kind of 'atomic bomb'. To begin with, he offered News Corp – publishers of *The Australian* newspaper and multiple tabloids – a huge scoop: they could be the first to report on the new petition and, more significantly, on the fact that the petition had the backing of some of the world's leading scientists. In return, there was an expectation that the story would feature as a front-page splash in all of the media giant's tabloid papers around Australia.

Peter Yates' style of leadership is unique. Team Folbigg met sporadically, and when it did so, more often than not, he would be away on a personal trip and dialing in from some far-flung location. On 1 March, three days before the burst of publicity he had helped to plan, he sent me and Professor Vinuesa an email from Australia's Red Centre, announcing his journey from Kata Tjuta (the Olgas) to Uluru (Ayers Rock) with a photo he had taken in the outback. How he managed to drink in the glorious landscape and focus on the launch was anyone's guess. But focus he did.

On the day in question, Wednesday, 3 March, the media operation unfolded with military precision. At 11.10 pm, the first online News Corp article was published. The embargoed petition was released soon afterwards by the Australian Academy of Science, and just after midnight on Thursday morning, News Corp had its own embargo lifted and published news of the petition in front page splashes around Australia. At 6 am, the Australian Science Media Centre sent out a press release to hundreds of journalists on its database. And at 7 am, TV stations started picking up on the story.

It was a huge moment for Kathy. In prison, she was told how the story was being picked up and given extensive coverage in every major newspaper around the country, and on radio, TV and social media.

By 2 pm on Thursday, Dan Wheelahan, the Academy's media manager, was telling Team Folbigg: 'So far today the story has been featured or mentioned in 18 print stories, 597 online news stories and on radio or TV 2056 times. And that's still with the evening news and current affairs stories and programs to come.' It was a phenomenal outcome.

'I'm really proud of Science Inc for having pulled that off,' Mr Yates told me later. 'I don't think that's happened before. I wanted science to be the hero. But I also wanted to make sure that the Attorney General's office realised that they were dealing with something that was completely different.'

I wrote a feature in *The Australian* to accompany the breaking news, headlined: 'Science on Folbigg Cannot Be Ignored'. The sub-heading was: 'Kathleen Folbigg was convicted in 2003 of killing her four children. Now, scientists believe she was innocent all along. Will she be freed?'

'What happened this week is unique in the annals of Australian criminal history,' my article began. 'A petition endorsed by 90 top scientists, medical practitioners and science advocates – among them, two Nobel laureates – was handed to the NSW Governor, calling for the pardon and immediate release of a woman convicted of killing all four of her children.'

The comments I reported from some of Australia's top scientists and signatories were blunt. Professor John Shine said: 'Given the scientific and medical evidence that now exists in this case, signing this petition was the right thing to do.'

'Expert advice should always be heard and listened to. It will always trump presumption,' Australia's former Chief Scientist, Professor Ian Chubb, said pointedly.

'The science in this particular case is compelling and cannot be ignored,' added human geneticist and researcher Professor Jozef Gecz.

Taken together, it was a powerful lineup of science's great and good, and their message was clear: scientific fact trumps judicial speculation and prejudice.

I quoted David Balding, Professor of Statistical Genetics at Melbourne University, who regarded Mr Tedeschi's use of the piglet analogy in his closing address to the jury at Kathy's trial as 'incredibly unprofessional', and 'pretty disgraceful'. He said: 'I think that's not a proper way for the state, the prosecution that represents the government and their people in principle, to behave.'

Echoing Professor Ray Hill from years before, Professor Balding pointed out that if cases of families with multiple children dying from natural causes are statistically rare, cases of mothers murdering their children, one after another, are also extremely rare.

The petition, signed by several Fellows of the Australian Academy of Science, highlighted a troubling gulf between science and the law; between those pre-eminent medical and scientific experts whose considered opinion was that Kathy's children had died from identifiable natural causes, and those who had pointedly rejected that view, and condemned her as a murderer.

The new petition argued that Mr Blanch 'made these findings based on his interpretation of Ms Folbigg's journal entries'. The petitioners asserted that the inquiry's findings ran 'counter to the scientific and medical evidence that now exists'.

It insisted that, based on evidence presented to the inquiry and the fresh scientific evidence obtained by the international group of experts that studied the *CALM2* mutation, 'a reasonable person should have doubt about Ms Folbigg killing her four children. Deciding otherwise rejects medical science and the law that sets the standard of proof.'

When the petition was lodged with the Governor of New South Wales, Kathy was serving out her sentence in Clarence Correctional Facility, where she had recently been attacked by another inmate.

The petition condemned the treatment meted out to her by some other prisoners, saying that Kathy had suffered 'and continues to suffer emotional and psychological trauma and physical abuse in custody'.

Buoyed by this unprecedented support from the scientific community, and in contrast to the deep dismay and despair which many had felt after the first inquiry, there was now a sense that this could be the breakthrough moment that her most loyal friends and supporters had been waiting for, for so long.

Surely now, they were saying, the fresh scientific evidence would be recognised as pivotal, pointing as it did to Kathy's innocence. The worldwide publicity produced a surge of hope that Kathy would soon be freed and allowed to start a new life.

But once again, as if she was bound to a wheel of torture turning endlessly, Kathy's hopes would be dashed.

At 10.10 am on Wednesday, 24 March, three weeks after the petition was formally submitted, Kathy entered a room at Clarence Correctional Facility, full of hope, and sat at a table, facing a camera linked to the Court of Appeal in Sydney. Eight minutes later, looking slightly bemused, she stood up and left.

In the interim, New South Wales Supreme Court Justice John Basten had taken less than forty-five seconds to dismiss the application made on Kathy's behalf the year before to quash the findings of the Blanch inquiry. Confusingly for many, the application to the Court of Appeal was completely unconnected to the petition, and the court had not considered the petition or the *Europace* paper.

Instead, in a scathing written judgment, the judges declared that: 'There was an ample basis, consistent with the scientific evidence, for the judicial officer to conclude that there was no reasonable doubt as to Ms Folbigg's guilt.'

The judges also suggested that: 'This was not a case in which the judicial officer's conclusion was at odds with the scientific evidence.'

In February, Kathy's legal team, led by Jeremy Morris, with newly recruited barrister Terence Ower assisting, had suggested that Reginald Blanch had exhibited 'apprehended bias' during the inquiry, and in some respects, had not been impartial.

However, as the hearings proceeded, this allegation was withdrawn.

Kathy's lawyers were hoping nevertheless to have the inquiry's findings overturned. Mr Morris argued that it had been wrong to redact the listening device transcript of the conversation between Craig and Kathy, where Craig explained how, in theory, he could have killed the children. And, that it was wrong to redact the reports from two of the expert medical witnesses, Professors Clancy and Goldwater.

Furthermore, Mr Morris argued, Mr Blanch should have reopened the inquiry to consider the further genetic evidence from Professor Schwartz after the hearings had ended. But this argument too was rejected, with the judges ruling that this did not amount to a denial of procedural fairness.

The judges also suggested that the scientific evidence put to the inquiry raised only a 'theoretical' possibility that there were innocent explanations for Sarah's and Laura's deaths.

But in a last-minute addendum to his report, after considering the evidence presented by Professor Schwartz and the data from the International Calmodulin Registry, Mr Blanch had acknowledged that 'Sarah and Laura may have had a cardiac condition and that raises a possibility it caused their deaths.' This was much more than a 'theoretical' possibility.

Moreover, in Laura's case at least, Mr Blanch had acknowledged that on the medical evidence in isolation, there existed a 'reasonable possibility the myocarditis found in Laura's heart at autopsy was fatal'.

The judges noted that Mr Blanch 'was required to consider evidence that, although the *CALM2* abnormality in Ms Folbigg and the two girls involved a change in an amino acid in the vicinity of Gly114, their circumstances departed from the reported cases of deaths associated with *CALM* abnormalities.'

Here, unquestionably, they were favouring the views of the Sydney team, and rejecting the opinions of the Canberra team, which was backed by the contemporary data recorded in the registry of calmodulin deaths which had been given to Mr Blanch by Professor Schwartz.

The grounds for appeal prevented the judges from considering the findings published in *Europace* and even if the judges had read the paper outside the court, they could not officially take it into account, because it was published after the Blanch inquiry.

Relying instead on the Sydney team's reservations and Mr Blanch's findings as to Kathy's credibility, the judges asserted that the deaths of Sarah and Laura were 'outliers' compared with those reported in the literature. The fact that Kathy's boys had carried a different genetic variant was also deemed to be unhelpful to her case, because it meant that no single genetic mutation could be held responsible for all four deaths.

The boys' genomes 'provided no common cause,' the judges wrote. 'When these matters were weighed with the inculpatory inferences derived from Ms Folbigg's diary entries and her evidence in seeking to present innocent explanations of them, there was an ample basis, consistent with the scientific evidence, for the judicial officer to conclude that there was no reasonable doubt as to Ms Folbigg's guilt.'

If the release of the petition had hit the media like an atomic bomb, the Appeal Court judgment came as a hammer blow, and as it sank in, scientists reacted with anger and dismay.

Professor Peter Schwartz weighed in, describing the judges' scientific commentary as 'simply wrong', and adding: 'It goes against the only serious data available, namely those of our International Calmodulin Registry.

'With over 100 patients enrolled, it is crystal clear that life-threatening or fatal events have occurred in infants and young children at rest or during sleep, and the majority occur without prior warning.'

The appeal court judges' conclusions implied that *CALM* mutations that are lethal in children are not inherited from healthy parents. But Professor Schwartz countered this argument as well, saying: 'It is widely accepted in genetics that highly symptomatic infants can inherit the disease-causing mutations from apparently healthy parents or parents with mild disease.'

As far as the scientists were concerned, the appeal court's decision went beyond the pale, and what happened next was unprecedented. That afternoon, the Australian Academy of Science issued a fiery statement directly contradicting the judges, saying: 'There are medical and scientific explanations for the death of each of Kathleen Folbigg's children.'

Academy President John Shine declared that: 'Experts from around the globe have offered an evidence-based explanation for the death of the Folbigg children. It is time that this evidence be brought to bear in the Folbigg case. Any statement suggesting a contrary view should be backed with data. The Folbigg case calls into question the ability for the legal system to assess the reliability of expert evidence.'

Professor Vinuesa went even further, describing Justice Blanch's conclusions about the genetic evidence she had uncovered as 'incorrect', and the inquiry's reasoning as 'non-scientific'.

Or in other words, the judges had got it wrong.

By now, it was clear that this was turning into a bare-knuckle fight between science and the law: on one side, the scientists, who believed that plausible natural causes of death had been established for all four of Kathy's children; and on the other, the judges, who didn't.

Professor Shine's contribution to this debate was pivotal, outspoken and, some would say, surprising. When I spoke to Anna-Maria Arabia about this, she described Professor Shine as 'methodical, measured, conservative and non-confrontational,' which made it even more surprising. But it was crystal clear that he held strong views about the case, and that he and Ms Arabia enjoyed a relationship of trust which allowed her to drive the Academy's involvement forward, with his blessing.

The scientists weren't backing down, and, despite the judgment of the appeal court, the petition remained a live issue to be considered by the Attorney General, Mark Speakman.

I wrote a news feature for *The Australian*, reflecting the anger felt by the Australian Academy of Science, and by the petition's signatories.

Professor Eugenie Lumbers from the University of Newcastle was one of those who spoke out, addressing head-on the tension between science and the law, saying: 'The conflict that exists between the legal system and science can be attributed to the rapid progress of new scientific knowledge. It is essential that the legal system takes a considered approach and places reliance on the expertise of scientists currently working in relevant specific areas of inquiry.'

The reprimands handed out to the appeal court judges marked a significant escalation in the increasingly frosty relationship between medical and scientific expert witnesses and the judges who assess their evidence.

I sought the opinions of two expert witnesses who had appeared on Kathy's behalf at the 2019 inquiry. Both openly criticised the way in which they and their evidence were treated.

Professor Robert Clancy objected to parts of his report being redacted, and said that, when questioned by Gail Furness, he was subjected to a 'vigour of inquiry' that he found 'aggressive and beyond anything I had experienced in over forty years as an expert witness'.

Professor Caroline Blackwell said her impression was that the inquiry 'was not aware of the complexity or the relevance of the information presented by Professor Clancy and myself'.

Professor John Hilton, long regarded as one of Australia's pre-eminent forensic pathologists, told me that the medical evidence 'certainly in one case, showed a clear-cut, obvious natural cause of death'. That case was Laura, Kathy's fourth child, where Professor Hilton and three other forensic pathologists all gave evidence to the inquiry that her death could be ascribed to myocarditis. Professor Hilton described it as a 'strong probability'.

Laura's myocarditis was also referred to by the cardiac geneticists who reviewed the case and who suggested that it may have triggered her underlying genetic condition, causing a cardiac arrest and her sudden death.

Professor Hilton's view was that, 'For some reason or other, people have found it terribly hard to get their heads around this. They didn't understand really what the medical evidence was saying.'

It was a troubling observation; if true, if it meant that those making the final judicial decisions didn't fully understand the science.

Law professor Gary Edmond, from the University of New South Wales, told me: 'If you were designing a system to facilitate an impartial review of a conviction, where the major issue is the biomedical evidence, would you appoint legally trained personnel to conduct, oversee and evaluate the evidence?

'Why do we have a legally trained chair, legally trained counsel assisting but no forensic pathologist, geneticist or statistician sitting on the panel?'

The appeal court decision came as an undeniable blow to Kathy and her team of lawyers, scientists and supporters, and particularly so, given that the petition which championed the fresh genetic evidence had been submitted so recently. Some of the media reports on the judges' ruling repeated the decades-old description of Kathy as a 'child killer', effectively wiping out the positive publicity created by the petition itself.

Her fate now lay in the hands of the governor of New South Wales, Margaret Beazley, herself a former justice in the Court of Appeal, and Attorney General Mark Speakman.

At the same time, voices were beginning to be raised against the judicial system that was keeping Kathy behind bars.

Professor Edmond argued that New South Wales 'should have an independent criminal cases review commission – like England, Scotland and New Zealand'.

He told me: 'At one level, given the medical evidence, the diary entries may not even be meaningful. If there is no medical evidence suggesting murder or even deliberate harm, does it matter that a woman has written self-deprecating and adverse self-accusations? The ambiguous diaries must be read subject to the medical evidence. If the medical evidence does not support murder, then ambiguous diaries cannot operate as a makeweight.'

Professor Blackwell agreed with this, saying: 'There have been significant advancements in science and medicine in the last eighteen years. This is particularly evident in the field of genetics, which has led to groundbreaking findings that could not have been envisioned almost two decades ago. The law needs to be open to this progress. It also requires scientists to support the legal system in their understanding of the true cause of all unexpected deaths.'

Solicitor Rhanee Rego and barrister Dr Robert Cavanagh, co-authors of the petition seeking Folbigg's release, put on a brave face, saying they believed that the appeal court's decision 'should not impact on the petition for pardon of Ms Folbigg, which is currently under consideration by the Governor. The petition deals with matters not considered by the NSW Court of Appeal.'

Ms Rego commented: 'One of the biggest tensions in our legal system is the varying levels of scientific literacy of those who preside over and appear in courtrooms. This can lead to fundamental errors in the assessment of scientific evidence ... We must be conscious to listen to those experts who represent their field of expertise and treat with caution those who do not.'

35

'DEAR MR SPEAKMAN ... PLEASE SOFTEN YOUR HEART'

Behind bars at Clarence Correctional Facility, and despite the distressing outcome of her appeal, Kathy could hardly believe her good fortune. Following the submission of the petition signed by Nobel laureates and other eminent scientists, her fellow inmates were treating her with a newfound respect. That, though, didn't dispel the impatience she felt at the time being taken by Mr Speakman to consider the petition.

Overall, it has to be said, the timing of Kathy's appeal and the fact of the judgment being handed down so close to the petition's launch was most unfortunate, and it reflected growing disagreements behind the scenes over the best legal strategy to adopt, following the outcome of the inquiry.

In 2005, after Kathy's first appeal was rejected, her lawyers had made an application to the High Court for special leave to appeal. Her arguments were put to the High Court judges by a legendary advocate, David Jackson QC, who was described after his death in 2023, as 'the finest constitutional and High Court barrister of a generation, indeed arguably since Federation'.

The application for special leave was rejected, with one of the judges, Justice Michael McHugh, making the highly questionable assertion that all of Kathy's children 'showed signs that were consistent with smothering with a pillow'. In fact, medical experts had confirmed to the trial that smothering an infant with a pillow may leave no signs at all.

Now, following the failure of Kathy's appeal against the findings of the Blanch inquiry, Stuart Gray briefed David Jackson once again to prepare a further application for special leave to appeal to the High Court. Mr Jackson, who worked pro bono on Kathy's behalf, was assisted by two new barristers, Eamonn O'Neill and Stephanie Gaussen. It was listed to be heard in December 2021.

The central point that Mr Jackson hoped to make to the High Court was that an inquiry should inquire. The application argued that once the new genetic material had been received by Mr Blanch – prior to his final report being published – the inquiry should have been reopened.

But the application never went ahead. Rather than risk another failure in another court, Kathy decided to pin her hopes on the petition, and instructed Mr Gray to discontinue her application for special leave to appeal. He duly did so, and Kathy appointed Rhanee Rego to be her instructing solicitor. From that point on, Ms Rego worked closely with Dr Cavanagh to progress the petition.

As Mark Speakman sought his own legal advice, the Australian Academy of Science offered to help him and his team understand the fresh genetic evidence, and its significance. Upsettingly for the scientists, Mr Speakman declined the offer.

Professor John Shine had written to the New South Wales Governor, Margaret Beazley, and to Mr Speakman at the end of April, offering to help set up an 'informal roundtable with you and your staff' to provide accurate, impartial advice on the science underlying the petition.

'The petitioners ... appreciate that scientific evidence is complex and fast evolving,' his letter said. 'It is in this spirit that the Australian Academy of Science wishes to offer you an opportunity to be briefed by scientists with expertise in genetics and statistics, some of whom are experts in *CALM* pathology and/or have been involved in the relevant studies. I am confident that gaining a comprehensive understanding of the scientific information available today would assist your consideration of this matter.'

Professor Shine listed eight pre-eminent experts in the field who, he said, would be available to give their own time, unpaid, to help the Attorney General's office to understand their area of expertise.

They included Professor Schwartz and Professor Toft Overgaard, the scientist who led the Danish team that had carried out experiments on the *CALM2* gene, confirming its pathogenic properties.

Those scientists had endorsed the petition, and Professor Shine made it clear that 'if there are other experts who you wish to nominate, I would be pleased to seek their participation'.

But Mr Speakman rebuffed the offer, telling the Academy: 'I do not propose to convene private consultations with individuals or organisations in relation to further information advanced in support of Ms Folbigg's petition.' Instead, he asked for any fresh evidence to be submitted in writing via Kathy's legal representatives.

The offer remained open. Professor Shine wrote to Kathy's lawyers, telling them that the Academy was still willing to facilitate a briefing for members of Mr Speakman's office and anyone providing advice to the Governor. 'Such a briefing has been offered by Australia's leading scientists in the field of cardiac genetics, genomics and statistics,' he assured the lawyers.

And, he told me: 'It is difficult to see how the Attorney General can adequately deliberate or arrive at an informed conclusion, without consulting scientific experts. It is hoped they will accept our offer.'

But Mr Speakman never did. This was the opposite of what an independent Criminal Cases Review Commission looking into the case would have done. Almost certainly, a CCRC would have bitten Professor Shine's arm off to obtain that kind of expert advice.

Ms Rego and Dr Cavanagh said they found it 'concerning' that Mr Speakman had turned down the offer. 'No just decision is capable of being determined without due consideration of all of the factual evidence, and any decision made without such due consideration is an opinion rather than a proper legally based decision,' they suggested.

Leon Kempler, Professor Vinuesa's friend and ally, was also highly critical of Mr Speakman, in comments made at her leave-taking party that same month, before she departed Australia to take up a new position at the Crick Institute in London. Mr Kempler questioned why the Governor, Margaret Beazley, who had been a Federal Court judge and was the first woman appointed as President of the New South Wales Court of Appeal, had to defer to Mr Speakman's advice.

On Sunday, 29 August, in response to Mr Speakman's refusal, Professor Shine announced that the Attorney General 'now has sufficient medical and scientific evidence before him that provides an alternative explanation for the deaths of the Folbigg children, that carries more weight than the circumstantial evidence used to convict her'.

He called on Attorneys General around Australia to consider legal reform that would empower the judiciary to identify the most qualified experts to provide evidence for any given case.

'To ensure miscarriages of justice like this are prevented in the future, it is imperative that evidence heard by the courts is accurate; is delivered by the most qualified expert; and draws on the most up-to-date science. This is particularly important in rapidly moving areas such as human genetics.

'We urge the NSW Attorney General to expedite this matter and advise the NSW Governor to pardon Kathleen Folbigg and release her from jail.'

Professor Elizabeth Blackburn, an Australian Nobel laureate, added her voice to the growing chorus, saying that it was profoundly wrong to deny justice by denying science. 'Do those who would deny Kathleen Folbigg's right to scientific evidence deny that the planet Earth revolves around the sun?' she asked.

Now more than ever, the battlelines were clearly drawn, for all to see, between science and the law – and only one of them could prevail.

The frustration within the scientific community was growing, and it was palpable. When I spoke to Professor Matthew Cook, who was part of the Canberra team, he told me: 'You know, we've got evidence now that is very solid, that there is a plausible natural cause of death for two of the children, that would seem to me to raise doubts about the conviction.'

Professor Cook talked about the nature of scientific inquiry, as it applied to the investigation of the Folbigg mutation. 'There was incremental progress,' he suggested. 'We had the bioinformatics information suggesting that we had a candidate that was plausible. And then there was empirical evidence that this genetic variant conferred a functional change in the protein. So, several steps in which the information that was being gathered was strengthened. And this is the nature of scientific inquiry, true findings are built upon because they lead to further positive findings.'

Professor Cook posed a rhetorical question: 'At what point do we pass the threshold for supporting evidence for a natural cause of death? There's definitely more information now in support of that than there was before. How much is enough?'

I also spoke again to Nicholas Cowdery, the former DPP, and this time round, it felt as if his attitude to Kathy's convictions had softened slightly. At the heart of this case, I suggested to him, was a woman who had spent the last eighteen years in prison. If in fact she hadn't killed her children, it was an extraordinary injustice.

'I have never pretended that the criminal justice process always gets the right decisions, that the results are always correct,' Mr Cowdery replied. 'If justice has miscarried in this case, as in any other case where it has happened, then it is a terrible thing to have done to the person at the receiving end.'

The 'person at the receiving end' was Kathy, and in August, she took matters into her own hands. She wrote a letter from jail to Mr Speakman, once again protesting her innocence, and voicing her regret at having stayed silent during her trial. 'I now have a voice,' she told him.

In her open letter, Kathy talked about the love and support of her lifelong friends, which had kept her going and given her the will to survive. She told Mr Speakman that the treatment meted out to her in prison had changed dramatically since the petition was lodged. It had radically changed her day-to-day existence. Now, she enjoyed the support of her fellow inmates.

In light of the fresh genetic evidence, Kathy begged Mr Speakman to 'please soften your heart' and, as he had previously done with Craig, to acknowledge her grief and suffering over the previous three decades – and not just the suffering endured by her former husband.

Kathy paid tribute to the scientists involved in her case, thanking them for having helped to remove the stigma of her as an 'evil monster'.

Kathy ended her letter by telling the Attorney General that she was tired, but not broken, and definitely not defeated, signing off 'with no hard feelings, but much respect.'

36

'IT'S TIME'

In October 2021, following months of work behind the scenes by Kathy's lawyers, it became apparent that the very diaries that helped to condemn her could hold the key to overturning her convictions.

It was an incredible turnaround, prompted in part by Tracy Chapman, who had urged Kathy's solicitor Rhanee Rego to consult an American expert called Professor James W. Pennebaker, to obtain his opinion on Kathy's journals, and on whether they amounted to 'virtual' admissions of guilt to killing her children.

At her trial, Mark Tedeschi had argued that Kathy's diaries were 'the strongest evidence the jury could possibly have for Ms Folbigg having murdered her four children'.

In his closing statement, he had told the jury that 'we don't have a machine to look into the minds of human beings, and thank goodness for that. But in this case we have something better than a machine to look into the mind of Kathleen Folbigg. We have her diaries which were a very intimate, personal and an exact analysis of what her thinking was during the time that she was trying to get pregnant with Laura, was pregnant with Laura, and in the early months of Laura's life.'

More recently, Reginald Blanch, who headed the 2019 inquiry into Kathy's convictions, said the evidence he had heard, including, most significantly, her own explanations of what the diary entries meant, had reinforced her guilt.

Now, four leading experts commissioned by Kathy's legal team had analysed the diaries and given their verdicts on what the journals contained.

'I am comfortable in describing Ms Folbigg as having been a very loving and attentive mother,' psychotherapist Dr Kamal Touma said. 'After reading and analysing the minute particulars of Ms Folbigg's diaries, and having met her for five analytical psychotherapy sessions, I cannot see anything in the diaries or from my sessions with Ms Folbigg to indicate that she harmed her children.'

At one level, this was an astounding conclusion for any expert to have reached. It was the complete opposite of what the jury at Kathy's trial, and numerous judges since then, had concluded.

Mark Tedeschi at Kathy's trial had re-voiced the diary entries to suggest that the only possible interpretation they carried was that she had deliberately killed her children. Justice Brian Sully at her first appeal in 2005 had said that a selection of entries, which he quoted, 'make chilling reading'.

And in his final report following the hearings at the 2019 inquiry, Reginald Blanch stated that: 'the evidence which has emerged at the Inquiry, particularly her own explanations and behaviour in respect of her diaries, makes her guilt of these offences even more certain'.

Dr Touma's contrary view was that Kathy was suffering from primary and secondary 'dissociation' following the traumas she endured in her childhood, including her mother's death at the hands of her father, when she was eighteen months old.

When it came to Kathy's own children dying, Dr Touma said: 'The painful aloneness of being dissociated with and from her feelings is illustrated by this simple heartbreaking entry in her diary the day her daughter Sarah died: MONDAY 30: SARAH LEFT US.'

Dr Touma rejected the notion that Kathy might have killed her children in severe dissociative, fugue-like states. 'Her dissociation is nowhere near the severity of a dissociative disorder that one would expect to observe with such phenomena,' he said. 'Nowhere in the diaries nor in my conversation with Ms Folbigg was this observable. I can comfortably exclude this hypothesis.'

When Dr Touma spoke to Kathy, he was particularly struck by how she spoke about her children.

'A written transcript cannot reflect what we may call the "musicality" of the moment where, immersed in associative thinking, she talked about her children,' he reported.

'This is the true memories she keeps of her children and wasn't since losing them able to access to express. This is not how a murderous mother would ever talk about her children.'

Dr Touma conducted five consultations with Kathy between June and August 2021, each lasting about forty-five minutes. On each occasion, Kathy was in a room at the prison, where she and Dr Touma, who was outside the prison, were able to see and hear each other via an audio-visual link.

In one of her sessions, Kathy spoke in detail about her four children.

'I don't have trouble now talking about … if I can remember funny stories or a personality trait that was amusing or something like that. I'm fine sharing that sort of stuff now,' she told Dr Touma.

'Each one of them was just a little bit different in each of their own way,' she recalled.

'Caleb might have been only nineteen days old, but he just came across as a little old soul. He was so serious when he stared at you. He had these such intense eyes; it was just sort of like "my gosh I think he's reading my brain" because he would just stare at you so intently and he was just placid and really calm. And you just sort of thought, "wow".

'I remember he had such long fingers, I just sort of thought, "piano player" – you instantly think of playing pianos or something because they've got these really long fingers and things.'

Patrick was very different.

'He would be rolling around the floor. I remember that I would quite often go into the living room and he would not be where I put him because he's gone and rolled somewhere ... investigating on his own with his hands ...

'With him there was no stopping him from discovering things even though he couldn't see. He was very tactile and hands-on.'

Sarah, Kathy remembered, was different again.

'I actually thought Sarah was probably a bit too much like me. I saw her as ... I anticipated she was going to be one hell of a handful because she was just cheeky. There was just cheek that would radiate from her. She was just ... if you turned around and called her name – her instant response was to poke her tongue out at you. And she just took such funny joy – it didn't matter what she was doing, there was fun.

'Having a bath was excitable, playing with toys was excitable, running around with dad was excitable. She was full on. We'd go to playgroup – as long as she could see me and she knew where I was, she would just take off and she would go and get into all sorts of stuff. I just sort of had visions of her being in the future as we were going to have to watch what she was up to.

'Laura was different again. She was very ... I already was starting to see that she was quite an empathetic and compassionate little kid, and she would quite happily share ... wanting to help in some fashion.

'They all had their own little things even at the ages that they were. But if you had tried to get me to share that sort of information with you in the first five, ten years maybe, I probably would have gone "nope, you're not having any of that – that's mine. I'm keeping that, you don't get to know any of that" ... I think it was just a subconscious thing, I would just go blank and just go "yeah, no, I'm not dealing with this. I'm not having these conversations ... I'm not going there".'

Kathy told Dr Touma: 'I realise now that it came across as me being incredibly cold and not caring. But it was what I did. I did that to protect myself more than anything else.'

A second expert, the US-based psychologist and textual analyst recommended by Tracy Chapman, Professor James W Pennebaker, said: 'I see absolutely no evidence to suggest that these were premeditated murders.'

Professor Pennebaker, who had helped the FBI and CIA understand the language of kidnappers, terrorists and violent criminals, added: 'I see no evidence that Kathleen Folbigg's language ... exhibited any signs of deception or attempts to cover anything up. I also see no sign that Folbigg is mentally unstable or is someone harbouring buried hostility or rage.'

A third expert, Associate Professor Janine Stevenson, a consultant psychiatrist, said: 'Nowhere in her journals does she use agency verbs, such as "I hurt her" ... Throughout the journal Ms Folbigg is detailing all the steps she took to ensure the safety of her children. There is no anger, no aggression, only self-doubt.'

And a fourth expert, Associate Professor of Linguistics David Butt, said: 'There is a likelihood that the courts and inquiry have misinterpreted the feelings of responsibility for not being a better mother as admissions of agency in the deaths of the children.'

Kathy's legal team also resubmitted the report written for the 2019 inquiry by clinical psychiatrist Dr Michael Diamond, who met Kathy in person and assessed her, in which he said: 'I found no evidence to support a view that Ms Folbigg has suffered from psychotic illness, severe mood disorder consistent with homicidal conduct or any other brain injury that might affect her conduct so as to carry out homicidal acts.'

Instead, Dr Diamond diagnosed Kathy as suffering from complex post-traumatic stress disorder. Dissociation is frequently observed with those who suffer from c–PTSD.

A sixth expert report, submitted by clinical psychologist Dr Sharmila Betts, who had written an earlier report for the 2015 petition, questioned how the diaries could be 'tantamount to confessions' as asserted by the prosecution at her trial. Her view was that 'the diaries do not contain any clear admission of guilt or confession of homicide'.

In 2019, Mr Blanch had dismissed the suggestion that expert psychiatrists or psychologists could help him understand Kathy's diaries.

He conceded that 'the diary entries contained no express admissions by Ms Folbigg to having killed her children,' but insisted that 'it is entirely proper in fact finding in circumstantial evidence cases for inferences to be drawn, and for individual pieces of evidence to be considered in combination, like strands in a cable'.

Mr Blanch acknowledged that 'aspects of her evidence had entered into areas which would be addressed appropriately by psychiatric reports,' but contended that: 'Even making every allowance for her deep-seated psychological subjective experiences and childhood trauma, and any emotional state she may have been in at the time of writing the various entries, it is impossible to give the diary entries any meaning other than their ordinary English meaning.'

Mr Blanch described the evidence Kathy gave about the meaning of her diaries, as 'a clearly deliberately designed attempt to obscure the fact that she had committed the offences,' and said he was 'satisfied the diary entries were written by a reasonably intelligent woman in plain language, carrying their plain meaning.

'Accordingly, neither Ms Folbigg's evidence before the Inquiry, nor the psychiatric assessment reports tendered in the Inquiry, causes me to interpret Ms Folbigg's diary entries other than in accordance with the ordinary English meaning of the words which she wrote.'

He concluded: 'I am satisfied that the plain meaning interpretation of the diary entries carries the character contended by the Crown at the trial, of virtual admissions of guilt for the deaths of Sarah, Patrick and Caleb, and admissions that she appreciated she was at risk of causing similarly the death of Laura.'

But the experts canvassed by Kathy's legal team took the opposite view.

Professor Butt said the 175 pages of Kathy's journals – which he studied – 'do not at all convince me that the claim of a single plain meaning is sound' and contended that the diaries had been 'cherry-picked' to focus only on 'those wordings that permitted some possibility of an interpretation of guilt.

'It is not reasonable to claim that the diaries of Kathleen Folbigg support only one "damning" interpretation,' he argued.

None of the new experts supported the view that the journals revealed an intent on Kathy's part to harm or murder her children, or that they carried any 'virtual' admissions.

'At first I did find some of her diary entries troubling but, when taken in the context of her mindset, that she basically hated herself and everything she did, they are a lot less troubling,' Associate Professor Stevenson said.

'It is not possible for a therapist, let alone a lay person, to interpret the meaning of writings in a diary. They are personal, idiosyncratic, expressing fleeting feelings, imaginings, and very influenced by the emotions of the minute … The "meaning" one day could be different the next, or there could be no meaning at all.'

Based on Associate Professor Stevenson's opinion, Kathy's lawyers argued that 'this makes the inculpatory interpretation of guilt by judges (and presumably the jurors at trial) highly likely to be wrong'.

In a direct challenge to Mr Blanch, the lawyers argued that he should have sought expert opinions to assist him instead of 'discounting Folbigg's explanations without the benefit of context'.

'It is clear that the courts and inquiry have misinterpreted Ms Folbigg's words. Nowhere in the diaries/journals are there confessions of murder and they should stop being used to suggest this.'

In an announcement designed to hammer home how flimsy the case against Kathy had become, Rhanee Rego and Dr Robert Cavanagh said: 'Experts now say that the diaries cannot be taken as confessions of murder or harm to any of her children. The only consideration is reasonable doubt. Every argument that has been used to suggest the guilt of Ms Folbigg has now been overcome and her convictions are untenable.

'Now no reasonable person can conclude that Ms Folbigg's guilt is established beyond reasonable doubt. It's time for Mark Speakman to recommend to the Governor that Kathleen Folbigg be released.'

37

WAITING FOR MR SPEAKMAN

One year after the petition had been lodged with the Governor of New South Wales, and five months after the diary experts had spoken, there was still no announcement from the Attorney General, Mark Speakman, on its outcome.

It was March 2022 and on Kathy's side, patience was wearing very thin. Anger was growing that it was taking so long for him to reach a decision.

In comments made much later, Mr Speakman explained that Kathy's lawyers had continued to provide material supporting the petition up until December 2021, and that senior and junior counsel were not briefed to advise him until after all of Kathy's submissions had been received.

In early March, Kathy's lawyers announced that they had recruited a former Commonwealth Solicitor General, David Bennett QC, to the team, in a renewed bid to push for her freedom. This felt like a major coup, and it showed that not every member of the legal establishment was opposed to Kathy's bid to have her convictions overturned.

Simultaneously, a third Nobel laureate, Australian National University Vice-Chancellor Professor Brian Schmidt, joined the other two laureates who had signed the petition, by co-signing a letter from the Australian Academy of Science to Mr Speakman petitioning for Kathy's release.

The strongly worded letter read: 'New scientific evidence explaining the deaths of her children now makes it patently clear that all four children died of natural causes, placing her innocence beyond reasonable doubt ... it is time that the NSW legal system also accepts that a miscarriage of justice has occurred.'

Mr Speakman, for his part, was still defending his refusal to accept an offer by the Academy to set up a panel of genetic experts to assist him in reaching his decision.

He announced that it would be 'inappropriate and unfair to the petitioner for the Attorney General to consider material provided by someone other than the petitioner or their legal representative or to hold private consultations with other members of the public'.

The Academy wrote back, telling the Attorney General: 'This offer still stands and is supported by Ms Folbigg and her legal representatives.'

Kathy, in a message from prison, again protested her innocence and spoke of losing her family in 'heartbreaking circumstances'.

'I'm frustrated because nobody appears to be listening to any of the well-educated and highly-experienced scientists, linguists, and medical and mental health experts involved in this case. This is just devastating and astonishing to me,' she wrote.

The petition by now had been endorsed by 150 scientists and science advocates. This included sixty-six fellows of the Royal Society of New South Wales who had added their support in April 2021.

The lawyers argued that for each of the children there were now clear natural causes of death, which were supported not just by the fresh genetic evidence uncovered by Professor Vinuesa and her team but endorsed, too, by some of Australia's foremost forensic pathologists. Those pathologists had joined forces with the geneticists, recognising that, because both Sarah and Laura carried the lethal *CALM* mutation, they had almost certainly suffered fatal cardiac arrhythmias which had been triggered by their 'intercurrent' infections – in Laura's case, by her myocarditis.

The pressure was building, and in mid-March Mr Speakman defended the delay at a committee hearing in the New South

Wales Parliament. He told his fellow MPs that he would have 'something to say' about the petition within a month.

Public interest in the case was also growing, and it demonstrated – if nothing else – that the public mood had shifted significantly. No longer was Kathy universally viewed as a monster. More and more journalists, commentators and members of the public were speaking up in her defence, asking why it was that a mother whose children had all – at least arguably – died from natural causes, was still, after nearly nineteen years, languishing behind bars.

On 5 March, I wrote a news feature for *The Australian* newspaper, under the headline: 'Nineteen Years in Maximum Security: Did Kathleen Folbigg Do It?'

The optimistic sub-heading read: 'The woman once viewed as Australia's most notorious child-killer, Kathleen Folbigg, has been in jail for nearly two decades. Now the weight of science could free her.'

The article pointed out that the responsibility for deciding on the petition lay primarily with Mr Speakman, rather than with the Governor, Margaret Beazley. Protocol dictated that she acted on the advice of Mr Speakman and the New South Wales Parliament's Executive Council, which is comprised of cabinet ministers who meet in secret.

There was no transparency whatsoever in the process, and this was compounded and confirmed by the failure of his office to address the issue openly. Instead, the Attorney General's office remained tight-lipped, saying only that the petition and its accompanying submissions were 'complex and voluminous', and that a decision would be reached as 'promptly' as possible.

'There has been compelling, fresh evidence for over a year now which supports Ms Folbigg's innocence,' her lawyers, Rhanee Rego and Dr Robert Cavanagh, complained.

'The delay is astounding, the process opaque and the lack of willingness to work with scientists, inexplicable. We very much hope the Attorney General provides his advice to the Governor soon and shows leadership by ending Australia's worst miscarriage of justice.'

Professor John Shine, President of the Australian Academy of Science, was, if anything, even more outspoken, describing Kathy's continued incarceration as 'untenable' and insisting: 'It is time that the NSW legal system accepts that a miscarriage of justice has occurred. The power rests with the NSW Attorney General to not only right this wrong but to bring about the legal reform required so that no person finds themselves in a similar situation.'

Mr Speakman's office observed that there were 5100 pages of submissions and other material provided as part of the petition, and 'consideration of that material and the updated grounds is a process that must be taken with great care and diligence, as is the case with all petitions. As such, the Attorney General has instructed the Crown Solicitor's Office to obtain the advice of senior and junior counsel on the matters raised in the petition.'

Kathy, the Academy and her legal team didn't buy this for one second. In their view, it had been an unreasonable delay, and it meant that in all, Kathy by this time had had to wait a total of over four years, while Mark Speakman and his predecessor Gabrielle Upton had lingered over Kathy's two petitions.

In a message from her prison cell, she complained: 'I am saddened and extremely disappointed that there is no response at the 12-month mark from Mr Speakman in relation to the pardon petition and the overwhelming supporting scientific and medical evidence ... I am an innocent woman, and a mother who has lost her family under heartbreaking circumstances, still sitting in a maximum-security prison after nearly 19 long and challenging years.'

Meanwhile, Dominic Perrottet, the Premier of New South Wales, had been lobbied publicly and privately by Peter Yates, the head of Team Folbigg.

'In my discussions with the Premier, I expressed my deep concern about the improper incarceration of Kathleen, and that whilst NSW is a state which supports and creates great science, in Kathleen Folbigg's case that support for the best science does not seem to have been found in the office of the Attorney General,' Mr Yates said.

On 8 May, Mother's Day in Australia, I wrote a feature for Sydney's *Sunday Telegraph* newspaper, highlighting the never-ending distress felt by Kathy on days like these. As an institutional veteran at Clarence Correctional Facility, she was determined to honour the memory of her own children by trying to help other women there who were struggling with not seeing their kids.

'Since my incarceration in 2003 I've really struggled to find meaning in my life,' Kathy said from prison. 'I'll always feel responsible for my children's wellbeing. I will always be their mother. So when our children died, we didn't just lose children that we loved. We lost all the years of promise we had looked forward to.

'The best I can do whilst I remain incarcerated is help other mums experiencing grief and loss in their own way, because we all experience it differently, and honour my children's memory in that way as that's the best I can do right now.'

Tracy Chapman, who had at least one phone conversation every day with Kathy, said: 'We were talking the other night about religion and beliefs and she made a beautiful comment about how her faith allows her to feel that her children are up there in heaven with other family that have passed and they're safe, happy and well cared for.

'It gives her comfort to know they're somewhere safe, even though it hurts terribly not to have seen them go through school, not to see what they might have chosen as a profession, who they might have married and how it might have been to be a nan.

'She's still a mother,' Tracy insisted.

'She gave birth to four children she loved and cared for well. Not a day goes by that they're not with her and she's grateful that her spiritual beliefs allow her to feel them in that way.'

'This year she is looking forward to not being taunted by other inmates about the deaths of her children. She's looking forward to supporting other mums on the day who are separated from their children by circumstance. Some mums in there really struggle with that,' Tracy said of her lifelong friend.

Kathy's supporters argued that with every Mother's Day that came around, the injustice of her incarceration only increased.

Mr Speakman, in a parliamentary hearing in March, had alluded to this when he said: 'I am conscious that, if there were to be a successful petition – I am not saying one way or the other whether it is successful – the utility of that success diminishes day by day if someone is sitting in prison waiting for that.

'I would anticipate being able to say something within a month,' he said – a deadline that wasn't met.

Professor Shine, meanwhile, drew Mr Speakman's attention to the fact that: 'Internationally, other mothers wrongly convicted of murdering their children based on the improbability that multiple infants can die in the one family from natural causes have been released.'

Kathy, he said, was 'the last known woman to remain in prison because of this discredited assumption. She remains incarcerated despite the new clear scientific evidence.

'I appreciate the time required for proper consideration of petitions of this kind, however any further delay calls into question how seriously the NSW Attorney General takes his responsibility to provide justice to the people of NSW.

'I again call on the NSW Attorney General to make an evidence-informed decision, based on the strong, new scientific evidence demonstrating Ms Folbigg's innocence, and release her from prison.'

Professor Shine said Mr Speakman 'would be widely applauded and would leave an extraordinary legacy if he also reformed the legal system to establish an independent body capable of identifying and correcting miscarriages of justice when compelling new evidence comes to light.'

To Kathy's supporters, an independent body would have helped to dispel their distrust in the legal process and the perception that cases like Kathy's were politicised. I was surprised when Nicholas Cowdery, the former DPP, told me that he thought the introduction of a Criminal Cases Review Commission, which would be entirely independent of government, was an idea worth exploring. 'It's working very well in the UK and in Scotland, and New Zealand has a similar body. It is planned for Canada. We should give serious consideration to setting up one here,' he suggested.

'Not acknowledging the new genetic evidence is also denying the NSW community the benefit of advances in science which could save lives,' Rhanee Rego said. 'Advances in genomics signal a new era in understanding formerly undetermined sudden and unexpected infant deaths. It can assist in preventing future deaths.'

Finally, on Wednesday, 18 May 2022, fourteen months after the second petition was lodged, Mr Speakman announced his decision. He declared to begin with that he wasn't going to pardon Kathy and release her. Given how long he had taken to consider the evidence, this was profoundly disappointing for Kathy, for her legal team, and for the Australian Academy of Science.

Instead, he announced that on his recommendation, the Governor had ordered a second inquiry which, he told the media, would focus on the fresh genetic evidence. As he had before, he expressed great sympathy for Kathy's former husband Craig, and no sympathy whatsoever for her.

Mr Speakman acknowledged that 'this new evidence, and its widespread endorsement by scientists, cannot be ignored'. But he went on to say that, 'It would not be appropriate for the Governor now simply to grant a pardon, or (for example) for the Governor or me to receive private briefings from experts with a view to considering granting a pardon, without that evidence being scrutinised independently in a public forum.' He added that 'Only a transparent, public and fair inquiry can provide a just resolution of the doubt or question raised by that new evidence.'

Anna-Maria Arabia, Chief Executive of the Australian Academy of Science, released a gracious and optimistic statement: 'We respect the Attorney General's decision and the legal process he has decided on, but the Academy has every confidence that the overwhelming scientific and medical evidence, which is beyond reasonable doubt, will see Kathleen Folbigg freed from jail.'

Professor Vinuesa, however, was less charitable, declaring the decision to be 'disappointing, given the strength of the medical and scientific findings, that Ms Folbigg has not been granted a pardon'. The evidence, she said, 'goes well beyond raising a reasonable doubt and instead provides the likely explanation for the natural deaths of Ms Folbigg's children'.

In reality, for at least seven years before this, the New South Wales government had possessed solid evidence that there were serious doubts surrounding Kathy's convictions. In 2015, Professor Stephen Cordner had concluded that: 'Ultimately, and simply, there is no forensic pathology support for the contention that any or all of these children have been killed, let alone smothered.'

To Professor Vinuesa, the decision not to grant a pardon carried a clear lesson. 'Today's decision points to the need for Australia to build a more scientifically sensitive and informed legal system.

'It must be capable of understanding advances in science and able to apply appropriately the information to legal cases. This will help reduce the likelihood of others enduring the miscarriage of justice that Kathleen Folbigg continues to face.'

One unanswered question now was whether the new inquiry would examine all of the exculpatory evidence, apart from the fresh genetic evidence. Rhanee Rego announced: 'We are confident that the overwhelming evidence will finally free Kathleen Folbigg and prove her innocence.'

In my opinion there was a political motive underlying Mr Speakman's decision to announce a second inquiry. By doing so, he had effectively delayed any final decision on Kathy's guilt or innocence until after the upcoming state election, which was due to take place the following March. All the political pundits agreed that the ruling Liberal Party would lose that election, and that in turn meant that Mr Speakman would no longer be the state's Attorney General.

It meant, in my view, that if the inquiry ruled in her favour, and if eventually she was pardoned and freed, he would not endure the discomfort of having to announce it.

Mr Speakman made a further comment, which didn't sit well with Kathy's growing band of supporters: 'I can well understand why members of the public may shake their heads and roll their eyes in disbelief about the number of chances Ms Folbigg has had to clear her name, and why does the justice system allow someone who has been convicted of multiple homicides yet another go?'

'But,' he added, 'the evidence clearly in my view reaches the necessary threshold for some kind of intervention; it certainly rises to the level of question or doubt.'

Mr Speakman declined to release the legal advice he had received, and when I attempted to obtain it under freedom of information legislation, my request was refused. He would tell me later that he couldn't 'waive the State's privilege' over the extensive legal advice he had obtained.

To my mind, that was the opposite of an open, transparent process. Everyone was left to guess at what that legal advice had said, what course of action it recommended, and whether he had followed that advice.

On the upside, the new inquiry would give Professors Vinuesa and Toft Overgaard the chance to present, in much greater detail than at the first inquiry, the complex genetic evidence.

Behind the scenes, Professor Toft Overgaard and his team were working furiously in the lab at Aalborg University in Denmark, conducting further experiments on the *CALM2* mutation, and analysing the results. Those experiments, it would later emerge, added even greater weight to the argument that the mutation was damaging and capable of triggering fatal arrhythmias in children while they slept.

Sometime before, I had interviewed Professor John Shine. At the time he commented, confidently, that: 'We have very strong, robust scientific evidence that the mutations in these children could certainly have played a major role in their susceptibility to sudden death.'

Describing Kathy as 'a victim of the genetic lottery', he said: 'She's extremely unlucky because the chance of having the particular mutation she's got is very, very low. It's almost non-existent in the rest of the population.

'However, once you have that mutation in the family, then your genetic blueprint has that mutation. And so the chance of passing that to your children and their children is incredibly high.'

Picking up on Mark Tedeschi's suggestion at Kathy's trial that 'It is probably more common that a person has been hit by lightning four times than what has happened to this family,' Professor Shine explained that: 'If you have four people randomly running around the earth, the chances of all four being hit by lightning are incredibly slim. However, if each of the four is given a very large lightning rod that they carry around, their chances increase significantly. And it's a bit like that. Once that mutation occurs in a family, then your chance of suffering the similar thing are 50 percent – incredibly high.'

This assertion, from one of the world's foremost genetic experts, drove a coach and horses through Meadow's Law, providing the most persuasive possible counter to the arguments put forward by Dr Janice Ophoven and others, that the chance of four children in the same family dying from natural causes, was astronomically unlikely.

But, even with the new science in this case, it wasn't going to be a walkover for Kathy or an automatic affirmation of the petition calling for her pardon and release.

Two separate hearings were to form the basis of this second inquiry: the first, in November, would examine the genetic evidence. The second hearing, planned for February 2023, would continue examining the genetic evidence, and would also hear from psychiatrists and psychologists who would give their opinions on the diaries that, at her trial, had helped to convict her.

It was an exercise that her supporters confidently predicted would bury, once and for all, the notion that the diaries contained 'virtual' admissions of guilt to having killed her children.

More than anything, it all came down to a single question: would the fresh genetic and psychiatric evidence raise reasonable doubt about Kathy's convictions?

38

IT'S ALL IN THE GENES

In November, as the second inquiry got underway, two new stars appeared from the scientific firmament to shine a light on the probable causes of Sarah's and Laura's deaths.

The two scientists were Professor Michael Toft Overgaard and his wife and colleague Professor Mette Nyegaard – both formidable specialists in their field. Professor Toft Overgaard is a professor in medical biotechnology, or 'protein science', while Mette Nyegaard is a professor in genomic medicine and genetics. Both are based at Aalborg University in Denmark.

When I spoke to the two professors at length, they explained how their unique professional partnership works. 'In every single cell we have in our bodies, we have these strings of DNA, and parts of this DNA are then, through a process, turned into proteins, which are the building blocks of the body. I study the DNA, and Michael studies the protein,' Professor Nyegaard told me.

The professor compared the effect of any mutation as being like the discovery of a 'typo' in a recipe. 'Part of our DNA is a recipe for proteins. If there's a typo in your cooking recipe, the dish turns out wrong. So basically I search for typos in the recipe, and Michael makes the dish so you can see if there's something wrong with the dish or not, caused by that typo.'

Taking the analogy one step further, Professor Toft Overgaard explained that it was like a recipe for bread; if you had a typo in the recipe that said you should add a kilogram of salt instead of a gram, you could predict that the outcome was going to be bad. At the 2019 inquiry, 'they had the recipe and the typo. We actually baked the bread and could taste, you know, this is very salty!'

As Professor Nyegaard explained to a joint symposium of the Australian Academy of Science and the Australian Academy of Law in November 2024, 'My focus is asking what mutations are causing disease, and Michael works with proteins; his focus is: what does the mutation do to the actual protein?'

It was only when I spoke to the two professors together, that I learned of yet another extraordinary twist of fate in Kathy's story.

In 2012, Professor Nyegaard carried out an investigation into a large Swedish family in which several family members had experienced seizures and adrenalin induced syncopes and two teenagers suffered sudden cardiac death during sports activities in school. She discovered a 'typo' in the family's *CALM1* gene – the very first calmodulin mutation that had ever been found, establishing that the mutation caused sudden cardiac death in young people.

Having done this, Professor Nyegaard convinced her husband to turn his laboratory into a calmodulin lab, in order to study the effect of calmodulin mutations on the protein. At the time, to use her analogy, 'there were no labs that I knew that could bake calmodulin bread.' As she later quipped: 'That's what husbands are for!'

That process took years, but what it meant for Kathy, was that when Professor Vinuesa asked Professor Toft Overgaard to carry out functional tests on the G114R mutation, he was able to do so quickly, because in Mette Nyegaard's words, 'the bakery was already built, and Michael had already baked a lot of bad bread!'

Significantly, where the clinicians at the first inquiry had argued that the mutation carried by Kathy and her daughters was a variant of 'unknown significance', or even potentially, benign, Professor Nyegaard, drawing on her own experience, took the opposite view, that there are no 'benign' calmodulin variants.

At the first inquiry, Professor Skinner and his colleagues had supported the use of the ACMG guidelines and its classification system to evaluate and classify the Folbigg variant. But the two professors would tell the second inquiry that, as the Canberra team had argued in their reports to the first inquiry, they 'respectfully' disagreed with this approach, because the guidelines were developed for use in clinical settings, in order to determine appropriate clinical action. They relied heavily on data already generated within the research community and were never intended as a tool to investigate novel links between variants and phenotypes – a person's visible physical characteristics.

In 2018, Professor Vinuesa and Dr Arsov discovered the G114R mutation, which was entirely new and at the first inquiry was predicted by the professor to be likely pathogenic.

What Professor Toft Overgaard and his team had now done, was to produce the protein in the laboratory and demonstrate that the mutation had a damaging effect on the protein's function. 'And we compared the damaging effect to other mutations that were known to be pathogenic, and it was similar in size.' Two other independent laboratories in Canada and the United States conducted different types of tests which also demonstrated that the mutation was damaging to the function of the calmodulin protein.

'We are part couple, part co-workers,' Michael Toft Overgaard told the producers of a documentary aired on the Danish channel TV2. 'We have this odd marriage where I find the mutations, and Michael examines them,' Mette Nyegaard explained. Michael, she said, was the messy one, while she was better organised.

But the couple's science was anything but messy; it was focused, forensic, detailed and precise. The calmodulin protein is vital to maintaining a regular, steady heartbeat. They had shown that the G114R mutation could disrupt the protein's normal functioning.

Both scientists had contributed to the *Europace* paper, which had concluded that the variant 'likely precipitated the natural deaths' of Sarah and Laura. Both children had suffered from infections just before they died, and the paper's authors concluded that: 'A fatal arrhythmic event may have been triggered by their intercurrent infections.'

This provided strong evidence that the *CALM2* mutation had killed the girls. But it was not yet definitive. Back in Denmark, following the publication of the *Europace* paper, Professor Toft Overgaard's team undertook further work in the lab to shore up or disprove the theory. In order to complete the experiments, the team had to replicate the *CALM2* genetic mutation in the laboratory, and then study its effect on different proteins. They discovered that the 'Folbigg mutation' had the same deleterious effect on the calmodulin protein as other lethal cardiac mutations which had previously been shown to cause sudden deaths of infants.

It was known that children with calmodulin mutations could die while exerting themselves, but dying in their sleep was much rarer. However, the scientists were aware of another gene that was known to interfere with the channel that allows molecules of sodium to move in and out of the heart's cells. This interference results, on occasion, in the ventricles – the lower chambers of the heart – beating abnormally fast, and in children dying in their sleep.

When Professor Toft Overgaard was sitting on the couch at home one day, studying the data, he suddenly realised that the G114R mutation identified in the two girls was located in the exact spot where calmodulin binds to the sodium channel. This triggered the thought that Sarah and Laura might have had Brugada syndrome, a rare genetic condition usually caused by an abnormality in the sodium channel that causes fainting and sudden cardiac arrest, often during periods of sleep, and triggered by a fever.

After showing his wife what he had found, she referred to it as 'The Sofa Moment'. The results clearly indicated that the Folbigg calmodulin variant impaired binding to the cardiac sodium channel, and therefore might impact on the function of the channel. To the two professors, it felt like an epiphany.

This happened on a Sunday, and the two professors were due to fly out to Australia the following Friday. If they were going to test the theory in the lab, and repeat the test, they would have to move fast.

The reason they could even attempt to do this in such a short time was because years had been spent setting up a robot in the lab to carry out some of the most complex tests. And, because they already had the funding to study different cardiac channels, they were able to go to the freezer and take out a sample of a sodium channel.

In an email headed 'A little bit urgent' written at 5 am, Professor Toft Overgaard asked Malene Brohus, a postdoctoral fellow in his team, and the first author listed on the *Europace* paper, to perform the same laboratory test with the sodium channel as she had already performed with the calcium and potassium channels.

On Monday evening, as he was driving, the professor received an email with the result, showing that the Folbigg mutation couldn't bind to the sodium channel. And on Wednesday the test was repeated twice, with the same results.

Heading this second inquiry was a former Chief Justice of New South Wales, Tom Bathurst, and his counsel assisting was a young silk, Sophie Callan SC.

When Professors Toft Overgaard and Nyegaard spoke with Ms Callan in an early morning call, it caused some panic for all concerned. The two professors were announcing this huge new development the day before they were due to step on a plane to fly to Sydney to present the results of their laboratory experiments.

Sophie Callan asked them to write a new report the same day containing the results of the new experiment. And the pressure was increased by the fact that Ms Callan and her team clearly had some reservations about the theory, given that Kathy herself appeared completely healthy, with few if any symptoms of Brugada syndrome.

In the mad rush to get the new report finished, Professor Toft Overgaard was still preparing it on his laptop on the way to the airport. 'I'm driving, Michael is writing next to me, so it's super stressful,' his wife told the Danish filmmakers. Even at this extremely late stage, as they sped to the airport, their colleagues back in the lab were generating more data to buttress their findings. And as the professor drafted the report on a Google Doc, simultaneously Mette's sister in Australia was working on the same document, correcting and editing Michael Toft Overgaard's English. 'It was insane!' Mette recalls.

The scientists knew that other experts who were giving evidence to the inquiry would be studying their report intently – and some of them would be highly sceptical. As they were waiting in Abu Dhabi airport, about to board the final leg to Sydney, Professor Toft Overgaard was still putting his final touches to the paper. Everyone else was onboard the flight, while Mette Nyegaard kept the gate open for her husband.

'I'm shouting to the guys: "You need to wait for this man!"' she recounted in the Danish documentary, laughing.

When the report was finally ready, the huge file had to be sent through what Professor Nyegaard describes as the airport's 'tiny' network. At the very last second, Professor Toft Overgaard managed to send it through, and boarded the plane. For the two scientists, the feeling of relief at finally completing their paper was mixed with disbelief that they were now the primary focus of the second inquiry. All eyes would be on them, and the stakes couldn't possibly be higher. Kathy's fate, to a great extent, lay in their hands.

'Suddenly we're focal points in the case,' Professor Nyegaard recalled. 'I've woken up thinking, "What have we got ourselves into?"'

What they had got themselves into was the unenviable task of persuading sceptical clinicians – and a judge – that their data demonstrated that the *CALM* mutation was damaging and therefore that it very likely had killed the two girls. If their data and their reasoning were shot down, it could have enormous negative consequences for Kathy, and for their reputations.

In Sydney, the day before they were due to give evidence, the Danish professors were still preparing their presentation. They were perplexed by the knowledge that there would be other experts, including cardiologists, at the inquiry, who would suggest that the mutation wasn't life-threatening, and who would argue that the fact that the laboratory experiments showed that the *CALM2* variant was pathogenic didn't mean that it had killed the two girls. The clinicians' view was that experiments carried out at a cellular level in the lab didn't necessarily translate into clinical effects in living, breathing human beings.

The two professors saw it as their duty to speak up and explain to the Commissioner, Tom Bathurst, why the disbelievers were wrong, and why the inquiry should respect the data they had acquired, and the conclusions they had reached about how deadly the variant was in real life.

'It is very hard to explain what we need to explain. It really is very complex,' Professor Toft Overgaard acknowledged.

But this was a huge understatement, and as an observer at the inquiry, what impressed me, during the hearings, was to watch the two professors calmly and methodically dig into the granular detail of calmodulin mutations, and the effect of those mutations on the heart's function, while all the time explaining it, not in their native tongue, but in English. I wasn't the only one who was impressed. Anna-Maria Arabia, CEO of the Australian Academy of Science, described it as 'one of the best forms of scientific communication I've ever seen in my life. It was outstanding – beyond measure.'

It was a genuinely stupendous effort, and Mr Bathurst congratulated them on their success in explaining extremely complex, novel concepts so clearly.

In their final report to the inquiry, the professors addressed head-on the criticisms and comments made by Professor Skinner and Professor Kirk in their report to the inquiry.

'Kathleen is currently the only person in the world – known to us – with a *CALM2* G114R mutation,' Professor Toft Overgaard and Professor Nyegaard wrote. 'Claiming that because she is alive then anyone with this mutation should also be alive is an example of "survivorship bias" and is an error of logic.'

Professors Skinner and Kirk had alluded to the existence of another G114R mutation carrier, in the *CALM1* gene, who was listed in the UK Biobank and was, apparently, still alive.

But where the Skinner report suggested that this supported their argument that the variant was not pathogenic, Professors Toft Overgaard and Nyegaard argued the opposite – that it demonstrated that a human carrying the mutation could survive, as Kathy had done. What the data didn't reveal was how many people with the variant had died. Nobody knew that.

A sign of how seriously Sophie Callan and the Commissioner Tom Bathurst took the fresh evidence produced by Professor Toft Overgaard and by Professor Nyegaard, was that after they had presented the results of their tests at the start of the inquiry in November 2022, the hearings were delayed for three months, in order to allow the other experts to assess the new data and draw their own conclusions. The inquiry reopened in February 2023.

From the outset of the second inquiry, Kathy's friends and supporters detected a very different tone in the way the Commissioner and his counsel assisting were approaching the issues under review. Where the first inquiry had been conducted almost like a trial, with Kathy herself being cross-examined relentlessly over two and a half days, this inquiry appeared more neutral, more open and more transparent.

Ms Callan, in her opening statement to the inquiry, made it clear that the conclusions reached by Reginald Blanch in the first inquiry were being set aside, and carried no weight in this inquiry. This inquiry would be entirely independent of the first inquiry.

Addressing Mr Bathurst, she told him: 'Your Honour's task as directed by Her Excellency, the Honourable Margaret Beazley ... is to form your own view as to whether there is a doubt in respect of Ms Folbigg's convictions.

'Accordingly, we submit that your Honour must put the findings and conclusions of the Blanch inquiry to one side. This inquiry is not a review of the Blanch inquiry on the merits or otherwise. Your Honour would similarly put aside the findings and conclusions made in respect of Ms Folbigg's convictions in proceedings previously dealt with in the Court of Criminal Appeal, the High Court, and more recently, the Court of Appeal.'

This, at the outset, felt like a huge victory for Kathy. Mr Bathurst and his team were approaching this second inquiry afresh and with an entirely open mind.

The inquiry was open from the outset to the possibility that the *CALM2* genetic mutation had led to Sarah's and Laura's deaths, and that there were natural causes of death for Caleb and Patrick as well. Professor Toft Overgaard would later describe the experience of giving evidence at the second inquiry in terms that were completely different to the Blanch inquiry. In contrast with how Professor Vinuesa had been treated at the first inquiry, Professors Toft Overgaard and Nyegaard were encouraged to explain their findings at length, in a non-adversarial environment, rather than being asked to give 'yes' or 'no' answers to questions from the counsel assisting.

There followed an extensive examination of the fresh genetic evidence, informed behind the scenes by the Australian Academy of Science, which acted as an independent scientific advisor to the inquiry. The Academy had recommended expert witnesses who could be called to give evidence, some of whom were accepted by counsel assisting, and some not, but in the opinion of the Academy's CEO Anna-Maria Arabia, 'the real benefit came towards the end, when all of the witnesses were giving their evidence, and every single day, before they were cross-examined by Sophie Callan and by Julia Roy, we were able to give them a list of questions and points that needed clarification'.

The Academy produced grids with potential lines of questioning, and points that needed elaboration or clarifying, which they gave to counsel assisting the inquiry. Not all the questions were put to the expert witnesses, but some were. Ms Arabia saw this as an expression of the Academy's independence and as a means of ensuring that the most accurate information from the most qualified experts was on the table, and that no stone had been left unturned when witnesses were cross-examined.

As the February hearings got underway, Professors Toft Overgaard and Nyegaard gave evidence again, laying out the results of more experiments they had carried out at their laboratory in Denmark. This hadn't altered their opinion.

'Our conclusion has not changed from our first report,' they wrote. 'In our opinion, based on the research data and the current understanding of human genetics, the *CALM2* G114R mutation is sufficiently deleterious to have caused the death of the two Folbigg daughters.'

The evidence given by the two Danish professors, however, didn't sail through unchallenged. They encountered headwinds from cardiologists and clinicians who were not at all convinced that the results they had achieved in the Danish lab were conclusive proof that the deaths of the girls had been caused by the genetic mutation.

The challenge they faced was that there were two entirely different types of expert in the room – the scientists and the physicians.

Professor Toft Overgaard would later observe that while clinicians were trained to give a definitive diagnosis of a patient, based on established medical evidence, scientists were trained to test a hypothesis and investigate the unknown, and the Folbigg mutation was unknown before the 2019 inquiry took place – it had never been seen before.

A further challenge was that for geneticists, the rarity of a mutation was usually evidence of its pathogenicity, while for clinicians and judges, a mutation which had not been previously reported carried less weight than mutations that had already been examined and proven to be pathogenic.

And a third challenge was that, because Kathy had been convicted of killing her children, the two scientists felt that the evidence they produced had to be even stronger than if Kathy had not been sent to prison. As Professor Nyegaard put it to me: 'Had she not been in jail, without a doubt people would have said, this is the explanation. We're happy. We found the explanation.'

Not all of the medical experts who gave evidence at the inquiry agreed with the professors' conclusions. At one end of the spectrum, Professor Schwartz strongly supported the theory that a mutation, or mutations in combination, had killed the girls. He highlighted a recent review of the children's genes which had identified a potential 'modifier' gene called *REM2* in all four children, which wasn't present in their mother and must therefore have been inherited from Craig.

While Professors Vinuesa and Cook were cautious about the possible effect of *REM2* in combination with the G114R mutation, Professor Schwartz was far more outspoken, telling the inquiry: 'All four Folbigg infants were found to carry a variant of the so-called "*REM2*" gene which has been clearly demonstrated to increase calcium entry in the cells: a most arrhythmogenic action.' He added: 'This variant is not present in the mother and was clearly inherited from the father. This new finding is a game changer.'

As if to emphasise the point, Professor Schwartz said the new findings showed that the two Folbigg girls 'had another genetic variant causing further increase in calcium current which is lighting the fuse into the barrel of dynamite ... These girls had a double hit as if they had two mutations, not just one. The combination of maternal and paternal DNA has represented a lethal cocktail.'

For their part, Professors Vinuesa and Cook noted that *REM2* presented a potential area for further study, but that it was premature to comment on whether it was in fact a modifying variant in this context.

At the other end of the spectrum was one of the cardiologists who opposed the *CALM2* theory: Dr Calum MacRae,

Professor of Medicine and Cardiology at Harvard Medical School, who had studied the genetics of human cardiac disease for almost thirty years. In a report he wrote for the inquiry he acknowledged that in general, he would support the view that a pathogenic variant would make arrhythmic events more likely if myocarditis was present. This was the scenario for Laura, if it was accepted that the *CALM2* variant was pathogenic.

But he also suggested that there did not appear to be a reasonable possibility that the variant caused Sarah's and Laura's deaths, given the medical and scientific data available. His written opinion was that 'A general estimate of the likelihood of all four siblings having died from independent causes is so unlikely as to be virtually impossible …'

When asked by one of the counsel assisting, Julia Roy, if he was familiar with Meadow's Law, he said that he was, and when asked if he could distinguish his reasoning from the reasoning underpinning Meadow's Law, he stated there was 'no difference in the reasoning, it's simply that probabilities are probabilities'. He added, 'the overall probability of seeing all four [deaths] in a single family suggests a shared influence – it doesn't exclude other possibilities. You're just looking at relative likelihoods, that's all.' Dr MacRae was the only cardiologist who expressed the view that the variant was not a 'reasonably possible' cause of the deaths of the two girls.

To some of those present, myself included, it seemed remarkable that an apparent adherent of Meadow's Law was being offered the opportunity to promote this line of reasoning, twenty years after the theory had been discredited.

If Professor Vinuesa's experience of the first inquiry was unpleasant, her experience of the second was, if anything, even worse, and stood in contrast to the welcome received at the inquiry by Professors Toft Overgaard and Nyegaard.

It was she who had first approached Professor Toft Overgaard, to ask him to carry out laboratory tests on the Folbigg mutation, and who had briefed many of the scientists who signed the second petition, which led directly to the second inquiry. It's fair to say that, without her efforts, the inquiry would not have happened.

After being questioned in what many who were present regarded as an overtly hostile fashion by Gail Furness at the first inquiry, she had no appetite to return to the witness box for a second round. But her initial private discussions with counsel assisting Sophie Callan led her to hope that her appearance at the inquiry would be far friendlier than her experience at the Blanch inquiry.

'We had two Zoom meetings before the actual inquiry,' the professor told me. The assurance she received from Ms Callan was, 'this is not going to feel at all like the first inquiry here. We just want to look at the science. We're going to talk to each of you individually. There's not going to be any confrontation.'

But just before she entered the courtroom to give evidence, the mood changed. Ms Callan approached Ms Vinuesa and – according to the professor – apologised in advance for the line of questioning she was going to put forward. There followed an extended series of questions to the professor about her alleged advocacy for Kathy, her public support for the view that Kathy was an innocent woman, and the suggestion that she might have crossed the line between advocacy and neutral scientific commentary.

Under questioning during the hearing, Professor Vinuesaa explained that: 'When I was first approached I had never heard of Ms Folbigg. To this date, I haven't been paid a cent for the work we've done. It's taken us numerous reports, numerous hours of my work, both during working hours and out of hours. I do this because I believe in the science that we do and I like to draw some conclusions on the science in the way that we can do it. I have no personal interest – I mean I do take personal interest in the cases that I work, but it's not about the individuals, it is about the science.'

She added: 'Our contribution was finding a variant that is verifiable; you can go back to Ms Folbigg's tissues and sequence that over and over again. That was our contribution, and that is infallible.'

Following on from this, Professor Vinuesa gave a short presentation, in which, significantly, she pointed out that for the three *CALM* genes, there had been a total of twenty-three 'missense' variants identified, six for *CALM1*, eight for *CALM2* and nine for *CALM3*. It was important to note, she said, that none had been classified as being benign.

In his final report, Mr Bathurst acknowledged that, in preparing her reports with Dr Arsov and Professor Cook, and in giving evidence before the inquiry, Professor Vinuesa 'sought to act objectively and impartially as an expert.' But she was left extremely unhappy by the experience, describing the experience to me afterwards as 'terrible' and the way in which she was questioned as aggressive and 'unwarranted'.

Almost all of the medical experts agreed with Sophie Callan that ascribing Sarah's and Laura's deaths to the G114R mutation was a 'reasonable possibility'. Professor Skinner wasn't present at the inquiry, but the co-author of their report, Professor Kirk, gave evidence, and Mr Bathurst summarised his views by writing that Professor Kirk, at the Inquiry, 'acknowledged that it was possible that the variant caused the deaths, and it was plausible that it could have caused the deaths, but he did not have enough evidence to say that it was likely that it caused the deaths. In that context, he withdrew the comment in his joint report with Professor Skinner dated 31 October 2022 that, in order for the variant to be included as a possible cause of the two deaths, they would have to accept that Ms Folbigg does indeed have evidence of *CALM* disease in the form of a partially concealed CPVT phenotype.

'Thus, contrary to his initial joint report, Professor Kirk was clearly of the view that the variant was a possible cause of the deaths of Sarah and Laura.'

Further medical evidence came from paediatric neurologist Dr Monique Ryan, a witness from the first inquiry, that Patrick, Kathy's second child may have died from a previously undiagnosed underlying neurogenetic disorder. 'More likely than not, he had an as-yet uncharacterised epileptic encephalopathy,' she suggested.

She was supported in this by another key witness, Professor Peter Fleming, an iconic British paediatrician and researcher, whose work has been credited with saving thousands of lives by pioneering the instruction to parents to put infants to sleep on their backs. Both Professor Fleming and Dr Ryan advanced the view that it was unlikely that Patrick's 'near-miss event', or ALTE, was caused by a 'hypoxic-ischaemic event' such as smothering and was more likely to have been caused by an unknown neurogenetic disorder. His death, it was suggested, could equally be characterised as a SUDEP (a sudden unexpected death in an individual with epilepsy).

Medically speaking, although no clear-cut natural cause of death existed for Caleb, the inquiry could not exclude the 'reasonable possibility' that Caleb died of unknown natural causes.

The final, and perhaps most crucial, consideration for the second inquiry was the meaning and significance of Kathy's journals, and here, for the very first time in the entire judicial chronology of Kathy's case, experts were called upon to offer their opinions about the diaries.

Eight experts submitted reports but were not called to give evidence, and a further three – two psychiatrists and a psychologist, called by the inquiry – gave evidence in person.

Crucially, none of the eleven experts suggested that any of Kathy's diary entries amounted to 'virtual' admissions by her that she had harmed or killed any of her children.

The psychologists and psychiatrists gave evidence that in their opinions, the diaries were manifestations of grief and despair and the guilt that any mother would feel over the death of one or more of their children – but they were not admissions to having harmed or killed the children.

One expert, psychologist Patrick Sheehan, made an intriguing suggestion about one of Kathy's diary entries which, in the past, had always been read to suggest that when Sarah died, she had left 'with a bit of help'.

Mr Sheehan was asked at the hearings whether he maintained there was an innocent explanation for this entry. His observation was that the writing in the diary was messy, in circumstances where it was scribbled out late at night in a state of distress. Mr Sheehan said it looked to him as if there was a full stop or comma after '& she left' which if so, changed the passage to read: 'I knew I was short tempered & cruel sometimes with her & she left. With a bit of help I don't want that ever to happen again.' Mr Sheehan also commented that in his opinion, the cross-examination that Kathy had endured at the first inquiry was 'quite brutal'.

In all, there were thirteen days of hearings at the second inquiry, starting in November 2022, and finishing at the end of April 2023.

On Day 11, as if the story of Kathleen Folbigg couldn't throw up any further surprises, a solicitor representing the Commissioner of Police delivered a bombshell. A box full of cassette tapes containing around 530 hours of secret recordings of Kathy and Craig at home had been discovered – but the police weren't revealing what was on the tapes.

The recordings appeared to have come from Operation Jetty – the secret operation to intercept phone conversations and to pick up conversations between Kathy and Craig in their home, before she was interviewed and later, arrested and charged. But mystery swirled around the fact that the existence of the box of tapes was only now being revealed, twenty years too late. A few of them contained recordings which had been transcribed and produced at the trial, but there were hundreds of hours of secret recordings which had not been produced at the trial, or at either inquiry, and it wasn't even clear whether the detectives had produced contemporaneous logs of the recordings, because those too had not been produced.

I was told that: 'The listening devices employed in this case were used lawfully for investigative purposes under the authority of a warrant issued by the Supreme Court.

'As is usual in such a trial, only the recordings, and transcripts of them, that were identified by the prosecutor (who is an independent office-holder) as relevant were tendered as evidence in the proceeding.

'It would appear that those tendered recordings were misplaced, and were not available by the time of the first inquiry despite efforts to locate them in that context.

'During the second inquiry, further attempts were made, and the tendered recordings were located at Muswellbrook Police Station. They were produced to the second inquiry accordingly.'

On 26 April, finally, Sophie Callan stood up to give her closing submission, in front of a court packed with counsel and with Kathy's friends and supporters. Kathy herself and her friends were quietly, if anxiously, optimistic but they had been down this road before with the Blanch inquiry, and there were no guarantees that Ms Callan would take a different view.

As the courtroom collectively held its breath, she told Mr Bathurst: 'On the whole of the body of evidence before this inquiry there is a reasonable doubt as to Ms Folbigg's guilt.' That one brief sentence would prove to be the statement that overturned two decades of injustice.

Crucially, Ms Callan revealed that the Director of Public Prosecutions had also accepted that the evidence brought to the inquiry raised 'reasonable doubt' over Kathy's convictions. There would be no push-back from the state's prosecutors.

Sitting next to Anna-Maria Arabia in court was the former President of the Australian Academy of Science, Professor John Shine, who reacted audibly, and with outrage to some of the details contained in the account of the case given by Ms Callan. 'But for me,' Ms Arabia told me, 'it was a moment of, "Gosh, I'm proud that the Academy's been involved in this way."'

The icing on the cake came from Mr Bathurst, who made it clear that he agreed with his counsel. 'In the present case …

there is a significant body of evidence now to suggest reasonable possibilities of identifiable natural causes of death,' he announced.

In complete contrast with the judgment reached by Mr Blanch, Mr Bathurst would later state: 'I do not regard the diaries as containing reliable admissions of guilt.' The diaries – maybe more than anything else – had persuaded the jury at Kathy's trial that she was guilty. But in 2003, not one single expert was called by her defence to suggest a different interpretation. Now, twenty years later, eleven experts, including three experts called to give evidence by the inquiry, had all agreed that the meaning of the diaries was an innocent one, and a senior judge concurred.

It was a stunning turnaround, but it also revealed the fragility of the law courts' ability to reach the right conclusion about a person's mental state. This was brought home to me in a conversation I had later on with Dr Betts, the clinical psychologist who concluded early on that Kathy's diaries were not admissions of guilt.

Dr Betts told me a story which until now has never been told in public. She said that some time after Kathy's conviction, she attended a Law Society presentation being given by the legal academic Gary Edmond, which was also attended by Peter Zahra, Kathy's senior counsel at her trial. After the presentation, she approached Mr Zahra and introduced herself, and told him that, in her opinion, Kathy's conviction was a 'tremendous injustice, and a wrongful conviction'.

'And he looked down at me, over the top of his glasses, and he said, "You would have no doubts if you had read the diaries." And he walked off.'

To say that I was stunned by this is an understatement – it left me speechless. Naively perhaps, I had always assumed that Kathy's defence team genuinely believed that she was innocent, and maybe some of them did. But clearly, not Peter Zahra. Sadly, he passed away in 2022 and I was unable to ask him about this, but Dr Betts' memory is very clear.

Mr Zahra's comment to Dr Betts did nothing to clear up the mystery of why Kathy's defence had not arranged for psychiatric evidence to be presented at her trial on her behalf. In July 2002, her solicitor Peter Krisenthal had written a letter to Doug Humphreys, the Director of Criminal Law at Legal Aid NSW, telling him, 'I believe we will need to obtain ... a comprehensive psychiatric evaluation of not only our client but also of the numerous entries made in diaries. There is a large body of diary entries which the Crown say are damaging, however it could equally be seen as being the ruminations of a grief struck parent.' The mystery remains as to why that never happened.

The only participant in the second inquiry who asserted that there was no reasonable doubt as to Kathy's guilt was her former husband, Craig.

Craig had refused to give a DNA sample in order to allow the scientists to establish whether his children had a 'de novo' mutation – that is, one not present in either parent, which are typically the most lethal and are known to account for two thirds of genetic disease in very sick children. Without both parents' genomes, it is impossible to identify these mutations, which in this case, might have thrown further light on the causes of death for Kathy's two boys. To Kathy's supporters, it seemed like sheer bloody-mindedness. It was something he could have done swiftly, at no cost to himself, and had he done so, he would have been applauded for helping the scientists establish a fuller genetic map of the family.

Damningly for him, his account of what occurred on the night that Sarah died was also not believed. Mr Bathurst, in his final report, agreed with Sophie Callan that there was no rational basis for preferring Craig's evidence over Kathy's as to what exactly happened that night.

'The evidence of Mr Folbigg varied from certainty that Sarah was in her bed, because he could see her by virtue of the streetlight, to certainty that she was not in her bed, to the intermediate position that he was not sure,' Mr Bathurst noted, adding: 'The reliability of his evidence is further affected by the statement that he was lying when he said "Kathy had kissed

Caleb on the night he died",' and comments he had made which were recorded by the listening devices planted by the police, and his statement that he had lied when he told his family and friends about Ms Folbigg grieving for Laura.

'In these circumstances, I am unable to accept Mr Folbigg's evidence in preference to that of Ms Folbigg as to what occurred on the evening of Sarah's death. In reaching this conclusion, I am conscious of the fact that Ms Folbigg's overall credibility is affected by the fact she lied to the Police when she stated she had not written in a diary since 9 May 1999 and her explanation of what she told the Police, given at the 2019 Inquiry was, to say the least, unconvincing.

'Notwithstanding this, for the reasons I have given, I am unable to accept the evidence of Mr Folbigg of the events which occurred on the night of Sarah's death, in preference to that of Ms Folbigg."

Mr Bathurst's opinion was that: 'Care must also be taken in dealing with certain aspects of Mr Folbigg's evidence regarding Ms Folbigg's relationship with her children.

'For example, his statement that Ms Folbigg appeared "devastated" after Sarah died, but she did not continue to be devastated seems to me to be an attempt to minimise the grief that Ms Folbigg suffered.'

Mr Bathurst noted that there were 'inconsistencies between his evidence concerning the morning of Laura's death and his statement to the Police and an inconsistency in his evidence that Ms Folbigg threw Sarah at him on the evening of her death.'

Added to which: 'It is also relevant that a considerable number of witnesses called at the trial and at this Inquiry gave evidence that Ms Folbigg was a loving mother who grieved for her children.'

Mr Bathurst referred in particular to the evidence given by Kathy's close friend Karren Hall and also, Megan Donegan's evidence.

Further, Dr Marley, the GP who attended to Patrick and Sarah, said he saw no signs of neglect, and that Kathy and Craig appeared to be caring and concerned parents.

'Counsel Assisting submitted that the evidence does not establish that Ms Folbigg was angry or frustrated towards her children on a consistent basis but rather tends to suggest that Ms Folbigg was, in general, a loving and caring mother towards her children.'

Damningly for Craig, Mr Bathurst concluded that: 'The evidence before the Inquiry, at most, demonstrates that Ms Folbigg was a loving and caring mother who occasionally became angry and frustrated with her children. That provides no support for the proposition that she killed her four children.'

Craig's counsel made some final submissions on his behalf which smacked of desperation. By this stage, even the Director of Public Prosecutions had acknowledged that the fresh evidence raised reasonable doubt as to Kathy's guilt.

But not Craig. His counsel made two quite bizarre submissions: first, in an unmistakeable echo of Meadow's Law, suggesting that the possibility of four deaths occurring from natural causes was one in a billion.

And secondly, even more disturbing, was a suggestion that there might be a genetic cause for Kathy murdering her children.

Mr Bathurst gave this notion very short shrift, saying: 'Suffice to say, this submission had no foundation in the evidence and was not permitted to be the subject of cross-examination of the genetic experts who gave evidence. The submission was rank speculation and should not have been made.'

His final comment was that Craig's submissions 'do not persuade me that there is not reasonable doubt that Ms Folbigg was guilty of the crimes for which she was convicted'.

39

FREE AT LAST

When it happened, it happened with unexpected speed. Kathy's twenty-year fight for justice came to a head, unexpectedly, almost in an instant.

Early on Monday, 5 June 2023, after twenty years behind bars, Kathy was pardoned unconditionally by the Governor of New South Wales, Margaret Beazley. One minute, she was going about her daily business inside Clarence Correctional Facility; the next, she was stepping into a van to be escorted out of the prison, and into the arms of her lifelong friend, Tracy Chapman, shaking in disbelief.

'My stuff's following me – they threw me out!' Kathy joked, adding: 'I am beyond happy – it's ridiculous.'

As Tracy admitted later, it was 'surreal'. And it showed. After fiercely hugging Kathy, she turned to the prison officer and hugged him too.

In one sense Kathy's sudden release ruined Tracy's carefully laid plans. She had spearheaded weeks of relentless media pressure on the state's new Attorney General, Michael Daley, in her efforts to have her friend freed, and further action was planned for the week when she was finally released. It proved to be unnecessary.

In a small flat Tracy and her husband, Phil, had prepared for her on their farm, Kathy was able to put on pyjamas and sleep for as long as she liked on a decent mattress. In Tracy's home, teeming with animals, she tucked into a T-bone steak. And in the field outside, Kathy and Tracy cuddled up to the horses that Tracy and Phil have taken care of for years.

For her, after two decades locked up in prison, these simple things were almost unimaginable luxuries, and for Kathy, they helped to start the long and difficult healing process.

Megan Donegan rushed from her home to be with Kathy and Tracy and for her, being with them both while they watched the TV coverage was 'the most emotional thing I have ever done. To watch a report about her dead babies, sitting there with her, everyone had tears rolling down their faces. It was too close to home; it was hard to watch,' she told me.

Six weeks earlier, on Wednesday, 26 April, Sophie Callan SC had stood up in the Sydney courtroom where the second inquiry was being heard, to deliver her final submission to Mr Bathurst. The words she spoke sent shudders through the New South Wales judiciary.

Ms Callan declared that after studying all of the evidence, it was open to Mr Bathurst to find 'reasonable doubt' as to Kathy's guilt.

At the same time, Sally Dowling SC, the New South Wales Director of Public Prosecutions, also acknowledged that there was reasonable doubt surrounding her convictions, although in a clear attempt at damage control, Dean Jordan SC, for the DPP, asserted that 'this substantial and extensive body of new evidence was unknown at the time of Ms Folbigg's trial'.

Rather than wait the months it would take him to prepare and publish his final report, Mr Bathurst provided a summary of his findings for the Attorney General on 2 June. He stated that he had reached 'a firm view that there was reasonable doubt as to the guilt of Ms Folbigg for each of the offences for which she was originally tried'. He recommended she be pardoned.

From that point, the Attorney General acted quickly. Mr Daley called a meeting of the Executive Council to obtain its agreement for his recommendation to the Governor that a pardon be granted.

It wasn't just Kathy and her friends and supporters who celebrated. The Governor's pardon represented an enormous victory for the lawyers who, on her behalf, had worked for years pro bono, and for those scientists who, in the teeth of fierce opposition from the state's legal establishment, dared to stand up and cast doubt on her convictions. Professor Chennupati Jagadish, the new President of the Australian Academy of Science, said: 'I am relieved that an unconditional pardon to Kathleen Folbigg has been granted and that science has been heard.'

The Governor's pardon also represented a triumph for Professor Vinuesa, who had refused to take Mr Blanch's verdict lying down, and for Professors Toft Overgaard and Nyegaard, the husband-and-wife team on the other side of the world, who finished the job, providing the empirical evidence that, from a scientific perspective, finally persuaded a judge that reasonable doubt surrounded Kathy's convictions.

In comments about Kathy's diary entries, Mr Bathurst said: 'Evidence suggests they were the writings of a grieving and possibly depressed mother, blaming herself for the death of each child, as distinct from admissions that she murdered or otherwise harmed them.'

Perhaps most significantly, Mr Bathurst emphasised in his summary that he was 'unable to accept … the proposition that Ms Folbigg was anything but a caring mother for her children'. It was a resounding validation of her qualities and commitment as a mother, and a strong rebuttal of all the allegations made at her trial by her former husband.

The announcement of Kathy's pardon and release was made by the Attorney General, Michael Daley. It came only after intense pressure was placed on him over a number of weeks to do so.

The pressure came from a broad and influential cross-section of lawyers and academics, as well as upper house MPs in the New South Wales Parliament, some of whom had issued passionate calls for her release in a debate the previous week.

At times, Kathy's supporters contended, the judicial hierarchy had been actively unhelpful.

Peter Yates, who headed Team Folbigg, condemned the lack of funding offered to her lawyers to do their job of representing her. 'The Attorney General's office and Legal Aid provided as little support as they could, even to the point of not being prepared to pay for travel and accommodation in Sydney during these inquiries for her Newcastle-based legal team.'

He continued: 'The result today brought together the science, through the endeavours of our great scientists, with huge support from the Australian Academy of Science; and the philanthropists, who have committed their skills and their financial resources in an extraordinary way.

'Without that, I don't think that this would have been possible.'

Kathy was free at last, but her life had effectively been destroyed. Branded as that most evil of criminals – a baby-killer – she had been deprived of her liberty, beaten up in prison, locked away in protective custody for much of her incarceration and vilified in the public's mind for decades.

She emerged from prison having lost the best years of her adult life, lastingly traumatised by her children's deaths, with not a cent to her name and no home she could call her own.

She had little else to look forward to beyond the welcome and warmth of those who resolutely refused to accept that she was guilty.

Five months after Kathy's release, in November 2023, Tom Bathurst handed down his final inquiry report, which ran to more than 600 pages.

Importantly, he couldn't say that Kathy had been proven innocent – for the simple reason that this was an impossibility. One of the challenges that had dogged her ever since she was charged with murdering her children, was that it was impossible to prove a negative – that she didn't kill her children, unless someone else confessed to doing so.

All she could do, and had always done, was to protest her innocence, and to allow the arguments supporting natural causes of death for each of her children to be made. But even here, she had always been at a disadvantage, because the deaths of two of her children, Caleb and Sarah, had been ascribed to SIDS, a diagnosis of exclusion, which always left open the possibility to prosecutors that she had actively hastened their deaths.

Now at last an inquiry had accepted that a genetic variant causing lethal cardiac arrhythmias had triggered the deaths of Sarah and Laura.

All Mr Bathurst could say, based on the fresh genetic and neurological evidence and the new interpretations of her diaries, was that reasonable doubt now existed.

'I have concluded that there is an identifiable cause of the death of Patrick, Sarah and Laura, and that it was more likely that Patrick's ALTE was caused by a neurogenetic disorder rather than suffocation,' Mr Bathurst declared in his report.

'Once that conclusion is reached, any probative force of the coincidence and tendency evidence is substantially diminished.

'Further, I have concluded that the relationship Ms Folbigg had with her children does not support the inference that she killed them.'

In one significant respect, Mr Bathurst was critical of the first inquiry, and the way in which Kathy had been cross-examined about her diaries. 'I have read and listened to the cross examination of Ms Folbigg at the 2019 Inquiry,' he wrote. 'It is fair to say that the object of the cross examination was to reinforce the finding of guilt and her examination by both Senior Counsel acting for the DPP and Senior Counsel for Mr Folbigg was openly hostile.'

If the aim of Mr Maxwell, who was acting for the DPP, and Ms Cunneen, who was acting for Craig Folbigg, was to wrestle a confession out of Kathy by browbeating her into submission, it hadn't worked. Mr Bathurst also wrote: 'Finally, I do not regard the diaries as containing reliable admissions of guilt.'

To this day, no clear cause of death has been established for Kathy's firstborn, but Mr Bathurst didn't suggest that he had been deliberately killed. 'Although no identifiable cause of Caleb's death was identified the matters to which I have referred in the previous paragraph mean that in his case the reasonable possibility that he died of unknown natural causes has not been excluded,' he wrote.

Even if it wasn't a full-throated declaration of Kathy's innocence, it was an unequivocal rebuttal of the conclusions reached by Reginald Blanch at the first inquiry, and of the circumstantial and coincidence evidence put forward at Kathy's trial. No longer did all the available evidence reinforce her guilt, as Mr Blanch had argued in 2019. Now, at last, a judge had accepted that the fresh evidence called her convictions into doubt, and, in agreement with his senior counsel Sophie Callan, Mr Bathurst went further than this, saying that in his opinion, Kathy was a loving, caring mother.

Crucially, Mr Bathurst granted Kathy's wish and the wish of her legal team by referring her case to the Court of Criminal Appeal. This could only mean one thing: that, barring extraordinary, unforeseen circumstances, Kathy's convictions would now be formally quashed, and she would finally be exonerated.

When Mr Bathurst handed down his report, Tracy Chapman told me: 'Kath thinks of her children every day and continues to grapple with the challenges of adjusting to life outside prison after twenty years of incarceration. Our hope is that the Court of Criminal Appeal will see the evidence with fresh eyes and exonerate Kathleen.'

Five weeks later, on Thursday, 14 December, the day Kathy had wished and waited for since May 2003 finally arrived.

Dressed in a purple top and hanging on to Tracy for dear life, Kathy joined her closest friends and supporters and her lawyers Dr Robert Cavanagh and Rhanee Rego at the Court of Criminal Appeal, inside the cavernous Supreme Court building in the centre of Sydney. Along with all the friends and supporters who had made it to the court, I gave her a hug and wished her well, as we trooped into the public gallery.

Minutes later, the three judges entered, bewigged and robed in red and white, and sat down. A court official solemnly declaimed the time-worn proclamation: 'All persons having any business before this honourable court now draw nigh and give your attendance.'

Chief Justice Andrew Bell began to read his judgment, tonelessly. It could have been a bus timetable he was reading out, and it was impossible to know what he was thinking, but the conclusion he and his two fellow judges had reached about Mr Bathurst's findings couldn't be clearer.

'Having ourselves reviewed the Report, we do so find, for similar reasons that led Mr Bathurst to the same conclusion.

'First and most significantly, the "substantial and extensive body of new scientific evidence" to which the Crown referred in written submissions and which was before Mr Bathurst and considered in the Report substantially diminished any probative force of what had been relied on at the original trial as powerful coincidence and tendency evidence.'

In layman's language, by demonstrating plausible natural causes of death for Patrick, Sarah and Laura, the scientists had demolished the coincidence evidence relied on at Kathy's trial to try to prove she had smothered her children.

'Secondly, in relation to the diary entries, it may readily be understood how certain entries, viewed in isolation, had a powerful influence on the original jury in a manner adverse to Ms Folbigg. Viewed in their full context, however, as they must be, and informed by the expert psychological and psychiatric expert evidence referred to extensively in the Report and which was not before the jury, we agree with Mr Bathurst's conclusion that the diary entries were not reliable admissions of guilt.'

This represented an enormous victory for Kathy. Where Reginald Blanch had ignored the context in which the diaries were written, and had insisted that the 'plain meaning' in her diaries could only mean one thing: that she had killed her first three children, here were four judges saying that wasn't the case, and that the entries she had written in her journals couldn't be interpreted as 'virtual' admissions of guilt.

'Thus,' Chief Justice Bell concluded, 'while the verdicts at trial were reasonably open on the evidence then available, there is now reasonable doubt as to Ms Folbigg's guilt.

'In these circumstances and as a consequence, it is appropriate that Ms Folbigg's convictions for: the manslaughter of Caleb Folbigg; maliciously inflicting grievous bodily harm upon Patrick Folbigg, with intent to do grievous bodily harm; the murder of Patrick Folbigg; the murder of Sarah Folbigg; and the murder of Laura Folbigg on 1 March 1999 be quashed.'

Chief Justice Bell took a moment to make one further order, directing the entry of verdicts of acquittal. With that, for Kathy, the presumption of innocence finally returned.

There was a short, stunned silence in court, as if no one could believe what had actually occurred. Then a gasp from Kathy, a round of applause from the public gallery, tears, laughter and hugs.

Everyone was taking in what had just happened, as if in slow motion. I walked over to a gaggle of Kathy's friends and supporters. The lawyers could barely contain their relief. Friends and supporters didn't. Anna-Maria Arabia had tears flowing down her cheeks.

Back in Newcastle, an ABC crew filmed Kathy's loyal first solicitor, Brian Doyle, watching the verdict on an online feed from the court. As the word 'quashed' was uttered, Mr Doyle smacked his fist into his hand, exclaiming, 'Yes!' Seconds later, he momentarily lost his composure. He gasped, his head dropped, and there were tears in his eyes as he was asked how he felt.

'It's been a long time. Justice for Kathleen Folbigg. But she had to do twenty years in jail to reach this stage,' he replied.

Mr Doyle was the first of Kathy's legal representatives to argue in court that her diaries were not confessions of guilt. Now his argument had been upheld by three of the most senior judges in the land. The vindication was sweet. 'This little lawyer from the country's views have been justified.'

Outside court, ten minutes later, Kathy, dabbing away her own tears, spoke to the media and her supporters: 'I hope that no one else will ever have to suffer what I suffered,' she said, her voice breaking. 'My children are here with me today, and they will be close to me for the rest of my life. I love my children and I always will.'

She ended with the words: 'Truth, and correct legal outcomes matter.'

I was reminded of Sally Clark's words when she was finally acquitted of murder in January 2003: 'There are no winners here. We have all lost out. We simply feel relief that our nightmare is finally at an end.'

A few hours later, not far from the court, a small, select group who had been invited by Kathy and by Peter Yates gathered for lunch in a room set aside at his club. It was billed as 'A Lunch to Celebrate Kathleen Folbigg and Team Folbigg – Mission Accomplished'.

The surroundings were formal, the atmosphere in the room much less so. On the menu, fittingly, was a seasonal offering of roast turkey and mince pies. And to drink, Jacquart Champagne, Clare Valley Riesling, Chardonnay, Pinot Noir and – in a tongue-in-cheek tribute to Kathy, the drink she most enjoyed before she went to jail – Kahlua. On her first evening following her release six months before, she had celebrated with Kahlua and Coke and a pizza. It was all a far cry from Clarence Correctional Facility.

The lunch was joyous, and everyone present, including Kathy and Tracy, spoke. But it wasn't a triumphal gathering. Emotional, yes, and suffused with happiness, friendship, relief and gratitude.

Tears flowed freely, and fulsome tributes were paid to the courage and determination of the scientists, to the years of unpaid effort put in by the lawyers on Kathy's behalf, and to the work carried out behind the scenes by 'Team Folbigg', without which, almost certainly, Kathy would still be in prison, serving out her sentence.

Kathy had emerged from prison as a horribly wronged woman, the victim of the most serious miscarriage of justice in Australia's recent criminal history; the mother who lost four children in succession, who was wrongfully charged with their murders, wrongfully convicted and subsequently vilified for heinous crimes she didn't commit.

The one word 'acquittal' represented a disaster for the New South Wales judiciary, which, through Kathy's trial, multiple appeals and the previous inquiry, had continued to assert her guilt, in the teeth of growing evidence that, in fact, she was an innocent woman. No fewer than twenty-one New South Wales judges had weighed in on the case, and only four in the end had concluded that Kathy's convictions could not be upheld.

The acquittal also represented a triumph for the Australian Academy of Science, which from 2020 onwards had put the case to a largely sceptical legal fraternity that a newly discovered genetic variant had triggered the deaths of Kathy's two daughters.

The Academy's efforts had been led by their CEO Anna-Maria Arabia, who was described to me by Professor Vinuesa as 'brave and determined'. It was she who, crucially, had introduced the professor to the former academy president, Professor John Shine, who had driven the efforts to get world-leading scientists on board with the second petition, who had requested permission for the academy to be legally represented at the second inquiry, and who had steered the Academy's media strategy, greatly enhancing its voice and visibility with a wider public audience. It was a mammoth and ultimately successful effort.

One notable absentee was Professor Vinuesa, who had moved to London to work at the Crick Institute, and when I spoke to Anna-Maria Arabia later on, she acknowledged the enormous contribution the professor had made to bringing about Kathy's exoneration. 'It took the team; without Peter, without all of us, it wouldn't have happened,' she told me, 'and it ought not be that way to deliver justice. But the star of the show, the Penelope Cruz in the Netflix series, is Carola Vinuesa.'

Despite the intense relief felt by everyone present at the lunch, there was also a keen sense that for Kathy herself, the moment was bitter-sweet. She could celebrate the outcome, but it would forever be overlaid with the sadness of her children's absence. In prison, Kathy said goodnight to them every evening, glancing at the newspaper clipping on the wall of her cell that carried their pictures.

Even though she was free, she had no idea where her children's remains were interred, because Craig had removed them from Singleton in a deliberate attempt to keep them away from her. It was just one more painful hurdle she would have to tackle, in order to be able to visit their memorial.

Rhanee Rego approached Craig's solicitor, Danny Eid, on Kathy's behalf, to demand to be told where her children's ashes lay. The answer given was that they had been scattered in the ocean by Craig at Sapphire Beach in northern New South Wales, a long way away from where Kathy and the children had lived. Mr Eid, meanwhile, had questioned the judges' decision to quash Kathy's convictions and acquit her, rather than ordering a retrial.

The suggestion was absurd – not least because so many of the witnesses who gave evidence at Kathy's trial had since passed away. No one – not the judges, nor even the DPP – had suggested that a retrial was appropriate. And it reflected badly on Craig.

EPILOGUE

On a glorious sunny day in August 2021, I drove with an old filmmaker friend and colleague, Ivan O'Mahoney, to Wentworth Falls in the Blue Mountains, outside Sydney, to record an interview with Professor John Hilton for a documentary we were hoping to make about Kathy's case.

Professor Hilton, who had always insisted that he was a neutral expert at Kathy's trial – and not a witness for the prosecution – had fallen ill, but that didn't dull his razor-sharp mind as we filmed with him over a long and testing day. It was the last recorded interview he gave before he passed away in November 2022.

Here was a man who, in March 1999, had uttered an oath on hearing that Laura was the fourth child to die in the Folbigg family, exclaiming that it was murder. When we saw him, graciously, he didn't deny having done so. 'This is, I suppose, the sort of reaction that most reasonably experienced pathologists would have had,' he told us.

Now, however, Meadow's Law was no longer in vogue and no longer supportable, and he was telling us that in Kathy's case, 'from a scientific point of view, or a medical point of view, it's a huge miscarriage of justice'. The wheel had turned full circle. And scientific truth had trumped legal intransigence.

In March 2024, Craig Folbigg died suddenly and unexpectedly after suffering a heart attack. He had been diagnosed with cancer a few months earlier.

For the Folbigg family, it was just one more terrible tragedy. For Kathy, Craig's sudden death wiped out any prospect of any kind of conversation or reconciliation – let alone a meeting of minds – between her and her former husband, following her acquittal.

Danny Eid released a statement on the family's behalf, saying that Craig 'was a dedicated, hardworking family man and he spent his last few years under enormous stress and pressure', and adding: 'He never stopped believing his children had been murdered.'

In my opinion, Craig was sadly misguided in that belief, and it seemed to me that once again, Voltaire's saying rang true: 'To the living we owe respect; to the dead we owe only the truth.' The respect so often denied to Kathy, now judged to be a loving, caring mother, had been deservedly restored, while the truth was that there was no evidence that her children were murdered, and Craig had been wrong all along to suggest that there was.

Kathy, through her tireless and fearless advocate Rhanee Rego, released a brief, gracious statement: 'There are only two people on this earth who knew what it felt like to lose Caleb, Patrick, Sarah and Laura. My condolences go to the loved ones Craig leaves behind.'

I'd been hoping to interview Craig and ask him whether he acknowledged the objective validity of the evidence uncovered by scientists, to support their view that Sarah's and Laura's deaths were triggered by a cardiac genetic variant, and whether he accepted the judges' view – in the end – that there were credible natural causes of death for his children.

But I think I know what his answer would have been.

Meanwhile, one year after her acquittal, Kathy still waits to be compensated for her wrongful conviction and incarceration, and as the victim of arguably the worst miscarriage of justice in recent Australian criminal history, she is still waiting to receive an apology.

Emma Cunliffe told me that when she first read the full acquittal judgment, 'I was looking for two things: I was looking, first of all, for an apology to Kathy, or at least, an acknowledgement of the ordeal that she had been through. It was striking by its absence; indeed, there was no expression of compassion for Kathleen at any point.

'The second striking thing about the acquittal judgment is that there is a complete failure to consider the question of whether the legal system itself has anything to learn from this case and, to take it a step further, to consider whether the legal system had played any contributing role in this wrongful conviction.'

In my view, Professor Cunliffe is right; instead of doing so, the state's Attorneys General buried their heads in the sand, pretending that Kathy's acquittal demonstrated that the legal system works.

Mark Speakman, who presided over years of delays before allowing her case to be reviewed, said there had been 'suggestions that we should have a kind of independent criminal review commission that might look at these sorts of cases', adding that 'I don't think that would've made any difference here.'

Mr Daley, who had the power, following Kathy's acquittal, to order a review of the legal processes undertaken in the case, instead waved away the opportunity to do so, saying, 'I am grateful as well and all citizens should be that the review provisions are available in New South Wales to ensure that where circumstances arise like these ones, justice can be ultimately done even if it takes a long time.'

That will come as no comfort to the woman who languished in jail for twenty years before her convictions were overturned.

Justice Michael Kirby, who turned down a High Court appeal by Kathy in 2005, told *The Guardian*, 'This isn't a rare case. We seem to be having lots of these cases of unjust convictions coming forward', while suggesting that an independent commission would act as a 'failsafe'. In a further comment to the *Law Society Journal*, Justice Kirby acknowledged that, 'You will never reduce totally the risk of miscarriage of justice, but we can do better.'

And what of Kathy herself?

Her loss has been by far the greatest, greater than any other recent victim of a wrongful conviction in Australia. For the rest of her life, as Sally Clark before her did when she was acquitted, she will struggle with the challenge of re-entering the 'real' world, with the task of maintaining her own mental health and wellbeing, and with the grief of losing her four precious children; Caleb, with the long, piano-playing fingers; Patrick, the risk-taker; Sarah, the cheeky one; and Laura, so loved by everyone.

She will live forever with the dismay of knowing what might have been.

Caleb, had he lived, would now be in his late thirties; Patrick one year younger; Sarah would be in her early thirties, and Laura would be in her late twenties – all with the very best of their lives ahead of them.

BIBLIOGRAPHY AND FURTHER READING

The Injustice Project (www.injustice.law/kathleen-folbigg) contains several articles explaining key issues in Kathy's case and republishes the petition from May 2015 that resulted in the first inquiry into her convictions in 2018 and 2019 (www.injustice.law/articles/folbigg-petition-to-governor-for-review). A second petition in March 2021, which resulted in the second inquiry, is also republished (www.injustice.law/articles/folbigg-petition-to-governor-for-pardon).

All of the transcripts and exhibits for Kathy's trial in 2003, and for the two inquiries into her convictions can be found on the 2022 Folbigg inquiry website (2022folbigginquiry.dcj.nsw.gov.au) together with the final reports from each inquiry. All of Kathy's journals and diaries were collated and published on that website. The Copyright and disclaimer notice for material appearing on the Folbigg inquiry website can be seen at dcj.nsw.gov.au/statements/copyright-and-disclaimer.html and unless a different form of attribution is specified for the material appearing on the website, material is © State of New South Wales (Department of Communities and Justice).

The ABC's *Australian Story* broadcast a double episode about Kathy's story in 2004, the year after she was convicted of killing all four of her children. In August 2018, a further episode was broadcast, which called her convictions into question (www.youtube.com/watch?v=fAcEQpGiV5w). Following Kathy's pardon and release in June 2023, they broadcast a further episode (iview.abc.net.au/show/australian-story/series/2023/video/NC2302Q016S00).

Chapter Title Quotes
1 'I'm Sorry Darling, I Had to Do It': Apology reportedly uttered by Thomas Britton after he had stabbed his wife to death.
4 'Mixed Feelings': On 3 June 1990, the day that Patrick was born, Kathy wrote in her diary that she had 'mixed feelings' as to whether she would cope as a mother.
5 'The Cheekiest One Ever': Kathy told Tracy Chapman that Sarah was 'the cheekiest one ever'.
6 'This Last One Has Broken Me': Letter from Kathy to Craig in 1995.
7 'The Biggest Party Ever!': In Kathy's police interview with Detective Senior Constable Bernie Ryan, Kathy talked about the party thrown for Laura on her first birthday.

8 'I've Had Three Go Already!': Kathy made this remark to the ambulance service on 1 March 1999.
9 'Four is Fucking Murder!': Remark reportedly made by Professor John Hilton, on being told of Laura's death.
10 'Obviously, I'm My Father's Daughter': Remark written by Kathy in her diary on 14 October 1996.
11 'All Night I've Been Thinking, Maybe I Killed the Kids': Remark by Craig Folbigg in a conversation with Kathy on 26 July 1999, secretly recorded by the police.
12 'With Three, You Yell "Murder!"': Comment by American forensic pathologist Dr Linda Norton in the Waneta Hoyt case, and quoted by police psychologist Rozalinda Garbutt in February 2000.
13 'I Couldn't Leave the Lady in the Lurch': Remark by Kathy's first solicitor Brian Doyle in conversations with the author.
15 'Honest to God': Remark by Craig Folbigg to police in May 1999: 'Everything that is recorded in this statement is the truth, honest to God.'
20 'A Scholar of Bias': Emma Cunliffe described herself as this to the author.
23 'An Eminently Fatal Case of Myocarditis': Description made by forensic pathologist Dr Matthew Orde to ABC's *Australian Story* regarding samples of Laura's heart.
24 'That's, as Mothers, What You Do': Remark by Kathy to Tracy Chapman in a phone call from prison, recorded for the ABC's *Australian Story*.
27 'It is an Appalling Situation': Remark by Reginald Blanch, Commissioner of the first inquiry into Kathy's convictions, on 18 March 2019.
28 'She Could be Part of that Small Number': Remark by Dr Allan Cala, chief medical witness at Kathy's trial, on 20 March 2019.
31 'The Ordinary, Plain Meaning': Phrase used by Gail Furness SC, counsel assisting the first inquiry into Kathy's convictions, on 1 May 2019.
32 'Hope Can Destroy One's Soul': Phrase included in a letter written to Emma Cunliffe by Kathy, following the publication of her book, *Murder, Medicine and Motherhood*.
35 'Dear Mr Speakman ... Please Soften Your Heart': From an open letter by Kathy to Mark Speakman, Attorney General of New South Wales, in August 2021.
36 'It's Time': Remark by Kathy's lawyers Rhanee Rego and Dr Robert Cavanagh for an article by the author for *The Australian* in October 2021.

Prologue
Much has been written about the tragic case of Sally Clark, and the mothers who were wronged by the false and damaging statistical speculations of Sir Roy Meadow. John Batt made the very strong comments noted here, for an article in *The Guardian* published on 17 March 2007, the day after Mrs Clark died. (Thair Shaikh, 'Sally Clark, mother wrongly convicted of killing her sons,

found dead at home', www.theguardian.com/society/2007/mar/17/childrens services.uknews)

For those who wish to understand the full story, John Batt's book, *Stolen Innocence* (Ebury Press, 2005), is essential reading.

And for a further detailed and forensic perspective on the case, see the paper written by Professor Stephen Cordner, and published in July 2005: *The Sally Clark Case, Professor Meadow and the GMC* (research.monash.edu/en/publications/the-sally-clark-case-professor-meadow-and-the-gmc).

1 'I'm Sorry Darling, I Had to Do It'
The horrific tale of Thomas Britton and the murder of Kathleen Donovan is detailed in extensive police and court documents from the day of his arrest in December 1968, through to his trial for murder in May 1969. Newspapers reported the trial, and earlier newspaper reports detailed his near-fatal attack on his wife, Margaret Britton, in 1954, for which he received a twelve-month prison sentence.

2 Neglected and Destitute
In August 2003, a story entitled 'The Homies', reported by this author, went to air on the ABC's *Four Corners* program. It highlighted the historical plight of young wards of state, the children society didn't want – kids like Kathleen Folbigg who had been orphaned or wrenched from broken families, and taken off to children's homes, as they waited for placements in foster families. For me, researching the story and filming with some of the 'homies' afforded a much clearer appreciation of the challenges faced by Kathy herself when she was sent to Bidura Children's Home, and to Corelli Babies' Home.

Over many decades, tens of thousands of Australian children were sent to state and charitable institutions to be raised by strangers. Some – like Kathy – were identified by numbers, not by their names. They were given menial chores to do, and discipline was harsh at best. Many endured extreme cruelty – emotional, physical and sexual.

One woman among many recalled her time as a state ward, suffering such abuse at Bidura Children's Home, after being 'charged' with having no fixed abode at the age of 14 months; she recorded her experience in an article she wrote for the *Sydney Morning Herald* (Caroline Caroll, 'Finally, we Forgotten Australians are believed', 16 November 2009, www.smh.com.au/politics/federal/finally-we-forgotten-australians-are-believed-20091116-igm8.html).

And a boy called Bryan Seymour who would go on to become a successful journalist described his experience at the Corelli Babies' Home in an article he too wrote for the *Sydney Morning Herald* ('Adoption: Who says you can safeguard a life by imposing a new identity?', 7 January 2016, www.smh.com.au/national/nsw/adoption-who-says-you-can-safeguard-a-life-by-imposing-a-new-identity-20160106-gm0gz5.html).

From the moment Kathy became a state ward, her life in children's homes and, later, in her foster home, was closely monitored and recorded by social workers from the state's child welfare department. Latterly, it operated as the Department of Community Services, or more colloquially, DoCS.

In 2003, three experts – consultant psychiatrist Dr Yvonne Skinner; forensic psychiatrist Dr Bruce Westmore, and forensic psychiatrist Dr Michael Giuffrida – were handed the records, to enable them to write their own detailed accounts of Kathy's upbringing.

In 2019, Dr Giuffrida wrote a second report for the first inquiry into Kathleen Folbigg's convictions, and consultant psychiatrist, Dr Michael Diamond, drew on the department's records for his own extensive report. This chapter draws on conversations and interviews with Kathy's friends, as well as the psychiatrists' reports, which can be viewed and read in the Exhibits section on the website for the 2022 Inquiry into the Convictions of Kathleen Megan Folbigg (2022folbigginquiry.dcj.nsw.gov.au/exhibits.html).

Kathy's foster sister, Lea Bown, and Lea's husband, Ted, later gave interviews to the ABC's *Australian Story*, from which their remarks were taken.

3 Charming and Seductive

Much of the account given by Kathy and Craig Folbigg of their early relationship, and the lives and deaths of their children, is taken from the lengthy police interview with Kathy that took place on 23 July 1999. A transcript of the interview can be accessed as Exhibit 19 of the 2022 inquiry into Kathleen Folbigg's convictions (2022folbigginquiry.dcj.nsw.gov.au/exhibits/exhibit-19.html).

Craig's own account of what occurred can be found in his statement to the police dated 23 May 1999, and in the interview he gave to the police on 19 April 2001. Transcripts of the statement and interview were not produced at the first inquiry into Kathy's convictions and were only produced by the NSW Commissioner of Police on 1 February 2023 – twenty years after her trial. They can be accessed at Exhibit 32 of the 2022 inquiry into Kathleen Folbigg's convictions (2022folbigginquiry.dcj.nsw.gov.au/content/dam/dcj/2022-folbigg-inquiry/documents/exhibits/exhibit-32/Exhibit_32_-_Additional_Evidence_Psychology_and_Psychiatry.pdf).

Medical documents relating to the lives and deaths of all four children can be found at Exhibit 2-H, (aka Exhibit H), the forensic pathology bundle, from the 2019 inquiry into the convictions of Kathleen Folbigg. This voluminous exhibit contains copies of birth and death certificates, letters to the coroner, statements from ambulance officers, and autopsy reports that were produced in advance of Kathy's trial in 2003. In the case of Caleb, this exhibit includes letters and notes written by consultant paediatrician Dr Barry Springthorpe (2019folbigginquiry.dcj.nsw.gov.au/content/dam/dcj/2022-folbigg-inquiry/documents/exhibits/exhibit-2/Exhibit_2-H.pdf).

Kathy's statement following the death of Caleb can be found in Exhibit 2-E of the exhibits tendered at her trial in 2003, along with letters written by Kathy to Craig, and by Craig to Kathy (2022folbigginquiry.dcj.nsw.gov.au/content/dam/dcj/2022-folbigg-inquiry/documents/exhibits/exhibit-2/Exhibit_2-E.pdf).

Further remarks, observations and comments in this chapter are taken from interviews that this author carried out with Kathy's lifelong friends Tracy Chapman and Megan Donegan for an episode of the ABC's *Australian Story* program, which went to air in August 2018.

4 'Mixed Feelings'

This chapter contains comments and observations taken from an interview with Megan Donegan as well as extracts from witness statements from doctors and ambulance officers, and letters and statements written following Patrick's death. As for chapter 3 sources, these letters and statements can be viewed at Exhibit 2-H (aka Exhibit H).

Much of the account by Kathy of the children's lives and deaths given in this and following chapters comes from the transcript of the lengthy interview given by her to the police on 23 July 1999. The transcript can be viewed at Exhibit 19-04 of the 2022 inquiry into Kathleen Folbigg's convictions (2022folbigginquiry.dcj.nsw.gov.au/content/dam/dcj/2022-folbigg-inquiry/documents/exhibits/exhibit-19/Exhibit_19_-_Video_footage_and_highlighted_transcript_of_ERISP_conducted_with_Ms_Folbigg_on_23_July_1999.pdf).

Footage of limited extracts from the filmed interview can be viewed via YouTube at Exhibits 19-01, 19-02 and 19-03, and at Exhibit 2-AZ.

www.youtube.com/watch?v=E21zEWlEY_U
www.youtube.com/watch?v=eR5XOn9jRjk
www.youtube.com/watch?v=c_Ff0cvTJ9s
www.youtube.com/watch?v=FPUhXh2CU8k

Further personal accounts of events and incidents in Kathy's life, her relationship with Craig, and the lives of her children, are contained in her journals. Exhibit 18 of the 2022 Folbigg inquiry website contains all the diaries Kathy wrote at the time, which were tendered to the inquiry (2022folbigginquiry.dcj.nsw.gov.au/content/dam/dcj/2022-folbigg-inquiry/documents/exhibits/exhibit-18/Exhibit_18_-_Original_Diaries_of_Kathleen_Folbigg.pdf).

Similarly, much of the account by Craig of the children's lives and deaths given in this and following chapters comes from two main sources: a statement he gave to the police dated 23 May 1999; and the transcript of an interview he gave to the police on 19 April 2001. Both the statement and the interview transcript are contained in Exhibit 32-09 and can be viewed on the 2022 inquiry website (see chapter 3 sources).

5 'The Cheekiest One Ever'
This chapter draws on the same sources as Chapter 4.

6 'This Last One Has Broken Me'
This chapter draws on the same sources as Chapter 4.

7 'The Biggest Party Ever!'
This chapter draws on the same sources as Chapter 4. In particular, Laura's sleep studies carried out by Dr Chris Seton can be found at Exhibit 2-H (aka Exhibit H), the forensic pathology bundle, from the 2019 inquiry into Kathleen Folbigg's convictions (see chapter 3 sources).

8 'I've Had Three Go Already!'
There is extensive material on the 2021 and 2022 Inquiry websites relating to Laura's death and its aftermath. As detailed above, much of this can be viewed at Exhibit 2-H (aka Exhibit H) as noted in chapter 3 sources.

A transcript of the call made by Kathy to the ambulance service following Laura's death was tendered at her trial and can be found at Exhibit 2-E (see chapter 3 sources).

Further accounts of what occurred (as in Chapter 4) are derived from Kathy's later police interview, and from Craig's statement to the police dated 23 May 1999; and the transcript of an interview he gave to the police on 19 April 2001.

Kathy's foster sister, Lea, and Lea's husband, Ted, later gave interviews to the ABC's *Australian Story*, from which their remarks are taken.

9 'Four is Fucking Murder!'
Professor Roy Meadow's book *ABC of Child Abuse*, which proved to be extremely influential, was published by BMJ Publishing Group in 1989, the same year that Dr Vincent JM DiMaio and his father, Dr Dominick DiMaio, published their textbook, *Forensic Pathology* (CRC Press).

For anyone who wishes to know more about the tragic case of Waneta Hoyt, *Trials of a Forensic Psychologist: A Casebook* (Wiley, 2008), by Charles Patrick Ewing, who played a part in the case, is essential reading. In Ewing's book he points out that Hoyt was deceived by the police into believing that the interview they wished to carry out with her was for research purposes. Kathy similarly believed that she was going to be helping the police to understand what had happened to her four children when she was invited to give the police an interview – and not that she would be accused of killing them all. In the case of Hoyt, as Ewing points out in his book: 'Everybody in the room but Waneta knew that she was a suspect.' The same can be said of Kathy when she entered the police station and agreed to be interviewed.

Mr Ewing conducted a psychological assessment of Mrs Hoyt, concluding that she suffered from 'long-standing, recurring episodes of serious depression as well as severe dependent and avoidant personality disorders.' Kathy too suffered long-standing, recurring episodes of serious depression.

In other respects, and in their individual circumstances, the two women were very different, but it is difficult to overestimate how significant the case of Waneta Hoyt proved to be within medical and forensic circles.

At Kathy's trial in 2003, Mr Tedeschi cross-examined Professor Roger Byard, the defence's leading medical expert about any cases he had heard of where three or more children in a family had died from natural causes. In his response, without naming her, the professor may have been alluding to the case of Waneta Hoyt, in the following terms:

Q. Have you from your discussions with your colleagues, either here in Australia or overseas, ever heard of a case of three or more children in the one family who have all died or suffered an ALTE suddenly, unexpectedly during a sleep period at home?

A. That's less easy to answer because there are cases that have been recorded in the literature of up to five deaths or more in a family that has been attributed to SIDS. These are cases from a number of years ago.

Q. Could I interrupt you there: Is it now considered by the medical profession that they were not SIDS?

A. I believe so, yes.

Q. So perhaps if I can refine my questions a little bit. Have you become aware from discussions with your colleagues of any case of three or more children present in one family who have all died of natural causes suddenly, unexpectedly during a sleep period at home?

A. I can't think of any cases.

The problem for Kathy's defence was that, when Kathy's trial took place, Mrs Hoyt had not had an opportunity to clear her name in an appeal, because in August 1998, she had died in prison from pancreatic cancer. At the time she was awaiting an appeal and because of this, under New York law, she was formally exonerated at her death.

That though, would have carried little weight at Kathy's trial.

Dr Allan Cala's interview, together with interviews with Lea and Ted Bown, and with Detective Inspector Ryan and Detective Sergeant Frith were featured in a two-part *Australian Story* episode, broadcast on the ABC and produced by Belinda Hawkins. The episodes went to air in 2004, and the transcripts of the two episodes can be viewed here (www.abc.net.au/news/2018-07-16/of-woman-born-march-15-2004/9998786).

Interviews with Joe Lavin and Robin Napper were carried out by the author, and as in previous chapters, significant details of what Craig alleged against his wife, and later retracted, can be found in his statement to the police dated 23 May 1999 (see chapter 4 sources).

10 'Obviously, I'm My Father's Daughter'

As in chapter 4 sources, transcripts of all of Kathy's diaries can be found in Exhibit 18 at the 2022 Folbigg Inquiry website.

Exhibit 2-F on the 2019 inquiry website contains complete transcripts of the evidence given at Kathy's trial. Three of Kathy's neighbours were called to give evidence by the Crown (2022folbigginquiry.dcj.nsw.gov.au/content/dam/dcj/2022-folbigg-inquiry/documents/exhibits/exhibit-2/Exhibit_2-F.pdf).

Transcripts of selected recordings from listening devices planted by the police in Kathy's home can be found at Exhibit 16 on the 2022 inquiry website (2022folbigginquiry.dcj.nsw.gov.au/content/dam/dcj/2022-folbigg-inquiry/documents/exhibits/exhibit-16/Exhibit_16_-_Other_documents_including_summaries_and_chronologies.pdf).

As in chapter 4 sources, a transcript of the police interview with Kathy which took place on 23 July 1999 can be accessed at Exhibit 19 of the 2022 inquiry into Kathleen Folbigg's convictions (2022folbigginquiry.dcj.nsw.gov.au/exhibits/exhibit-19.html).

11 'All Night I've Been Thinking, Maybe I Killed the Kids'

As in chapter 10 sources, transcripts of some of the conversations between Kathy and Craig, which were secretly recorded by the police, can be found at Exhibit 16 on the 2022 inquiry website.

12 'With Three, You Yell "Murder!"'

The statements and reports from Dr Allan Cala, Dr Susan Beal, Dr Janice Ophoven, and Professor Peter Berry can be found at Exhibit 2-H (aka Exhibit H), the forensic pathology bundle, from the 2019 inquiry into the convictions of Kathleen Folbigg (see chapter 3 sources).

The report written by police psychologist Rozalinda Garbutt can be found at Exhibit 23 (2022folbigginquiry.dcj.nsw.gov.au/content/dam/dcj/2022-folbigg-inquiry/documents/exhibits/exhibit-23/Exhibit_23_-_Rozalinda_Garbutt.pdf).

The interview given by Craig to the police on 19 April 2001 can be found at Exhibit 32 of the 2022 inquiry into Kathleen Folbigg's convictions (see chapter 3 sources).

13 'I Couldn't Leave the Lady in the Lurch'

The report produced by Professor Peter Herdson can be found at Exhibit 2-H (aka Exhibit H), the forensic pathology bundle, from the 2019 inquiry into the convictions of Kathleen Folbigg (see chapter 3 sources).

Details of Kathy's committal hearing are contained in contemporaneous newspaper accounts.

14 The Trial

Kathy's trial was held not far from the old Darlinghurst Gaol, which opened in 1841 and which, for a while, held public hangings within the walls of the prison. Accounts differ as to whether the total number of men and women hanged at the gaol was 76 or 79. The gaol closed in 1914, and one of the most colourful accounts of its history can be found at www.aguidetoaustralianbushranging.com/2020/10/21/spotlight-historic-old-gaol-darlinghurst-closed-1914/

As noted in the *Dictionary of Sydney* (archived in 2021 and published by the State Library of New South Wales: dictionaryofsydney.org/entry/darlinghurst_gaol), one of the most well-known inmates to be hanged there was Jimmy Governor in 1901, later immortalised as Jimmy Blacksmith in Thomas Keneally's novel, *The Chant of Jimmy Blacksmith*.

Fortunately for Kathy, the last woman to be hanged at the gaol was Louisa Collins in January 1889, after she was convicted of poisoning both of her husbands with arsenic. As in Kathy's case, much of the evidence used against Louisa was circumstantial. Her story is told in Caroline Overington's *Last Woman Hanged* (HarperCollins, 2014). On 19 February 1951, just sixteen years before Kathy was born, Jean Lee became the last woman to be hanged in Australia. Her case is worth noting because, like Kathy, her conviction for murder was highly contentious.

In the event, by 1985 all Australian jurisdictions had abolished the death penalty, and in 2010 the Australian government passed legislation prohibiting the reintroduction of capital punishment.

Exhibit 2-F on the 2022 inquiry website (see chapter 10 sources) contains complete transcripts of the evidence given at Kathy's trial.

15 'Honest to God'

As for chapter 14, Exhibit 2-F on the 2022 inquiry website (see chapter 10 sources) contains complete transcripts of the evidence given at Kathy's trial.

16 The Verdict

The original video footage, filmed by Craig, of Laura playing in and around the family pool on 28 February 1999 can be viewed at Exhibit 2-E, Tab K, and on YouTube (www.youtube.com/watch?v=1yCgU8Bf9oM).

Matthew Benns is the author of *When the Bough Breaks: The true story of child killer Kathleen Folbigg* (Bantam, 2003). He was interviewed by this writer for an episode of the ABC's *Australian Story* in August 2018.

Other quotes and recollections are taken from conversations between Kathy and Tracy Chapman, which, with their agreement, were recorded for an episode of *Australian Story* in August 2018.

As for chapter 14, Exhibit 2-F on the 2022 inquiry website (see chapter 10 sources) contains complete transcripts of the evidence given at Kathy's trial.

17 Behind Bars

As for chapter 16, some quotes and recollections in this chapter are taken from conversations between Kathy and Tracy Chapman, which, with their agreement, were recorded for an episode of *Australian Story* in August 2018.

Details of the sentence handed down on Kathy in October 2003, together with the judgement of Justice Barr, can be found online (www.austlii.edu.au/cgi-bin/viewdoc/au/cases/nsw/NSWSC/2003/895.html).

The report written by forensic psychiatrist Dr Michael Giuffrida for consideration by Justice Barr at her sentencing, is Exhibit 2-BD on the Folbigg 2022 inquiry website (2022folbigginquiry.dcj.nsw.gov.au/content/dam/dcj/2022-folbigg-inquiry/documents/exhibits/exhibit-2/Exhibit_2-BD.pdf).

Justice Brian Sully's judgment in Kathy's appeal against her convictions and sentence in 2005 can be found online (www.austlii.edu.au/cgi-bin/viewdoc/au/cases/nsw/NSWCCA/2005/23.html).

As for chapter 14, Exhibit 2-F on the 2022 inquiry website (see chapter 10 sources) contains complete transcripts of the evidence given at Kathy's trial, including those exchanges which took place in the absence of the jury.

The judgment in Kathy's second appeal was handed down in December 2007, and can be found online (www.austlii.edu.au/cgi-bin/viewdoc/au/cases/nsw/NSWCCA/2007/371.html).

Anne Henderson's book, *An Angel in the Court: The Life of Major Joyce Harmer* (HarperCollins, 2006), tells the story of the part played by Joyce and her husband, Hilton, in supporting Kathy during the ordeal of her trial and subsequent imprisonment.

18 The Champion Bridge Player

In 2008, Gordon Wood was sent to jail for 17 years for the murder of his girlfriend Caroline Byrne. Three years later, the ABC's *Four Corners* program broadcast an investigation into the controversial case, as it was being appealed and key expert evidence given at the trial re-examined. The program, reported by this writer, went to air in October 2011, and in 2012 Mr Wood was acquitted after spending more than three years behind bars.

The *Four Corners* story 'Trial and Error' is available online (www.abc.net.au/news/2011-10-27/trial-and-error/3612532).

The judgment of the Appeal Court in the case of Gordon Wood is available online (www.austlii.edu.au/cgi-bin/viewdoc/au/cases/nsw/NSWCCA/2012/21.html).

Also see *The Death of Innocents: A true story of murder, medicine and high stake science* by Richard Firstman and Jamie Talan (Bantam Books, 1997).

19 Mothers in the Dock

A Cry in the Dark, also released under the title *Evil Angels*, is a 1988 film, directed by Fred Schepisi and starring Meryl Streep as Lindy Chamberlain, and

Sam Neill as her husband, Michael. The Hollywood movie ensured that the story of Azaria Chamberlain and how she was taken by a dingo in August 1980 reached a worldwide audience.

For those who wish to understand the full story of Sally Clark, John Batt's *Stolen Innocence* (see Prologue notes) is essential reading. And for a further detailed and forensic perspective on the case, see 'The Sally Clark Case, Professor Meadow and the GMC' by Stephen Cordner (*Australian Journal of Forensic Sciences*, 2005, Volume 37, Issue 2, research.monash.edu/en/publications/the-sally-clark-case-professor-meadow-and-the-gmc).

The summary judgment at Sally Clark's appeal is available online (www.inference.org.uk/sallyclark/CA2003.html) as is the full judgment (www.inference.org.uk/sallyclark/Judgment03.html).

The judgment of Lord Justice Judge at Angela Cannings' appeal could equally apply to Kathy's case, where no forensic evidence of her having harmed or killed any of her children was offered to the jury at her trial.

Lord Judge told the court: 'If murder cannot be proved, the conviction cannot be safe. In a criminal case, it is simply not enough to be able to establish even a high probability of guilt. Unless we are sure of guilt the dreadful possibility always remains that a mother, already brutally scarred by the unexplained death or deaths of her babies, may find herself in prison for life for killing them when she should not be there at all. In our community, and in any civilised community, that is abhorrent.' (See www.bailii.org/ew/cases/EWCA/Crim/2004/1.html.)

Carol Matthey was presented for trial for the murder of four of her children, but in a pre-trial judgment handed down in October 2007, Justice John Coldrey concluded: 'Obviously, in consequence of the exclusion of a number of pieces of evidence, and the arguably doubtful probative value of much of that remaining (which may well become the subject of further exclusionary rulings) it will be necessary for the Crown to reassess the viability of this prosecution.' Following this, the case against her was dropped (see www.austlii.edu.au/cgi-bin/viewdoc/au/cases/vic/VSC/2007/398.html).

In his judgment, Justice Coldrey commented that 'Relatively unique cases such as the present one may be seen to present real challenges for the legal process in dealing with expert medical opinion. This conjunction of law and medicine and "the challenge of achieving a legally and medically fair result in a trial that is based largely on circumstantial evidence" was the subject of a recent article in the *Australian Journal of Forensic Sciences* entitled "The Case of Kathleen Folbigg: How did justice and medicine fare?"

'The authors from the School of Psychology, University of New South Wales, examined the medical evidence given at the Folbigg trial. In assessing the impact of the medical evidence, the authors are critical of the trial of the four cases together.'

'The Case of Kathleen Folbigg: How did justice and medicine fare?'

(Sharmila Betts and Jane Goodman-Delahunty, 2007, Volume 39, Issue 1) argued that: 'The case of Kathleen Folbigg encapsulates the challenge of achieving a legally and medically fair result in a trial that is based largely on circumstantial evidence' and warned about 'the complexities and pitfalls in managing medical and other expert evidence in multiple infant death trials' (see www.tandfonline.com/doi/full/10.1080/00450610701324916).

20 'A Scholar of Bias'
Emma Cunliffe's book *Murder, Medicine and Motherhood* (Hart Publishing, 2011) was the first to make the case that Kathy's convictions in 2003 amounted to a miscarriage of justice. Matthew Benns' book *When the Bough Breaks: The true story of child killer Kathleen Folbigg* (Bantam, 2003) had been published shortly after her trial, and didn't question her guilt.

21 The Fightback Begins
Following the publication of Emma Cunliffe's book (see chapter 20 sources), the fight to free Kathy began in earnest from Newcastle, where many of her friends and supporters lived, and where a team of barristers began to work on her behalf, aided by students and academics from the University of Newcastle's Legal Centre. Also helping to raise the profile of the case, and the fight for a judicial review, was the *Newcastle Herald*, which over the years has published multiple articles about the case.

A summary of the Legal Centre's role in Kathy's case is available online (www.newcastle.edu.au/hippocampus/story/2023/fight-for-justice) and the *Newcastle Herald* reported on Helen Cummings' fight to free Kathy in an article by Joanne McCarthy on 4 February 2003, 'Crusade to Free Kathleen Folbigg' (www.newcastleherald.com.au/story/1278171/crusade-to-free-kathleen-folbigg/).

22 The Petition
A full copy of the 2015 petition, delivered on Kathy's behalf to the Governor of New South Wales, is available online (www.injustice.law/articles/folbigg-petition-to-governor-for-review/).

Four reports were appended to the petition. They included an extensive review of the forensic pathology records and evidence relating to the deaths of all four children, which was written by Professor Stephen Cordner, then Professor of Forensic Pathology (International), Monash University, and Head, International Programmes at the Victorian Institute of Forensic Medicine (VJFM).

Professor Cordner's report, together with a peer review of his report by Michael S Pollanen MD, Chief Forensic Pathologist for Ontario, can be found as Exhibit 2-C on the 2019 inquiry website (2019folbigginquiry.dcj.nsw.gov.au/content/dam/dcj/2022-folbigg-inquiry/documents/exhibits/exhibit-2/Exhibit_2-C.pdf).

A third report which was appended to the petition, by British Professor of Mathematics Ray Hill, can be found as Exhibit 14 of the 2022 inquiry (2022folbigginquiry.dcj.nsw.gov.au/content/dam/dcj/2022-folbigg-inquiry/documents/exhibits/exhibit-14/Exhibit_14_-_Additional_Evidence_Cardiology_and_Genetics.pdf).

Exhibit 24 of the 2022 inquiry contains an update to the Psychological Report on Kathleen Folbigg dated 18 April 2014, which is written by clinical psychologist Dr Sharmila Betts, and which was also appended to the 2015 petition (2022folbigginquiry.dcj.nsw.gov.au/content/dam/dcj/2022-folbigg-inquiry/documents/exhibits/exhibit-24/Exhibit_24_-_Dr_Sharmila_Betts.pdf).

23 'An Eminently Fatal Case of Myocarditis'
Dr Orde's comments in this chapter were made in interviews recorded for the ABC's *Australian Story* program, and in conversations with the author.

24 'That's, as Mothers, What You Do'
Kathy and Tracy's conversations were recorded by the ABC's *Australian Story* and featured in an episode that went to air on Monday 13 August 2018. It was the first time Kathy had spoken publicly about her children, her diaries, her convictions, and her life in prison.

The episode is available online (www.youtube.com/watch?v=fAcEQpGiV5w).

25 Eureka!
Exhibit AE from the 2019 inquiry contains the 'pedigree' of Kathy and her children, taken by Dr Todor Arsov when he visited her in Silverwater prison on 8 October 2018 (2019folbigginquiry.dcj.nsw.gov.au/documents/Exhibit_AE_-_Pedigree.pdf).

Exhibit AG from the 2019 inquiry contains the report written by Professor Carola Vinuesa, following her own and Dr Arsov's discovery of the *CALM2* genetic mutation on 2 December 2018 (2019folbigginquiry.dcj.nsw.gov.au/documents/Exhibit_AG_-_Report_of_Professor_Carola_Vinuesa.pdf).

26 An Inquiry at Last
The 2019 inquiry into Kathy's convictions had at its disposal an enormous volume of research, reports, witness statements and submissions. It included all of the evidence and transcripts from Kathy's trial in 2003, together with substantial fresh evidence in the field of genetics.

The hearings themselves covered three separate subject areas: in the week from 18 March 2019, evidence relating to forensic pathology, SIDS, Sudden Unexpected Death in Infancy (SUDI), immunology and microbiology was heard by the inquiry.

In the week beginning 15 April, evidence relating to genetics, cardiology and neurology was discussed. And in the week beginning 29 April, Kathy gave evidence to the inquiry about the entries she had written in her diaries, and those diaries she had disposed of.

For anyone interested in exploring the inquiry in detail, all of this is contained on the website entitled *2019 Inquiry into the Convictions of Kathleen Megan Folbigg* (2019folbigginquiry.dcj.nsw.gov.au/hearings.html).

Transcripts of the eleven days of substantive hearings at the 2019 inquiry can be found as Exhibit 4 on the 2022 inquiry website (2022folbigginquiry.dcj.nsw.gov.au/content/dam/dcj/2022-folbigg-inquiry/documents/exhibits/exhibit-4/Exhibit_04_-_Transcripts_of_the_substantive_hearing_in_the_2019_Inquiry.pdf).

Separate daily transcripts are stored on the 2019 inquiry website.

On 18 March, the first day of the substantive hearings, senior counsel assisting the inquiry, Gail Furness SC, gave her opening statement (2019folbigginquiry.dcj.nsw.gov.au/documents/FINAL_-_Transcript_of_18_March_2019.pdf).

The exchanges between Mr Blanch and Mr Morris on the subject of the diaries, and Kathy giving evidence about them, took place at the second directions hearing on 12 December 2018. A transcript of the hearing is available online (2019folbigginquiry.dcj.nsw.gov.au/documents/Transcript_of_Inquiry_-_Directions_Hearing_12_December_2018.pdf).

27 'It is an Appalling Situation'
The author's exclusive report on the fresh evidence that was presented to the 2019 inquiry was published on the ABC website on 18 March 2019, the first day of the substantive hearings: 'Kathleen Folbigg Inquiry to Consider Fresh Evidence in Wrongful Conviction Case' (www.abc.net.au/news/2019-03-18/kathleen-folbigg-new-evidence-suggests-wrongly-convicted-killing/10910200).

The article referenced four reports in particular. The first was a report by Professor Monique Ryan, Director, Department of Neurology, Royal Children's Hospital, which is contained in Exhibit AJ on the inquiry website (2019folbigginquiry.dcj.nsw.gov.au/documents/Exhibit_AJ_-_Expert_report_of_Professor_Monique_Ryan.pdf). The second was by consulting forensic pathologist Professor Johan Duflou, which is contained in Exhibit L on the inquiry website (2019folbigginquiry.dcj.nsw.gov.au/documents/Exhibit_L-Expert_report_of_Professor_Johan_Duflou.pdf). The third report was written by Professor Robert Clancy, and is contained in Exhibit W on the inquiry website (2019folbigginquiry.dcj.nsw.gov.au/documents/Exhibit_W-Expert_reports_of_Emeritus_Professor_Robert_Clancy_AM_dated_13_March_2019_and_17_March_2019.pdf). The fourth report referred to was written by Professor Caroline Blackwell, then Conjoint Professor at the University of Newcastle School of Biomedical Sciences and Pharmacy, and is contained in Exhibit T on the inquiry website

(2019folbigginquiry.dcj.nsw.gov.au/documents/Exhibit_T-Expert_report_of_ Professor_Cecelia_Blackwell_dated_5_March_2019.pdf).

28 'She Could be Part of that Small Number'

Transcripts for days two, three and four of the substantive hearings, at which expert forensic pathologists gave evidence, can be found at:

2019folbigginquiry.dcj.nsw.gov.au/documents/FINAL_-_Transcript_of_19_March_2019.pdf

2019folbigginquiry.dcj.nsw.gov.au/documents/FINAL_-_Transcript_of_20_March_2019.pdf

2019folbigginquiry.dcj.nsw.gov.au/documents/FINAL_-_Transcript_of_21_March_2019.pdf

29 The CALM Before the Storm

Beginning on 15 April 2019, three days of hearings took place into the genetic and neurological evidence before the inquiry. Transcripts of each day's hearings can be found at:

2019folbigginquiry.dcj.nsw.gov.au/documents/FINAL_-_Transcript_of_15_April_2019.pdf

2019folbigginquiry.dcj.nsw.gov.au/documents/FINAL_-_Transcript_of_16_April_2019.pdf

2019folbigginquiry.dcj.nsw.gov.au/documents/FINAL_-_Transcript_of_17_April_2019_Redacted.pdf

Some of the terminology used by the scientists is difficult, at best, to understand. For anyone who would find it helpful to read a basic primer of genetics, there are several useful sources, including by the National Human Genome Research Institute: www.genome.gov/about-genomics/fact-sheets/A-Brief-Guide-to-Genomics

www.genome.gov/about-genomics/fact-sheets/Genetics-vs-Genomics

The Melbourne Genomics Health Alliance publishes a helpful glossary of terms used in genetics and genomics, arranged alphabetically from 'allele to zygosity' (www.melbournegenomics.org.au/guide-genomics/genomics-explained/what-genomic-test/genomics-glossary).

Pages 542–550 (Annexure G) of the 2019 Folbigg inquiry final report contain a glossary of medical terms used during the inquiry (2019folbigginquiry.dcj.nsw.gov.au/documents/Report_of_the_Inquiry_into_the_convictions_of_Kathleen_Megan_Folbigg.pdf).

Pages 427–459 of the 2022 Folbigg inquiry final report contain a more detailed glossary of terms used during both inquiries (2022folbigginquiry.dcj.nsw.gov.au/content/dam/dcj/2022-folbigg-inquiry/documents/Report_of_the_2022_Inquiry_into_the_convictions_of_Kathleen_Megan_Folbigg.pdf).

Multiple reports and written responses were submitted to the 2019 inquiry by experts from the Sydney and Canberra teams, all of which are included in different exhibits tendered to the inquiry (2019folbigginquiry.dcj.nsw.gov.au/documents/exhibits.html). A selection of these reports, letters and responses includes:

    Exhibit AG: Report of Professor Carola Vinuesa, 2 December 2018

    Exhibit AB: Report of Dr Michael Buckley, 25 February 2019

    Exhibit AF: Joint report of the Canberra genetics team, 29 March 2019

    Exhibit Z: Joint report of the Sydney genetics team, 29 March 2019

    Exhibit Y: Expert report of Professor Jonathan Skinner, 31 March 2019

    Exhibit AX: Written response to joint expert report of Professors Vinuesa and Professor Cook, 9 April 2019

    Exhibit AY: Written reply to response of Professor Kirk and Dr Buckley, 12 April 2019

    Exhibit BL: Letter from Dr Hariharan Raju, 18 April 2019

    Exhibit BJ: Supplementary report of Professor Jonathan Skinner, 24 April 2019

    Exhibit BK: Letter from Professor Jonathan Skinner to the Inquiry, 30 April 2019

The following documents were submitted after the inquiry hearings had ended:

    Exhibit BT: Letter from Professor Peter Schwartz to Professor Vinuesa, 29 June 2019

    Exhibit BU: Lia Crotti et al: 'Calmodulin Mutations and Life-Threatening Cardiac Arrhythmias: Insights from the International Calmodulinopathy Registry'

    Exhibit BV: Supplementary report of Professor Jonathan Skinner, Professor Edwin Kirk and Dr Michael Buckley, 5 July 2019

    Exhibit BW: Response from Professor Carola Vinuesa, Professor Matthew Cook, Professor Peter Schwarz, Professor Michael Toft Overgaard and Dr Todor Arsov to the 5 July supplementary report, 11 July 2019

30 Under Siege

The transcript for the first day of hearings, when Kathy was cross-examined about her diaries, is available online (2019folbigginquiry.dcj.nsw.gov.au/documents/FINAL_-_Transcript_of_29_April_2019.pdf).

31 'The Ordinary, Plain Meaning'

The transcripts for the second and third days of hearings, when Kathy was cross-examined about her diaries, are also available online:

    2019folbigginquiry.dcj.nsw.gov.au/documents/FINAL_-_Transcript_of_30_April_2019.pdf

    2019folbigginquiry.dcj.nsw.gov.au/documents/FINAL_-_Transcript_of_1_May_2019.pdf

32 'Hope Can Destroy One's Soul'

The final report of the 2019 inquiry, released on 22 July 2019, is available online (2019folbigginquiry.dcj.nsw.gov.au/documents/Report_of_the_Inquiry_into_the_convictions_of_Kathleen_Megan_Folbigg.pdf).

33 Europace

The *Europace* paper, 'Infanticide vs Inherited Cardiac Arrhythmias' (Brohus et al, 17 November 2020, Volume 23, Issue 3), can be accessed as Exhibit 15 of the 2022 inquiry (2022folbigginquiry.dcj.nsw.gov.au/content/dam/dcj/2022-folbigg-inquiry/documents/exhibits/exhibit-15/Exhibit_15_-_Journal_and_other_articles.pdf).

34 A Nobel Cause

On 2 March 2021, a petition signed by Dr Robert Cavanagh and Rhanee Rego on Kathy's behalf, and endorsed by 90 scientists, medical practitioners and science advocates, including two Nobel laureates, was delivered to the Governor of New South Wales, seeking Kathy's immediate pardon and release from jail. The petition is available online (www.injustice.law/articles/folbigg-petition-to-governor-for-pardon/).

35 'Dear Mr Speakman ... Please Soften Your Heart'

The *Daily Telegraph* reported on Kathy's four-page letter to NSW Attorney-General Mark Speakman on 29 August 2021, 'Convicted Child Killer Kathleen Folbigg Pens Four-Page Letter Begging for a Pardon' by this author. The contents of that article are replicated on The Injustice Project website (www.injustice.law/articles/daily-telegraph-convicted-child-killer-kathleen-folbigg-pens-four-page-letter-begging-for-a-pardon/).

36 'It's Time'

The reports written by Dr Touma (Exhibit 29), Professor Pennebaker (Exhibit 25), Associate Professor Janine Stevenson (Exhibit 27), and Associate Professor David Butt (Exhibit 28), can be found on the 2022 inquiry website (2022folbigginquiry.dcj.nsw.gov.au/exhibits.html). In addition, Dr Michael Diamond's report, written originally for the 2019 inquiry, can be found at page 43 of Exhibit 16.

Exhibit 24 of the 2022 inquiry contains an update to the Psychological Report on Kathleen Folbigg dated 18 April 2014, which was written by clinical psychologist Dr Sharmila Betts, and which was originally appended to the 2015 petition.

37 Waiting for Mr Speakman

On 8 May 2022, the *Daily Telegraph* published an article written by the author, laying out the various options open to Mr Speakman, in considering the petition that had been lodged with the Governor of New South Wales in March 2021. The article, 'Paths to Freedom for Kathleen Folbigg Revealed' was published on Mother's Day (www.dailytelegraph.com.au/truecrimeaustralia/could-this-be-the-last-mothers-day-in-prison-for-convicted-child-killer-kathleen-folbigg/news-story/9b6023ff64cda466ee79725ba8159758).

On 18 May, Mr Speakman announced a second inquiry into Kathy's convictions, to be conducted by the retired Chief Justice of New South Wales, the Hon Thomas Bathurst AC QC (dcj.nsw.gov.au/documents/news-and-media/media-statements/2022/speakman-statement-kathleen-megan-folbigg.pdf).

38 It's All in the Genes

Transcripts of the four directions hearings, and the thirteen days of substantive hearings of the 2022 inquiry into Kathy's convictions, are available through the inquiry website (2022folbigginquiry.dcj.nsw.gov.au/transcripts.html).

The Danish TV documentary featuring Professors Toft Overgaard and Nyegaard is also available online (play.tv2.dk/serie/mysteriet-om-de-doede-boern-tv2).

39 Free at Last

The final report of the 2022 inquiry into Kathy's convictions, released on 8 November 2023, is available online (2022folbigginquiry.dcj.nsw.gov.au/content/dam/dcj/2022-folbigg-inquiry/documents/Report_of_the_2022_Inquiry_into_the_convictions_of_Kathleen_Megan_Folbigg.pdf).

The judgment of the NSW Court of Criminal Appeal on 14 December 2023, quashing Kathy's convictions and entering a verdict of acquittal in respect of all five charges for which she had previously been convicted, is also available online (www.austlii.edu.au/cgi-bin/viewdoc/au/cases/nsw/NSWCCA/2023/325.html).

ACKNOWLEDGEMENTS

Many people, some of whom do not wish to be credited, helped me in the research and writing of this book. I was aided on a personal level by some who know Kathy well, and on a professional level by many in the worlds of law, science, medicine and genetics.

My particular thanks go to Peter Gill, who set me off on this extraordinary trail; to Emma Cunliffe, without whose insights Kathy's wrongful convictions might never have been seriously questioned; to Helen Cummings, who so generously, introduced me to Kathy; and to the tenacious Tracy Chapman and Megan Donegan, who trusted me and the ABC to tell Kathy's story truthfully and who encouraged me to persist in highlighting her story over many years. And Kathy herself, who also trusted *Australian Story* to enable her voice to be heard when she chose to go public on television for the first time.

Dr Robert Cavanagh, Rhanee Rego and Isabel Reed, all brilliant and indefatigable lawyers, took me into their confidence while working tirelessly to take Kathy's case forward; they and other members of Kathy's legal teams offered invaluable insights into the evidence underpinning Kathy's prosecution and identified and informed me about where the fault lines in that evidence lay. I had many long conversations with law professor Ray Watterson, and I thank him for his constant encouragement over many years.

At the ABC, Caitlin Shea, *Australian Story*'s Executive Producer, commissioned the episode that called Kathy's convictions into question and helped to trigger the judicial process that followed. The brilliant production team was led by Caitlin and by supervising producer Jennifer Feller, and the story was edited by Andrew Cooke, and filmed by Quentin Davis with sound by Anthony Frisina.

My ambition to write a book about Kathy's case was supported from the outset by Tracy Chapman, and also by Stuart Neal and Sharon Guest, and I thank them for their encouragement. I am also lastingly grateful to Ivan O'Mahoney, a good friend and former ABC colleague, with whom I discussed this story over many years, and with whom I filmed several key interviews for a planned documentary. I have drawn on those interviews for my book.

Later, another former ABC colleague, Suzanne Smith, herself an accomplished author, introduced me to her publisher at HarperCollins, Jude McGee, who took the brave step of commissioning the book. Helen Littleton took over as publisher and showed remarkable forbearance as I missed almost every deadline, as did my former publisher, the endlessly creative and enthusiastic Georgia Frances King.

Many thanks too, to the legal team at HarperCollins, Simon Stubbs and Alisdair Doctor; to my reassuringly calm editor, Shannon Kelly, to my copyeditor John Mapps and to my proofreader Nikola Lusk.

At the Australian Society of Authors, particular thanks go to Victoria Chylek and to former CEO Olivia Lanchester, for their valuable detailed advice. At the Australian Academy of Science, thanks to Chief Executive Anna-Maria Arabia, and in her media office, to Dan Wheelahan and Paul Richards.

Many thanks too to Juliette Brodsky, who helped me with my research into Kathy's early life, and who, as Media Liaison Officer at the Supreme Court of New South Wales, with her colleague, Media Manager Chris Winslow, helped steer me through the thicket of formal applications to publish various court documents. Thanks too to Dr Justin Cahill, Principal Solicitor, Open Government Information and Privacy at the NSW Department of Communities and Justice, for his thorough, careful advice.

Many personal friends and many of those with whom I have shared a workspace while writing have supported me and lightened my mood when needed – most notably Kate Barnes, Jane Curry, Andrew Thalis, Dale Masters, Paul Davidson, Stephanie Allen, Georgina Jarvis, Angus Hannan and Christine Abad. Big thanks to them and also, to David Wallace, Dr Robert Cavanagh and Professor Stephen Cordner, who gave up hours of their time to review my manuscript, make corrections, and offer helpful suggestions.

All of those mentioned have been endlessly generous; none is responsible for any inadvertent mistakes or misjudgements I may have made.

Finally, I can't thank enough my beautiful partner, Tracey, our amazing boy, Oscar, and my two extraordinary daughters, Jess and Tess – all of whom now know this story back to front and, in Oscar's case, in far more detail than I ever wanted him to. Your grace, good humour and unending encouragement have been inspirational.